BLIND CONSCIENCE

Margot O'Neill is a senior reporter with ABC TV's *Lateline* program, and has worked on a variety of programs including *Four Corners*. She has been a television, radio and newspaper journalist in Australia and overseas for 25 years. O'Neill won two Walkley Awards, the United Nations of Australia Media Peace Award, the national Human Rights Award for Television, and has been nominated for three Logie Awards. She reported extensively on issues surrounding immigration detention and in 2005, with the *Lateline* team, won awards for a program on Vivian Solon, an Australian citizen wrongfully deported to the Philippines.

To my late Dad, who always believed in striving for more.

To Mum, whose strong heart always urges me on.

To my family, Ken, Charlotte and Molly, whose love and support make my life bloom.

BLIND
CONSCIENCE

Margot O'Neill

NEWSOUTH

A New South book

Published by
University of New South Wales Press Ltd
University of New South Wales
Sydney NSW 2052
AUSTRALIA
www.unswpress.com.au

National Library of Australia
Cataloguing-in-Publication entry
Author: O'Neill, Margot.
Title: Blind conscience/Margot O'Neill.
ISBN: 978 086840 853 8 (pbk.)
Subjects: Refugees – Australia – Government policy.
        Refugees – Australia – Social aspects.
        Refugees – Australia – Public opinion.
Dewey Number: 305.9069140994

Some names in this book have been altered to protect the identities of the people involved. 'Mohsen', 'Hassan', 'Toby', 'Anna' and 'Nicholas' are pseudonyms.

Design Josephine Pajor-Markus
Author photograph Hilary Cam

Contents

Acknowledgments

So many people shared their time, and often their tears, to tell the stories in this book. It was always a privilege to hear them. I thank them all.

But there would be no telling any of their stories without the impossibly patient and nurturing Phillipa McGuinness from UNSW Press, whose enthusiasm, advice and well-disguised panic got me through.

Likewise the truly amazing Alanna Hector (née Sherry) who somehow juggled two toddlers and a monster list of fact checking with lightning speed and grace.

Thanks also to Jessica Perini whose steady, deft editing helped wrestle the monster into shape.

And to a bunch of unfortunate friends who agreed to read the manuscript: Bobby Waterman, whose passion for the narrative was so heartening, Paula McNamara, who helped part the clouds on story structure, Rob Bryant, who pointed to the cliff's edge of hyperbole; Kate Legge and Lisa McGregor who helped pull the author through the rough surf of actually starting; and lawyers Kerry Murphy and Nick Poynder and my colleague Brett Evans who offered helpful advice.

Others also went far beyond their interviews to offer support: the indomitable Ngareta Rossell, who first got me thinking about such a book; the inspiring Zachary Steel; the insightful Paris Aristotle; the gracious Highfields; and the ruthlessly efficient Michael Kapel.

But thanks to *everyone* in the book for all the follow-up checking and research that entailed digging into memories, diaries, filing cabinets, books, letters and medical and legal reports for late night emails: Julian Burnside and Kate Durham, Petro Georgiou, Bruce Baird, Judi Moylan, Russell Broadbent, Ian Rintoul, Aamer Sultan, Anne and Gerard Henderson, Louise Newman, Marion Le, Damien Lawson, John Forrest, Pamela Curr, Eric Vadarlis, Michaela Byers, Jacquie Everitt, Jo Szwarc and Dale West.

And to all those who gave me their valuable time and insights along the way: Phil Glendenning, Robert Manne, Margaret Piper, Jeremy and Jane Moore, Paul Boylen, Andrew Bartlett, Kate Gauthier, Maqsood Alshams, Anne Coombs, Richard Bailey, my niece Ariane Welch, Diana Goldrick, Carmen Lawrence, Lisa D'Ambra, Claire O'Connor, Chris Stanton, Diane Gosden and Howard Glenn.

As well as other authors who blazed the trail and whose material and insights were fundamental, like Peter Mares in *Borderline* and David Marr and Marian Wilkinson in their brilliant *Dark Victory*.

Also to Philip Ruddock, for agreeing to be interviewed despite knowing the tenor of the book.

Thanks especially to the ABC's John Cameron and Tim Palmer who allowed me to extend my deadline one or two (or three or four …) times to finish the book before returning to work. To Peter Charley and John Bruce for giving me time off in the first place. And to Tony Jones for his contagious enthusiasm for tackling big projects.

Likewise all the team from UNSW Press: Heather Cam, Nella Soeterboek, Gabriella Sterio and Uthpala Gunethilake. As well as Cathy Solomon for such speedy transcripts. And the immigration department for helping with statistics.

And last but not at all least, my extended family: Mum who told me to 'get on with it!'; my sisters D'arne and Carolyn who helped me talk through moments of doubt; Natalie Hurrell who kept my home going through the clinches; my beautiful kids, Charlotte and Molly, who both put up with take-out dinners (although I think they preferred them!) And my darling husband, Ken Hudson, who saw me through this from the first twinkle of an idea to the very last draft with unswerving devotion and encouragement. (Well, he said he was happy to read it that 99th time!)

In short, we're all very glad it's finally done!
I hope it honours all those who inspired it.

Preface

When I first spoke to refugee advocates, I remember thinking *they must be exaggerating*. Who could believe that Australia locked up children in desert camps? That they were called by numbers instead of names? Or that people, without being convicted of a crime, were put away sometimes for years, even though some were being mentally destroyed?

As a journalist of 25 years standing, who now works on ABC TV's *Lateline* program, I was wary of such dramatic claims by frantic activists. I responded slowly, too slowly. Some other journalists, notably on *Four Corners*, were already investigating the treatment of asylum seekers.

For me, the turning point was listening to Farshid Kheirollahpoor, a smart, articulate and warm-hearted Iranian refugee. As he described vividly the sad sickness he had seen engulfing a two-year-old toddler in Port Hedland, it was if the air around him turned thick and black. I just knew what he was saying was true. We had to break the interview to find some cleaner air.

The same toxic moments washed through a four-hour interview I conducted for *Lateline* with Woomera's longstanding GP, Dr Simon Lockwood, who for the first time poured out all he had seen. We would take breaks and try to chat brightly, but end up staring away. Whatever the government's policy argument or bureaucratic rationale, in those moments we all knew we were talking about deliberate cruelty to powerless people. It leaves you feeling angry and ashamed. Because it was state-sponsored, it also leaves you feeling a little scared.

Not here. Not in 'fair go' Australia.

My journalism was spurred on by the public intervention of Australia's medical profession, initially led by some brave detention centre nurses, as well as the psychologist and researcher Zachary Steel, followed by one of Australia's leading psychiatrists, Dr Louise Newman. Many other medicos also stepped forward to decry what was happening in Australian immigration detention centres to thousands of asylum seekers and their children. I was astonished to see their evidence of systematic psychological damage repeatedly dismissed by the federal government and mental illness labelled 'inappropriate behaviour'.

As I followed the stories of neglect and despair, I got to know some of the thousands of Australians, many of them women who were middle class and middle aged with grown children, who came to dominate a new wave of refugee advocacy. I watched as they upended their lives to focus on helping those held in detention. It was remarkable to me how determinedly mobilised they became, despite having little political experience. It seemed so simple to them. This was a crisis of humanity. It could not be allowed to stand.

But standing up on this issue meant getting stampeded by the herd of public support for the government's policies. These were turbulent and confusing times. Islamist terrorist attacks against the West had prompted fear and loathing. The phenomenon of Pauline Hanson's 'One Nation' party was stealing angry and disaffected voters from Australia's major parties. It stirred together bitterness over economic displacement with anti-immigrant sentiment. When boat people fleeing tyrannical Middle East regimes began arriving, of whom more than 90 percent from Afghanistan and Iraq were refugees, the federal government saw an opportunity to drown out Pauline Hanson once and for all. It turned up the political rhetoric: harsh measures were adopted ostensibly because thousands more were on their way, entire villages were packing up, they might be terrorists, they even throw their own children overboard!

I watched refugee advocates yell out 'No! We can't treat people like this!' At first it was like shouting into a gale. They were marginalised as naïve do-gooders, who didn't understand that Australia needed hard men to guard its borders. Still they argued, protested and lobbied. They abandoned holidays, nice restaurants and weekend rest. They gave their all. Some became obsessed. They lost friends, colleagues, money and sometimes they even lost hope. But they found new friends and new networks and, sometimes, they discovered a new purpose.

In an otherwise tragic story, they inspired me. There have been other books touching on the pain and bravery of some of the refugees who now live alongside us in Australia. I wrote this book to tell at least some of the stories of the Australians who resisted the government's refugee policies. They are a diverse bunch. From the radical activist many people prefer to ignore; to the middle-aged woman many people underestimate; to the psychologist who saw too many broken minds and the trauma rehabilitation specialist who watched a monster unfold inside government; and the successful barrister who took on cases, even though he knew he'd lose.

And the small group of Liberal politicians who fought an epic political battle against one of the country's most successful prime ministers. Together they forced the government to finally curb the worst excesses of the policy. They provide a gripping insiders' account of toe-to-toe political showdowns.

The book is based on the advocates' stories, largely in their own words. They all chose different means of protest, and sometimes strongly disagreed with each other. The interviews proved cathartic for many, prompting emotional moments even for some of the politicians. They offer powerful and confronting testimony about what happened. They also reveal compelling accounts of the refugee underground and desert escapes.

I needed to include an interview with former immigration minister, Philip Ruddock, at the end of the book, because I wanted to know why and how this had all happened. You can judge for yourself whether he provides any new insights. He is always willing to discuss the issues.

There are hundreds more stories of individual advocates from Perth to Brisbane and scores of regional towns in between, which are not told in this book. Like the courageous campaign by Phil Glendenning and the Edmund Rice Centre to track down the people Australia deported back to danger, sometimes with shoddier travel documents than those used by people smugglers. Or the relentless internet advocacy of Jack Smit or the commitment of former Democrats leader and senator, Andrew Bartlett. Or the feisty Woomera Lawyers' Group muscling its way into Woomera, taking the government to court, and never taking a backward step. Or the extraordinary devotion of a pharmacist, Elaine Smith, to those marooned on Nauru. And so many more.

It sounds corny, but the advocates were not campaigning just for the refugees in detention camps, but for all of us who didn't have the time, or the inclination, to fight to ensure that Australia didn't throw its humanity overboard.

Prologue

Petro Georgiou sees a sudden burst of camera lights as his car approaches the arched iron gates. Through the drizzle of a Canberra winter's night the small TV spotlights zigzag, as cameramen jostle to capture one brief shot in what has become a cliffhanger story.

Poor bastards, Petro thinks. *Cold, wet and fast approaching their deadlines.* He doesn't stop; he is focussing on the cliff's edge.

There is little conversation inside the two white, chauffeur-driven government sedans carrying Petro and three of his Liberal Party parliamentary colleagues as they turn into the prime ministerial residence known as the Lodge.

Petro is fairly confident that his three colleagues can hold firm. But he is expecting a rough night.

The prime minister, John Howard, is at the peak of his power. It is June 2005. He has been re-elected for a third time and the Liberal/ National government has won control of both houses of parliament for the first time in more than 20 years. This is a prime minister who can expect gratitude from his backbenchers. Instead he is facing an audacious revolt.

Petro has played out in his mind how the meeting might unfold.

John Howard had been an adroit negotiator in their earlier meetings; attentive, apparently willing to address at least some of their concerns.

But Petro and his gang of three are not asking for minor concessions. They want to overturn one of John Howard's pivotal policies:

the indefinite mandatory detention of all asylum seekers including children. It's a policy that the prime minister has personally fanned as a potent vote-winner over two elections.

Almost 12 000 asylum seekers arrived on Australia's coastal door-step in 152 vessels between 1999 and 2002. The numbers were minis-cule compared to many European, African, Middle Eastern and Asian countries, which see tens or even hundreds of thousands of asylum seekers each year. At the time there were nearly 15 million refugees worldwide marooned in makeshift, overcrowded camps or as a power-less underclass in mostly impoverished countries. The largest number of refugees was from Afghanistan (nearly four million), followed by Burundi (554 000) and Iraq (530 000).

But it was the largest human tide of seaborne asylum seekers in Australian history and John Howard's government warned 10 000 (or maybe more) were on their way. 'Whole [Middle Eastern] villages are packing up … If it was a national emergency several weeks ago, it's gone up something like 10 points on the Richter scale,' says immigra-tion minister, Philip Ruddock.

The government thundered that Australia's historic generosity towards refugees had made it a soft target for a new breed of organ-ised criminals: the people smugglers. Floodgates were opening to the world.

Public alarm was spurred on because the latest wave of boat people was not from the Asia–Pacific region, but from a more distant corner of the globe: the Middle East in particular, Afghanistan and Iraq. After the September 11 terrorist attacks on the World Trade Centre in the United States in 2001, government ministers played up the possibility that Muslim terrorists could be hiding among the boat people: 'it can be a pipeline for terrorists', says defence minister, Peter Reith. Most terror experts laughed at the idea and no boat people were rejected on security grounds by the Australian Security Intelligence Organisa-tion (ASIO) by August 2002. (Many were actually persecuted ethnic minorities like Afghan Hazaras or non-Muslims, like the Sabian Mandaeans, an ancient Gnostic religion pre-dating Judaism, Christi-anity and Islam.)

The fall of governments in Iraq and Afghanistan would eventually stem the flow. In the meantime, with surging public support, the government introduced a range of dramatic interventions including rapidly expanding the number of detention camps in remote desert and island locations (for example, Woomera in South Australia and Christmas Island in the Indian Ocean).

That took care of those already here. Then the government introduced new laws designed to stop asylum seekers from reaching Australia at all by making it a smaller target. In a territorial crash diet in September 2001 and again in July 2005, the government excised more than 4000 islands from Australia's migration zone in a sweeping northern arc from the Pacific to the Indian oceans. Most boat people had landed at faraway outcrops like Ashmore Reef, 840 kilometres west of Darwin. Now they would have to make it all the way to the mainland before triggering Australia's protection obligations towards them.

'Once we had brought people ashore and they were in the migration zone – [Australia's international legal] obligations kick in and – it was game, set, match,' the immigration minister, Philip Ruddock, explained.

Australia is a signatory to the 1951 United Nations' *Convention relating to the Status of Refugees*, which had come into being to provide a more humane international response to those fleeing murderous regimes like Germany's Nazis. Under the convention it is not illegal to seek sanctuary without legitimate travel documents or authorisation.

The most common routes to becoming a recognised refugee in Australia are first, join the so-called overseas 'queue' by making it to either a United Nations' High Commission for Refugees (UNHCR) office or refugee camp, which most refugees don't. Then hope you are selected for resettlement, which most refugees aren't. Each year worldwide less then 0.1 percent of all UNHCR refugees are chosen for resettlement in developed countries, of which Australia takes about 6000. Australia also often extends humanitarian visas to some members of a refugee's family (about 7000 a year). Chances of success by waiting in the queue? Negligible.

Or you can try to make it to Australia yourself.

For most countries, asylum is the only method of refugee resettlement. Worldwide, more than a million people applied for asylum once they managed to reach another country in 2000. In Australia, those found to be refugees were assured of a permanent visa, welfare, work rights and eventually full citizenship. But the deal was proving too attractive, according to the government. There was too much 'pull factor' to Australia. The government was muscling up the 'bugger off' factor.

It downgraded permanent visas for all refugees who arrived without authorisation. These people were now placed on three-year temporary visas with less welfare support, no rights to citizenship, overseas travel or family reunion. It seeded Australia's own refugee underclass.

But still they came. In fact, boats were now teeming with women and children. They were taking their chances on the high seas to try to reach their husbands already in Australia, or to ensure their family would stay together.

So the government sent out the navy.

The idea of turning refugee boats back at sea had been routinely derided by modern-day governments as the extremist rantings of redneck shock jocks. John Howard seemed to recoil at the suggestion of a refugee blockade in early August 2001.

'We are a humanitarian country. We don't turn people back into the sea, we don't turn unseaworthy boats which are likely to capsize and the people on them drown. We can't behave in that manner,' he said during a radio interview.

His reticence was short-lived. With a tough election looming on the horizon perhaps more ominously than refugee boats, Australian sailors were ordered to impede, turn around and tow away any Suspected Illegal Entry Vessel (SIEV) from 3 September 2001. This 'border protection program' was called 'Operation Relex'.

It involved, in words quoted from Australian warship logs, orders to make 'close quarters manoeuvring' or to 'aggressively board' asylum seeker boats.

In one case the Australian warship HMAS *Adelaide* fired three cannon shots and 23 rounds of machine gun fire near one heaving, flimsy vessel carrying 223 men, women and children. In all, Operation Relex would intercept 12 such boats by the end of December 2001, four of which were escorted back to Indonesia. Two women drowned on another boat that sank. Its remaining passengers and crew were rescued by the Australian navy. The occupants of two more boats were also rescued.

In a staggering tragedy in October 2001, more than 350 people including nearly 300 women and children trying to rejoin husbands and fathers, died when their boat, known as SIEV X, sank before reaching the naval blockade.

In the unlikely event that any boat made it through the gauntlet, or was left on places like Ashmore Reef, the coup de grâce was that Australia would take them back across the water for processing on Nauru. This was a remote rocky outcrop in the Pacific Ocean, and a virtually bankrupt state. Another lonely outpost was opened on Papua New Guinea's Manus Island. Forcibly transferring asylum seekers to these off-shore camps became known as the 'Pacific Solution'.

It meant the government overturned decades of providing safe haven within Australia to refugees who made it there. Instead, Australia now defined its protection obligations as not sending asylum seekers back home; at least not until they had been processed somewhere else. And for those found to be refugees, as more than 90 percent of Afghans and Iraqis were, they would be shipped off to a third country. Well, that was the electorally popular rhetoric. In fact, no other government would co-operate (except New Zealand briefly), so most of the refugees ended up back in Australia, living among Australians.

With the flow of refugees into Indonesia easing and with all boats being turned back from Australia, people smugglers struggled to find new clients. The tide of boats soon stopped.

'We shall decide who comes to this country and the circumstances in which they come,' John Howard famously declared.

John Howard had protected Australia. He had won two elections and cowed the Labor Party. So exactly why should he change anything?

Petro Georgiou knew John Howard would not yield on such a popular policy, even though mandatory detention had not been a deterrent. The largest number of asylum seekers had begun arriving seven years after mandatory detention had been first introduced in 1992. Petro knew that the camps weren't just about sending a message to people smugglers. They were a potent political billboard for Australian voters.

Detention camps were the most visible domestic weapon against boat people; big hoops of razor wire glinting in the desert sun. They gave expression to Australian resolve. It was a satisfying response for many voters; boat people triggered a deep anxiety about their island nation being overrun by foreigners. It made the government look like it was in control of these so-called 'illegal' intruders, punishing them, deterring others.

But Petro had an ace up his sleeve, and now might be the time to play it. The first half of 2005 had seen a string of shocking scandals inside detention centres, including nearly 250 cases of wrongful detention. Among them a mentally ill Australian resident Cornelia Rau was detained, and a mentally ill Australian mother, Vivian Solon, was wrongfully deported. The scandals had begun to undermine confidence in how the policy was being managed. Was Australia being necessarily tough? Or had it become unnecessarily cruel?

Petro was fond of exhorting his staff, 'Don't tell me about the first step in a campaign. I want to know the last step!' The endgame was everything.

Regarded as having one of the best tactical minds in politics, the 57-year-old Greek immigrant, with his signature trouser braces and grandfather spectacles, had first earned his ruthless political reputation as a young advisor to the then Liberal Opposition leader, Malcolm Fraser. This was during the controversial dismissal of the Whitlam Labor government in 1975. He later sprang to national prominence as state director of the Liberal Party in Victoria 1989–94, when he was the chief architect of legendary victories with former premier, Jeff Kennett.

Beating the Australian Labor Party is one thing. Tackling your own prime minister and most of your own party is quite another. But Petro's gritty reputation had been well-earned. Even as a six-year-old new arrival with no English, he'd refused to answer his Australian teachers when they decided his name should be 'Peter' not 'Petro'.

He emerged from the backrooms of machine politics to enter the Commonwealth parliament in 1994, in the affluent inner-eastern Melbourne seat of Kooyong. It is a blue-blood Liberal electorate whose members expect to produce national leaders such as their former Liberal Party leaders, Andrew Peacock, and Robert Menzies (Australia's longest serving prime minister). There were some pursed lips about their new member, 'the Greek', especially when he failed to rise through the ranks.

Petro was widely tipped to become a minister when John Howard won government in 1996. But when the call came it was only for the more junior role of parliamentary secretary. Petro turned it down. There would be no more offers from John Howard.

The two had never been close, although they'd known each other since the days of the Fraser government in the 1970s. John Howard as a frustrated treasurer who would later castigate Fraser's leadership, Petro Georgiou as a high-ranking staffer who remained loyal. Petro also worked for John Howard's greatest Liberal Party nemesis, Andrew Peacock, against whom Howard fought four bruising leadership battles.

But their schism is more than just factional. John Howard is a social conservative who dislikes terms such as 'multiculturalism' and who, as Opposition leader, had suggested in 1988 that Australia slow down the rate of Asian immigration.

Petro Georgiou, on the other hand, was at the centre of introducing multicultural institutions like the Special Broadcasting Service (SBS) and went on to chair the Australian Institute of Multicultural Affairs after leaving Malcolm Fraser's office.

Of course if he had become a minister, Petro probably wouldn't be greeting John Howard tonight amid the chocolate-brown leather couches of the Lodge. Ministers don't lead political rebellions, unless they're trying to behead the leader. This was strictly a backbench play.

Petro peers over his glasses at his colleagues as they shake off the Canberra cold near a fire. He knows there will be a price to pay for what they are doing. This prime minister will not allow such a brazen rebellion to go unpunished (no matter how much he talks publicly about the Liberal Party being a broad church). Behind the smiling spin, vendettas will be hatched against them.

Near Petro sits the stylish West Australian former real estate agent with the polished vowels, Judi Moylan. She's been in parliament since 1993 and served as Minister for Family Services and then for the Status of Women in the Howard government before being dumped. Passionate and determined, she'd had her eyes opened to the richness of refugee contributions to Australia as a young girl during Sunday family lunches.

Her father, a railroad supervisor in a West Australian country town, invited many of his 'new Australian' employees home despite community prejudice. 'I guess I learned about their stories. And about how silly were some of the attitudes in town questioning why they couldn't speak English and so on. "They'll never assimilate." That sort of thing. They said the same about the Asians. And now it's the Afghans and the Iraqis.' Judi is the one most likely to lose her cool with the prime minister.

Alongside her is the tall, elegant and affable former New South Wales deputy Liberal leader, Bruce Baird, who oversaw Sydney's successful Olympic bid. He's now in federal parliament representing a relatively conservative electorate, which would be the scene of the Cronulla race riots at the end of 2005. His presence has been a simple matter of conscience since he first visited detention centres in 2000. 'I couldn't believe what I saw. I couldn't believe the despair and the terrible conditions. I'm a practising Christian. This is where the rubber hits the road for me.' But he is a realist and thinks their little group should take the best deal being offered by the prime minister, and stop pushing for more.

And there's the representative from rural Victoria, Russell Broadbent, a former singer in a club band called the True Tones, who went on to become a director of his family's retail company and Pakenham shire president. He is now clinging for dear life to one of the most marginal and volatile seats in parliament. It had changed hands four out of the last five elections. Russell Broadbent has already been elected and defeated twice. He has the most to lose and is the least likely to be here. But by 2005 he can't ignore his conscience, even though John Howard has personally pressured him to abandon Petro's rebellion.

'What are you doing with this chardonnay sipping set?' the prime minister had yelled at him. 'They don't represent the same kind of people as you! Their seats are not like yours!! Why are you here? You don't belong in this group!' It was the only time John Howard shouted, Russell Broadbent says.

Russell says he stepped forward after a constituent who'd become involved with detainees came to see him. 'She sat in my office and told me about two young boys she was trying to help inside detention. She cried and cried. She was not some abusive activist, she was genu-ine. I realised then that the mood for change had spread to my own constituency. I had wanted reform, but I was in the most marginal seat in Victoria. I had to be careful. But that meeting changed my world for me. When Petro rang to ask me to join in and meet with the PM, I was ready.'

Each time they meet, however, Russell Broadbent has to fetch his own chair. A little gesture from the prime minister to remind him he shouldn't be there, he thinks. Russell tends to say the least. But he is still here.

As they join the prime minister for their historic showdown, Petro Georgiou observes wryly that 'quite a lot's been done to the place' since he'd been there with Malcolm Fraser (who'd become one of John Howard's sharpest critics on refugee policy). Petro wants to puncture the prime ministerial grandeur of their surrounds, lest it encourage meekness in his colleagues.

Petro had visited the Lodge many times in the 1970s as a young staffer to Fraser. He'd even attended meetings there about the fate of more than 135 000 Vietnamese refugees to be absorbed into Australia, a couple of thousand of whom had been Australia's first boat people. At the time, the immigration department suggested the federal government build Australia's first detention centres. Prime Minister Fraser dismissed the idea and instead, with the United Nations, helped forge regional agreements to resettle a share of the Vietnamese crowded into camps in Hong Kong, Indonesia, Malaysia and Thailand. The policy worked and the boats stopped coming.

There are no prime ministerial or departmental staff in the room tonight as they sit down over cappuccinos. There's also no immigration minister, Amanda Vanstone, who is sidelined throughout the negotiations. John Howard wants to deal with this rebellion himself. And the prime minister is 'well versed in everything we needed to talk about', says Bruce Baird. As is Petro Georgiou whom the group agree should be the lead negotiator. But that breaks down over the next two and a half hours, as the rebels and the prime minister gnaw at each other's positions with increasing frustration.

The rebels argue that the boats have stopped, the crisis has passed. Now it's time to deal with some of the unintentional consequences of such a harsh and rigid policy. Like the women and children languishing behind the razor wire. The men facing a lifetime of being locked up, even though they've never been convicted of a crime. Not to mention the horrific mental devastation enveloping long-term detainees.

It's easy to imagine how combustible such discussions with a group of rebels would have been under former Labor prime ministers, Bob Hawke or Paul Keating. Language would have flowed purple.

But Bruce Baird says John Howard is always civil, although there are awkward moments when he 'tries to stare you down'.

But the underlying intensity occasionally cracks the polite veneer of the meetings they've held with John Howard.

West Australian MP Judi Moylan has to hold herself in check whenever the prime minister refers to refugees as 'stock'.

'How much stock do we have?' the prime minister asks, in what she assumes is an administrative aside.

Other meetings would see these two clash. On one occasion Judi Moylan abruptly stands ready to walk out because 'it is clear, prime minister, you are not serious about these discussions and that I have wasted my time over the last six months!' The others look to Petro to see if he is also ready to walk out. He sits calmly reading and making notes. The prime minister suggests a short break. The crisis passes. Negotiations resume.

On another occasion Judi Moylan slams down her notes on the table declaring that she is 'sick of being called a political terrorist!' because she disagrees with the government's detention policies. Prime Minister Howard shoots back that he is 'sick of being told I have no compassion!'

At the Lodge tonight, as the meeting drags on without any sign of a breakthrough, John Howard's irritation with the rebels becomes palpable. His twitching impatience grows more pronounced. He makes it plain that he will not dismantle a policy so resoundingly endorsed by the electorate. They should take what is on offer and back off.

Bruce Baird thinks 'Ok, maybe we should.' It would involve time limits on processing refugee applications; significantly better than the open-ended decision-making that prompted many detention riots. But it would not involve overturning the locking up of children or indefinite detention or any regular independent review of detainees. Everyone waits to see what Petro Georgiou will do.

'He was the masterful poker player in these discussions,' says Bruce Baird.

Petro has started this fight knowing the last step. He hasn't been sure if or when he would take it, until tonight. But he realises their efforts have hit the wall. Despite six months of discussions, the prime minister is still offering only incremental reforms and more discussions.

So he will play his ace. It is a trigger that could ultimately split the government on the floor of the parliament. A private member's bill to free all asylum seekers and demolish the system that locks them up.

Petro knows he's unlikely to get the numbers to pass the bill into law. But if it comes to a vote, no one can predict how many Liberals might break ranks to support it. The government won't be rolled, but it will look unstable.

John Howard can't let that happen. He's slogged through the mucky trenches of Liberal Party leadership battles five times. The mantra 'disunity is death in politics' has nearly been his political epitaph. He won't let Petro split the party. And Petro knows that.

'That's it,' Petro says sharply, rising to leave. 'I'm introducing my bill tomorrow.'

'Let's be clear about this Petro,' John Howard replies just as sharply. 'If you do this, you will embarrass your government and you will embarrass your party.'

The intensity and directness of what comes next surprises even Petro's three colleagues.

'I'll tell you what's embarrassing, John,' says Petro. 'Three years ago you agreed to let out a three-month-old baby who'd been born in detention. She's now three years old and she's smashing her head against a wall inside Villawood. That's an embarrassment to the party, John.

'We've got psychiatric patients I went to you about, who should have been released for treatment, but instead that was blocked by the department and now a court has found the government has breached its duty of care to these people. That's what I call an embarrassment to the party.

'And we've got 140 people locked up for three years or more with no convictions and no evidence that they pose a threat to anyone. Let me tell you, John, *that's* an embarrassment! I'm introducing the bill tomorrow.'

John Howard tries to defuse the confrontation. 'Petro let's all back up here a bit.'

But the fuse is lit. John Howard has failed to break the rebellion. But can Petro Georgiou break the system holding refugees and their children in indefinite detention?

By now, thousands of Australians have joined refugee advocacy groups to oppose John Howard's hard line. For many, Petro's push has put the nation's conscience on trial. But it has been a long, lonely and often traumatic journey to this point for many activists. Australia has been locking up refugee families for more than ten years.

CHAPTER 1
One placard

There is no media waiting for Ian Rintoul and his small group as they arrive at the Villawood immigration detention centre. Just four people have managed to find their way to the centre, which is buried in the industrial back streets of Sydney's far flung western suburbs. They have come to be part of one of the first protests outside a detention centre.

Ian Rintoul sucks in his breath. It is November 1999. The mass movement against the detention of refugees and their children is two years away; Petro Georgiou's parliamentary rebellion is six years away.

But it isn't surprising that Ian Rintoul is here so early. He has keen political antennae for dissent. Not the 'Excuse me, Mr Speaker' variety, but the grass-roots, out-in-the-street kind.

A founding member of the International Socialist Organisation (ISO), he reckons he's been arrested up to 60 times in a medley of protests against wars in Vietnam, Yugoslavia and Iraq, as well as confrontations over apartheid, the waterfront dispute and globalisation.

Before the refugee issue, he was darting around the country disrupting what he believed were racist rallies by the independent Queensland MP, Pauline Hanson, also from his hometown of Ipswich. He judged his success by whether she was forced to abandon her speech. It seemed like conspicuous hypocrisy from a man quick to demand free speech for his own unpopular views. He says he had to shut down

Hansonism because migrants, especially Muslims, were being increasingly assaulted. Bullies had to be stopped.

There are those who hold prayer vigils. Ian Rintoul prefers 'direct action' and has spent a lifetime building a fat ASIO file while perfecting the art of street marches, rallies, picket lines and outdoor speeches to highlight often ostracised causes.

Dismissed by politicians and the media as a loony left-wing ratbag, he understands the caricature he cuts. Here is a man in his 50s who still hangs out with university students, counting recruits like an old missionary.

He could even pass for one. Tall, thin and bearded with glasses, he's the personification of the ageing revolutionary, still dreaming of a workers' paradise. Shouldn't he have grown up and got a job?

Many of his baby boomer cohorts are gorging on the fruits of international consumerism and queuing their kids for private schools, while Ian Rintoul is often on the dole scrounging money to help organise the next student picket line.

But that's where political vitality exists, he says. Trade unionists and students tend to embody what he calls the 'radical impulse' necessary to create mass protests and push for change. And when Ian Rintoul talks about change, he isn't talking about legislative reform. The ISO, which he helped co-found in the 1970s, boasted on its website that it wanted to 'smash' the capitalist parliamentary system in Australia. He downplays the possibility of a 'violent overthrow of the government'. But he doesn't rule it out.

He also acknowledges this is 'unlikely to happen in my lifetime'. After all, communism has a bad name after blood-soaked failures just about everywhere in the world. But he is a dogged idealist, who says that only proves it hasn't been done right *yet*. And he has been absolutely certain of this since he was 16 years old.

While many adolescents rate surreptitious alcohol and drugs as life changing experiences, for Ian Rintoul it was a communist anti-Vietnam War leaflet dropped at Ipswich high school when he was in Year 11.

Without the knowledge of his parents, who were not politically active, he took a train to Brisbane to find the headquarters of the then

Communist Party of Australia (CPA). An eager, young Ian Rintoul arrived in the doorway of a tiny, cluttered room above a bookshop to find just one weary activist who waved his wide-eyed passion away. 'Leave your name and address,' he was told.

He never heard from the CPA again. But like a budding actor who'd seen his first play, Ian Rintoul suddenly knew his life's purpose.

So here he is, more than 30 years later, outside Villawood high-lighting another injustice, because it might help more people see that the whole system is rotten.

He and his little group decide to walk up to the detention centre's side gates. They cross an open field dotted with abandoned hostels. This is where previous waves of Italian and Greek immigrants had awaited their transition to a new life.

One section of brown brick bungalows and demountable buildings had been more recently fenced off. A security perimeter is patrolled by guards and topped by barbed wire and cameras. It looks like a makeshift suburban prison; more chicken coop than steel bars. But the message is clear: Villawood's gateway into Australia is now locked.

Few people know or care about the mandatory detention of boat people. Most polls show overwhelming support for even tougher measures.

There is virtually no public debate on the issue with both major political parties in lock-step. They attack the credibility of boat people, while also promoting Australia's generosity to 'real' refugees.

The 'real' refugees are those chosen by the government from overseas camps, they say. There's an excellent resettlement program including welfare, language training, family reunion and psychologi-cal counselling.

But those refugees who turn up uninvited by boat can expect an increasingly punitive response.

There had been a similar panic when the first boat people (not counting the First Fleet) washed up on Australia's vast northern coast-line in the late 1970s after the end of the Vietnam War. One newspa-per warned of an impending 'tide of human flotsam'.

The then federal Australian Labor Party president, Bob Hawke, stated, 'Of course we should have compassion, but people who are coming in this way are not the only people in the world who have rights to our compassion. Any sovereign country has the right to determine how it will exercise its compassion and how it will increase its population.'

Liberal prime minister, Malcolm Fraser defused the crisis. He set up a program that would ultimately absorb nearly 150 000 Indo-Chinese selected from the region's teeming refugee camps over the next decade. It was the biggest intake of Asians ever seen in Australia, and a dramatic demonstration that it had truly shed its White Australia Policy. It was also the largest per capita intake of 'boat people' of any nation on earth.

Malcolm Fraser knew the giant risk involved. The public was skittish and easily stampeded on Asian migration.

But because 'the political parties were united ... Australians accepted the policy as right for the nation,' Fraser has said. In April 1979, then immigration minister Michael MacKellar announced that 'refugees arriving by boat are no longer considered queue jumpers'.

Despite the scale and success of the Vietnamese resettlement program, the Labor government introduced mandatory detention in May 1992. This happened after nearly 450 Cambodian, Vietnamese and Chinese asylum seekers staggered ashore over three years as part of Australia's second wave of boat people.

It was done at least partly because officials feared a major outflow from China, especially following Australia's embrace of more than 25 000 Chinese students and others in 1989.

What a difference leadership makes. Bob Hawke's emotions flowed openly as he offered them the chance to stay in Australia after the Chinese government's massacre in Tiananmen Square of mainly young pro-democracy activists. The students would all ultimately be given permanent residence without a public backlash.

But the welcome mat was withdrawn just two years later when 56 Chinese people landed on the far north coast of West Australia. They somehow survived the desert and mountains of the remote Kimberleys before reaching help. 'They've made Superman look like a Sheila,' said local police Sergeant Michael Harper.

That was the problem as far as government officials were concerned. Fears of a flood of hardy and determined boat people from China were reignited.

Mandatory detention 'puts it all beyond doubt, very clear, that if you come here and want to come to Australia, you'll have to enter in a proper way,' said the then immigration minister, Gerry Hand.

It started off modestly enough. Detention was supposed to be for a maximum of nine months. It was a useful policy plug for nearly 250 inconvenient Cambodians who insisted they were fleeing on-going civil unrest and violence. At the time, Australia had brokered a United Nations sanctioned peace deal in Cambodia. Australian foreign minister, Senator Gareth Evans, was nominated for the 1992 Nobel Peace Prize. The idea of Cambodian refugees was not acceptable, especially since the peace plan included the repatriation of 300 000 Cambodian refugees on the Thai border.

Prime Minister Bob Hawke and Senator Evans were adamant that the Australian orchestrated peace plan was working. The Cambodians should all go home. Bob Hawke declared they were economic refugees and wouldn't be allowed to 'jump the queue' of Australia's orderly migration program. 'Bob is not your uncle ... People just can't pull up stumps, get in a boat and lob in Australia ... that's not on,' he said.

To help motivate the Cambodians to go home, the Labor government modified a disused working camp to create the first remote detention centre in Port Hedland, in Western Australia. A small iron ore mining town surrounded by red desert, Port Hedland's temperatures in summer can reach more than 45 degrees. In its first year nearly 300 people were held there, the majority Cambodians.

The whole system almost fell apart early when the Federal Court found the detention of some of the asylum seekers was illegal, because it exceeded nine months. The Labor government responded quickly by passing laws to get rid of the time limit. Although few advocates realised it at the time, the government now had the power to lock up boat people forever; a power subsequently confirmed in 2004 by the High Court.

Australia's unique system of indefinite, non-reviewable mandatory detention of all boat people, including children, was born. It would reach full maturity under John Howard's Coalition, which swept to power in 1996.

One of the earliest opponents of the detention regime's effects on children, refugee advocate and migration agent, Marion Le, says there was little public outcry at the time.

'I remember in 1994 I gave a speech at the National Press Club after I'd won a refugee advocacy award,' says Marion Le. 'I did like a 20 minute outraged outpouring about what was going in Port Hedland with the Chinese and Cambodians. It was living hell then as well, and there were so many, many children and babies. I made a plea for one little Cambodian girl I'd met in Port Hedland named Dina to go free. I said "Let Dina go free!" and the media picked it up. Philip Ruddock was there and he was really on side in those days when he was in Opposition. He congratulated me on the award and on my speech. The media rang the next day to say Dina was freed. But for so long I felt like a lone voice.'

When the third and biggest wave of boat people broke on Australian shores after 1998, the Howard government enthusiastically expanded Labor's architecture adding new desert and island camps. Dedicated immigration detention centres already existed in Sydney (Villawood) and Melbourne (Maribyrnong) as well as at Port Hedland and Perth airport. Now the government would recommission a detention facility at Curtin on the vast military base outside Derby in West Australia, and open new camps at Woomera, on the former rocket testing range in outback South Australia, Cocos (Keeling) Islands and Christmas Island northwest of the Western Australian coast, and Baxter, outside Port Augusta in South Australia. They also drastically curtailed the rights of refugees by introducing temporary protection visas and reducing access to health and welfare support.

Public enthusiasm for such dramatic measures was fuelled by abusive language towards asylum seekers by both major parties. Even before clambering off their rickety boats they were deemed undeserving queue jumpers, illegals, designer label refugees, economic opportunists, rich, accomplices in organised crime and manipulative liars. Sometimes the rhetoric sounded petty.

PHILIP RUDDOCK: We've even had them putting orders to us. I think one group asked for Pert two-in-one shampoo. They have high expectations.

PHILIP: It's amazing, isn't it, that we're dealing with a group of people who seem to have in large part access to mobile phones which many would see as a luxury within the context of Australia. Many pensioners would perhaps like to be able to afford to buy a mobile phone.

Calls for greater empathy for those fleeing monstrous regimes like the Taliban in Afghanistan and Saddam Hussein's Iraq were slapped down by the strong men now guarding Australia's borders. Public dissent was consigned to the margins. That's a space Ian Rintoul knows well.

The group holds aloft one placard reading 'Free The Refugees'. Suddenly the gates open and a dozen guards march out to form a human barrier.

'Get back,' they warn the protesters. 'This is Commonwealth property.'

Security at immigration detention centres had been privatised in 1997 and the service provision contracted out to Australasian Correctional Management (ACM). This was a subsidiary of the giant American security conglomerate, Wackenhut.

At the time, Wackenhut was moving into the management of US private prisons. This was a market it would later abandon following a series of controversies involving prisoner abuse and neglect.

George Wackenhut, the company's founding father and a former FBI agent, had welcomed Australia's tough new immigration policies saying that Australia is 'really starting to punish people as they should have all along'.

ACM also had prison contracts in New South Wales, Victoria and Queensland since 1991. What it knew best was how to maintain discipline for adult male prisoners who understood the rules of incarceration, including when they would get out. The company had little expertise in how to deal with traumatised asylum seekers and their children who often had little or no English and no idea if they would get out at all.

Former ACM operations manager at Woomera from early 2000 to July 2001, Allan Clifton, says many ACM guards were hired straight off long-term dole queues and given just four weeks of training. This mainly focussed on physical restraint and control.

'They were totally unsuited for the work they would have to do. They had no real maturity, no work experience, not enough life experience,' Allan Clifton, an ex-prison guard from both public and private prisons in Victoria, has said. Many of the new, young guards would often declare angrily that detainees didn't show them enough respect.

At Woomera some guards would sing to rejected asylum seekers, 'Leavin' on a jet plane, Goin' back to see Saddam Hussein.' Or deride them as 'sand niggers' and 'dune coons'.

The federal government also gave priority to security over welfare in its contract with ACM. Even though it repeatedly stressed that immigration detention was not a punishment, but an administrative measure not comparable to imprisonment.

Yet while the immigration department imposed clear penalties for security breaches such as riots and escapes, there were no similar penalties if ACM breached a detainee's medical, legal or welfare needs. It was a recipe for perpetual discontent among a fearful and disoriented population. And it was dealt with by an improperly trained and authoritarian staff.

Detainees were given numbers instead of names. There were musters four times a day, including checks on detainees in the middle of the night. At one detention centre a single mother had to stand in line outside the medical centre, even in the rain, while holding a febrile child to obtain one dose of Panadol. ACM had ruled that no medicine could be taken back to a detainee's room. No exceptions. Women also had to queue to ask often male guards for sanitary napkins.

Pressures inside the camps were mounting as the number of detainees soared around the country from less than 3000 in June 1998 to more than 8000 by June 2000.

By the time Ian Rintoul arrives at Villawood's gates there have already been some incidents. These included violent outbursts by disturbed individuals, as well as the beginnings of more organised protests such as hunger strikes and passive resistance. ACM responded forcefully from the start. It would transfer some hunger strikers from Villawood to isolation cells in the remote Port Hedland detention centre. And at Woomera, ACM would unleash tear gas and water cannon during protests that also involved children. It was the first time a water cannon had been used in Australia. This was despite the potential for serious injury like shearing off skin.

Stories leaking out about protests and ACM's brutal response have drawn Ian to Villawood. He and others have been in telephone contact with some of the detainees. He wants to try to talk to them through the wire fences and let them see they have Australian supporters. Surely the public will respond if they hear first-hand accounts of inhumane treatment.

What Ian Rintoul doesn't know that morning as he sees Villawood's fences for the first time, is how, like Petro Georgiou, the refugee issue is about to transform his political life. It will not be just another entry on his protest menu. It will become virtually his sole campaigning focus. Eventually it will wrench him away from his beloved party, the International Socialist Organisation, after 27 years, and shatter lifelong comradeships.

But for now he does what he knows best. He remonstrates with the guards. 'We just want to talk to some of the refugees. We have the right to show them support.'

The guards hold the line. Ian shouts out to the detainees: 'WE KNOW WHAT'S BEEN GOING ON INSIDE AND WE SUPPORT YOU!'

Bewildered detainees stare back at him.

'WE WANT YOU TO BE FREE!' he yells. 'WE PROMISE TO TELL THE REST OF AUSTRALIA ABOUT THIS!'

There's a stand-off for 45 minutes before police arrive. Ian Rintoul decides the first protest outside Villawood has come to an end. He also knows it will not be the last. He will come back with more people and more placards. And translators. Next time, they will not be so easily pushed away.

But as he and his little group retreat to their cars, Ian wonders whether the refugee issue can ever attract the same energy and numbers as the anti-Hanson rallies. *We have to find a way to break through to a wider audience*, he thinks. *We have to get out of the margins.*

◎

Trish Highfield is at home on Sydney's middle-class northern beaches when she puts on the evening news. Staring at her, through wire are tiny children, in the Australian desert.

She stares hard in disbelief. The hot air shimmers around their little faces as they cling to fencing in the Port Hedland immigration detention camp. It is 1998.

The last time she'd seen anything similar was when the gaunt, haunted faces of young Bosnian men stared out from behind wire-fenced camps guarded by the Serbian military. But these pictures are of children in Australia.

She turns to her husband, a veteran ABC radio broadcaster, John Highfield. Does he know that children are locked up like this? How many are there? And why is it in such a harsh, remote place? He doesn't know.

As a trained childcare worker, Trish Highfield knows this kind of treatment can devastate children. *The government must know too*, she thinks. The past decade have seen a flood of revelations about the life-long trauma caused by child abuse and family upheaval.

Her local Catholic Social Justice group had attended support meetings for Aboriginal groups trying to overcome the effects of the Stolen Generation. (So-called because children had been systemati-cally taken by the government from their Aboriginal parents.) Trish had sat stricken while listening to stories about families torn apart and children's lives broken. *But now we know better*, she thinks.

She contacts Father Walter McNamara, the parish priest in Port Hedland. She has questions about how the government is catering for the children. He cuts her off bluntly. The immigration detention centre 'is a gulag', he tells her. 'There are human rights abuses here. What are *you* going to do about it?'

Do? What can she do? Surely there are established refugee and child support groups already 'doing' something?

Trish had travelled widely to support her husband's international reporting career. Three times she was based in London while John Highfield covered stories across Europe and the Middle East for the ABC. These included the civil war in Northern Ireland and Israel's invasion of Lebanon.

But while it meant long hours and constant travel for him, Trish focussed her energies on raising their son, maintaining a home and where possible, volunteering to help homeless youths or disadvantaged families with young children.

She is not a front-line campaigner. Or a trail-blazer. But in Australia she is a member of her local Catholic Social Justice group. She also regularly attends meetings for the Social Justice in Early Childhood Group, which campaigns for disadvantaged families. She is a dedicated if low-key participant, describing herself as shy and lacking confidence in public. But Trish Highfield is steely determined when it comes to children's welfare.

With Father McNamara's words etched on her conscience, and with the endorsement of the Social Justice in Early Childhood Group behind her, Trish contacts various groups over the next 12 months to find out who is advocating for children in detention. To her astonishment no one has specific information about them.

At the time refugees dominate the news (although that is not what they are called). They are instead referred to as part of an armada of illegal immigrants gathering on the northern horizon. No one mentions children. So she writes to the immigration minister, Philip Ruddock, with a list of questions about children in detention. She receives a surprisingly earnest reply from Senator Kay Patterson, parliamentary secretary to the minister, in April 1999.

'Let me assure you,' the letter states, 'that the government is as concerned as you that children held in immigration detention are appropriately cared for.'

There are 64 children in detention, including one child without any family, Senator Patterson says.

'Specific arrangements are put in place to ensure their special needs are appropriately catered for. Children in all centres have access to a range of services including educational facilities and health and welfare services. They are encouraged to participate in a variety of physical and cultural activities to ensure that their developmental needs are appropriately met.

'… Educational programs include pre-school and school curriculum-based programs which focus on English as a second language …'

Senior officials review cases each fortnight, particularly those involving children.

'I can assure you that all efforts are made to ensure detention of children is a last resort and for the shortest possible period … The emphasis is on sensitive treatment of the detainee population …'

Trish Highfield is somewhat relieved. At least the government seems to understand that it needs to provide specialist medical, recreational and educational support. After all, this isn't Bosnia.

But the footage of those small, sad faces behind the detention wire stay with her.

◎

Jump to 2000. Australia is ablaze with gold-medalled images of national pride as Sydney's Olympic Games get underway. A small army of nearly 50 000 volunteers have been assembled to smooth the way for half a million ticket holders. Their unfailing good humour is to be one of the outstanding successes of the Games.

But it is all 'bah, humbug!' for Ian Rintoul. He sees the Olympics as a generally revolting celebration of Australia's smug mythology of egalitarianism. He spends his time trying to muster enough volunteers to help prick the national euphoria.

The day before the Opening Ceremony, Sydney pulses with anticipation and excitement. While the Olympic torch is cheered by thousands down the main street of the inner-western suburb of Newtown, Ian and about 25 stalwarts chant anti-racist and anti-government slogans.

'Stop wasting our money! What about our schools and hospitals?

Free the refugees!'

'Bugger off!' is a common reaction.

Just like any thick-skinned politician on the hustings, Ian Rintoul is unflappable. 'I find that engaging with angry people by putting the political argument is usually disarming. I say "You can rip my placard off me but it won't change the fact that the government is spending millions of dollars on things like this rather than health and education."'

It has been 12 months since his first visit to Villawood and still he is frustrated in his efforts to generate greater support. He's helped form a new group, the Refugee Action Collective (later Coalition) known as RAC, and has doorknocked the usual suspects in trade unions and student groups to boost numbers at rallies.

Traditional advocates like the Refugee Council of Australia are too constrained. 'The Refugee Council was very concerned with its role as a policy advisor to the government, so it was very cautious, very, very cautious about saying anything at all. They wouldn't do anything publicly with us. They wouldn't support our statements or our protests. We were on our own.'

Approaches to many ethnic community groups are also rebuffed. 'They didn't want to know about us,' he says. 'They didn't want to upset their contacts with the immigration department, because some of their members were waiting to hear about applications for family members to come to Australia.'

There is one powerful, albeit brief, exception. The chairman of the New South Wales Ethnic Communities Council, an Italian business-man Salvatore Scevola, addresses several RAC rallies despite opposi-tion from within his organisation. He is sacked within a year.

'They didn't want to rock the boat,' Salvatore Scevola says. 'Our core funding came from the state and federal governments. Philip Ruddock threatened to withdraw funding unless I shut up.'

He claims the threat was made directly by Mr Ruddock at an offi-cial function. This was after Scevola criticised the government's poli-cies in the newspaper of the peak national ethnic body, the Federation of Ethnic Community Councils of Australia (FECCA).

'Ruddock was really frothing at the mouth saying we carried these articles about refugees and about what the Australian Democrats were doing, but not the message from the minister. He said he would have to reassess funding for FECCA if it couldn't be more balanced.

'I remember we were standing with the French and Egyptian consuls. I said I hadn't realised I was living in a fascist state where we had to only say what the government wanted. And both the consuls quickly excused themselves from the conversation.'

Salvatore Scevola is removed as chairman in December 2001 for allegedly working against the interests of the organisation. He had publicly criticised the organisation for rejecting membership applications from some Muslim groups. He believes his removal was payback for attacking the government's refugee policies. He's now studying for the priesthood.

'It was an appalling experience,' says Salvatore Scevola. 'I felt like an isolated voice. But someone has to speak up for these poor people.'

The Refugee Council of Australia is also put on notice by the immigration minister, Philip Ruddock, after its president, Margaret Piper, criticises the government's policy of mandatory detention, following a riot in Woomera in 2000.

The riots, Margaret Piper says, were 'symptomatic of a policy that is causing enormous suffering to the people who are being detained and is forcing them into a situation where they feel they need to take desperate steps to make people aware of their situation'.

Philip Ruddock responds angrily in parliament. 'Some people have attempted to justify what has happened here ... The one organisation that should know far better than most, because it is funded to have expertise in these matters, is the Refugee Council of Australia ... If any organisation, no matter how worthy they are, knowingly misrepresents the situation, that is to be addressed and I will continue to address it.'

The message for all advocacy groups is clear: work with the government, not against it. While the government can up the ante against asylum seekers with increasingly harsh policies, advocates are expected to continue to respond through the same time-consuming back channels.

Not so Ian Rintoul's Refugee Action Collective (RAC). It continues to roll out a steady if lonely diet of sit-ins, pickets, rallies and press releases. A picket outside immigration minister Philip Ruddock's office draws five people; a sit-in at the foyer of the Refugee Review Tribunal (RRT) is more successful with about 30 students.

'I find that these actions are always worth it because there's people who hate what's happening, but think they're the only ones until they see us, even if there's only a few of us handing out leaflets. But yeah, I was wondering whether this thing was ever going to take off.'

Then in 2000, the pressure cooker inside detention centres blows. For the first time there are mass organised protests by detainees including hunger strikes and break-outs.

More than 700 boat people at three remote detention centres stage walk-outs, including 500 from Woomera, who sit-in at the nearby township.

'We could erect around detention centres the sorts of protective screens that they had in Hong Kong, palisade fences,' says Philip Ruddock. 'You could make a detention facility which is essentially for administrative detention for unlawful arrivals into a high security gaol ... we determined not to do that.'

Within a year Philip Ruddock orders the erection of palisade fences and razor wire.

The Australian public gets its first sense of the bizarre nature of remote detention centres when several nurses from Woomera claim that ACM has failed to properly investigate concerns that a young boy is being abused. It sparks a media sensation. While no evidence of sexual abuse is found, there is evidence that some officials concealed a file about the allegations. The nurses break their ACM contracts, which forbid any public comment to lambast conditions inside Woomera.

'There was intimidation – there was intimidation to the nurse on duty that night because she had already written an incident report which stated, and fair enough too, that it was alleged that the boy had been anally raped. She was made to tear up that report,' says Marie Quinn, a Woomera nurse at the time.

Ian Rintoul finally senses a groundswell of interest. He is increasingly quoted in the media about what he says is happening inside detention centres based on telephone conversations with some inmates. As another rally approaches, this time outside the immigration office in Parramatta, he is confident RAC will finally attract more than the usual two dozen protestors.

◎

It is a sticky, hot Saturday when Trish Highfield catches a bus and a train for over two hours to get from Sydney's north to its western hub at Parramatta. Most people are at home watching Kieren Perkins finish a brave second in the 1500 metres swimming race. *What am I doing?* she thinks as the journey stretches out into the thickening heat. *Here I am heading off to a rally probably full of radicals, some of whom might become violent!* The only rally she'd ever been to before was with a couple of Catholic nuns. They held a prayer vigil and lit candles for the East Timorese.

After hearing about the RAC rally, Trish had decided to go to Parramatta in the hope of finding someone who would have more information about children in detention.

As her train pulls in she can see mainly young protestors gathering near the Parramatta railway station with banners proclaiming the International Socialist Organisation. Riot police are gathering as well.

Trish nervously approaches one of the organisers who directs her to a middle-aged lawyer named Heather who has clients inside Villawood. Heather instantly understands what Trish is trying to find out. Finally someone who can help.

Just a week ago, she tells Trish, she was at Villawood when two Yemeni asylum seekers tried to escape over the barbed wire, but became ensnared in its claws.

'They were cut to ribbons in front of everyone, including children. There was blood everywhere. The guards were telling them to hold still, to stop moving and making it worse. They took them on stretchers to an ambulance.

'Look, even the guards are upset by what's happening to these people. You must do whatever you can.'

'I know. I'm just not sure what,' Trish says.

'You should go to Villawood.'

Trish had not realised this was even possible. But Heather explains that you can go as a visitor if you have the name of someone inside. She offers to find a parent for Trish to visit. Trish can ring them and set it up.

'I'm not going back,' Heather says. 'This has been just awful. I've taken a job overseas.' In later years, Trish Highfield would understand that kind of burn out.

The squeal of megaphones signals that the protest march is getting underway. Ian Rintoul is encouraged that 100 people have turned up. After all, Kieren Perkins is swimming his way into history on TV. They begin marching to the offices of the immigration department.

'FREE THE REFUGEES! LOCK UP PHILIP RUDDOCK!'

Trish locks eyes with a police camera filming the march. She feels awkward and anxious. She looks around in vain for Heather. Little does she know that she will never see the lawyer again. She walks a few blocks then quietly peels off and heads back to the station.

The following Friday Trish is sitting by her phone holding a scrap of paper with the telephone number of Villawood immigration detention centre stage two and a detainee's name: Mr Heman Baban. Baban is a 22-year-old Iraqi Kurd, a single father with a three-year-old son. She hadn't realised you could just ring detainees. She takes a deep breath.

'Mr Baban? My name is Trish Highfield. A lawyer, Heather, gave me your name. I'm an early childhood professional.'

'Yes, Trish, how are you?' He sounds clear, polite. Good English.

'Thank you, I'm well. I'm wondering about the conditions in Villawood for children. For instance, is there any shade cloth in their play area?'

'Cloth?'

'Yes, shade cloth to protect them from the sun. And soft fall under the play equipment to protect them if they fall? I'm trying to understand what the children have there.'

There's a pause.

'My child has been locked in solitary cell with me. He was not allowed out to play, only to toilet twice a day. He had to urinate on some clothes in a corner. We were in Port Hedland.'

The faces of Port Hedland's caged children come flooding back to Trish.

'Mr Baban are you saying your child was locked in solitary confinement? I don't understand. Why would anyone do that?'

'I do not mean to upset you. But this is what happened. We were having protest, hunger strike, in Villawood. The guards came in the night with handcuffs. They tried to put my son in handcuffs. They took us on a plane for a long time. We were put in small room in Port Hedland. We had no food or drink until the next day. I was locked up with my son for 13 days. This is what happened.'

Trish Highfield ends the conversation in a daze. She has made no arrangement to visit him in Villawood. She doesn't know if she can believe this man. She is troubled by his admission that he was on a hunger strike while he had sole responsibility for a young child. As disbelief and alarm tumble in her head, she dials the office of the immigration minister.

A ministerial staffer listens patiently. 'You shouldn't get involved with these people,' Trish is cautioned. 'They often try to manipulate you if their cases have failed.' But the staffer promises to raise the allegations with the minister and to call Trish back next week.

That weekend Olympic marathon runners pound their way around Sydney's picturesque beach suburbs as the city prepares to farewell the Games. Sunday night's final embrace of the world's athletes at the Closing Ceremony is designed to reinforce Olympic principles of 'mutual understanding with a spirit of friendship, solidarity and fair play'. The city is aglow with goodwill.

Trish Highfield can't sleep. By Sunday morning, she knows she has to go to Villawood to meet Mr Baban. She rushes to the beach to collect sea shells and coloured glass, which she puts in a bag with some limes and children's books and other knick-knacks.

With so many trains diverted to the Olympics, it takes three hours before she finally arrives in the deserted streets of Sydney's far west. Within minutes, she is hopelessly lost. Villawood's visiting hours are about to end. In desperation, she flags down a car to ask directions.

There are some extraordinary coincidences in her refugee work that Trish Highfield says propelled her on. Like the large German woman who is driving the car that stops to pick her up this very day.

Not only does the woman know the Villawood detention centre, she had once lived in the hostels as a new migrant, and then worked there as a cook. She insists on driving Trish to the entrance. 'It's a different place now,' she says, becoming teary as she speaks of the difficulties faced by children. 'It's terrible. I hope you can do something. Please, do whatever you can.' Trish waves goodbye and turns to see the detention centre for the first time.

Cages. Lots of farmyard cages. A white utility truck moves slowly around the perimeter towards her. The guard driving stares at her from behind sunglasses. She signs in at the main entrance; her name, address, occupation, who she is here to see. Through one cage. Her bag is searched. 'Oh that's nice,' says a guard. 'You've brought something for that little boy. He needs something nice.' Through another cage and into a bigger cage containing a small, dusty, hot yard with plastic chairs, a rusted swing and a broken climbing frame. So much for shade cloth.

A guard unlocks a gate from a residential compound to let Heman Baban and his son through. Trish's trained eye assesses the child immediately. He is pale and stressed, and clinging to his young, anxious father. She opens her bag of gifts. Mr Baban takes the limes, a favourite Middle Eastern food, and consumes the aroma over and over. 'Thank you, thank you,' he says. 'This is the first time anyone has given me a gift in a long, long time.'

She takes out a book about animals to read to his little boy, Bawan. Trish has a special interest in children's literature and story telling. But as she points to animal pictures and tries to entertain him with animal noises, she realises the child has no idea what they are. The only picture he seems to comprehend is of a kitten.

'We've been in here since he was one,' Heman says. 'He's never seen animals. A guard sneaked in a kitten for him to play with one day. He loved it. That was a good day.'

Bawan points at the picture of a kitten and smiles. Trish pulls out the sea shells and coloured glass to distract him while she asks his father to tell her again about what happened in Port Hedland.

Heman retells the story with great detail and intensity. He begins to hyperventilate while describing how the guards dragged him by the hair and then grabbed his son who'd become hysterical. And then slumped and exhausted, he describes how he and Bawan are left in a small, locked room for 13 days.

'How did you try to protect your child in that room?' Trish asks.

'I just talked to him, talked to him, talked to him. I take him to another place with my words.'

Trish stays for 45 minutes playing, soothing and smiling with Bawan who enjoys exploring everything inside her gift bag.

As she gets up to leave, he reaches out to her. 'Me go too? Me go?' He wants he and his Dad to go out the locked gate as well.

'I'm sorry. I'll come back again. I'll come back to see you soon,' she says.

Heman picks up his little boy to watch Trish go out through the cages and reappear outside the perimeter fence. As she heads towards the road leading back to the train station they walk alongside her on the inside of the fence. 'I'll be back. I can't promise anything. But I will be back and I will try to do something about this,' she says to Heman. She blows kisses to little Bawan who waves shyly. Once the young father and his son are out of sight Trish breaks down.

'I knew he was telling the truth. I knew it. It was horrifying to me.'

That night Sydney farewells its Olympic love affair with music and fireworks. Athletes and visitors from around the world hug each other goodbye. A new song has been written for the event, proclaiming the common humanity of all. 'We are one! We are one!' the chorus declares.

The ministerial staffer calls Trish as promised. 'I've investigated what you told me, Trish, and I'm sorry to say I've found that this Mr Baban is a bit of a dodgy character so you should leave him alone. He's not eligible to be considered as a refugee. He has the right to appeal but he's going to be knocked back.'

'Oh?'

'What you should know, Trish, is that he's been an agitator in Villawood and when he went on a hunger strike he wasn't feeding his own child. When they were in Port Hedland the children were allowed into the hall and outside. They were given toys and books as well. But Mr Baban refused to co-operate. He urinated on a guard's head. He chose to not let his child out of that room. You shouldn't take on individual cases like this. The government has the proper resources to deal with these people.'

None of this jibes with Mr Baban's account. Trish asks whether the child can receive counselling and some respite from detention such as attending pre-school. She also questions whether locking up any child is appropriate.

'Well why didn't he leave the child with his mother instead of bringing him to Australia?' the staffer snaps.

Trish considers the logic of hurting a child because of parental action. Then she snaps.

'I think I should tell you that since we last spoke I've been out to Villawood and met Mr Baban and his child and I observed good interactions between them. I saw good parenting skills. I also should tell you that the guards who spoke to me showed no antipathy towards Mr Baban. I found him to be a polite, educated man and I have to say that I believe his story. So you need to know this: from this day on I will be making as many people aware of what is happening to children in detention as it is in my power to reach. I will not stop until something is done!'

Trish puts down the phone. Her life will never be the same again. She isn't sure how she is going to do it, but she knows she is about to become a campaigner, a trail-blazer if that's what it takes. She has to find a way to show people what is really happening to these children and their families. If only she had proof.

CHAPTER 2

Proof

It's not often a devoted research scientist finds himself in a hot, crowded, inner-city bar bursting with emotion, alcohol and politics. Well, not clinical research psychologist, Zachary Steel.

The angular, softly-spoken academic has left his toddler and a pile of statistics he needs to analyse at home, more than an hour away, to be here at a left-wing salon known as 'Politics in the Pub'.

More blood sport than debate club, speakers are invited to address a single topic followed by questions at an open microphone. At least, that's the version given to rookie participants. One regular speaker compares the open microphone session to 'wrestling with snakes. It's conspiracy theories at 40 paces among the hard core. And no matter what the issue, it's always the fault of the conservatives!!'

Zachary looks around the upstairs bar of the Gaelic Club that hosts 'Politics in the Pub' in Sydney's Surry Hills. It is a ragtag group of 100 or so mainly older academics, writers and activists, with wardrobes and ideological agendas that need urgent updating. *Tonight at least, they'll hear something new*, he thinks.

As one of Australia's key researchers into refugee mental health issues, Zachary Steel is quantifying what he believes is a psychiatric catastrophe inside Australia's burgeoning detention camps. His appeals through government channels have been ignored.

So now, in February 2001, he has decided to campaign publicly about his research to try to change what he believes is dangerous government policy.

It is unchartered territory for Zachary, who is more comfortable entering a pile of statistics into a computer model than downloading in a pub.

'You know why I took the [research] job?' Zachary recalls. 'Because they were doing some structural equation modelling and I like statistics. I wasn't interested in politics at all.'

Zachary's outstanding abilities as a researcher make him a sought-after commodity, and his work is widely published. But it is also a deeply personal quest. He's managed to survive a turbulent youth, which left him homeless and alone as a teenager. He'd found his way to Sydney's City Mission where he'd finished high school and went on to university. Other youths, his friends at the shelter, weren't so lucky. Most of them are now in gaol or dead.

Zachary had been drawn to psychology and statistical research, where he'd found at least some clarity in the science of quantifying social behaviour.

Now he is ready to throw himself into the mayhem of the Gaelic Club. He walks up to the microphone.

'I don't know that anywhere else has ever recorded the kind of astronomically high rates of mental illness that we seem to be seeing inside these immigration detention centres. At least not in peacetime in a western country. I think it's directly related to the policy of mandatory detention itself, and to the authoritarian conditions inside the camps. I think Australia is systematically, and in some cases, irreparably damaging some of the most vulnerable people in the world. But we need to do more research. Let me take you through what we know so far.'

By the time he sits down 20 minutes later, he's detailed the calamity emerging behind the razor wire. He is excited to see a long line queue up for the open session.

'Comrades!' the first respondent begins. 'The workers must unite against the racist fascist government of John Howard!'

'This is another example of the architecture of the fascist state!'

The speakers get progressively louder.

'WE MUST RESIST THESE BOURGEOIS RACIST ATTACKS
TO DIVIDE THE WORKERS!'

And on and on it goes. Yelling at the conservative prime minister,
John Howard, at the bourgeoisie, sometimes even at each other.

Zachary sits in bewilderment. 'There was this real disconnect
between what I said and then their slogans, which seemed to be something they'd been saying for 20 years. You know, like this was just
another evil example of the system they'd been fighting forever. And
they worked themselves up into such a rage. It was bizarre. All I could
think was, "What *are* you all talking about?"'

Here is a group that Zachary Steel had assumed would get the
message and help fire activism against indisputably harmful government policies. If they don't get it, what hope is there? It has been hard
enough just getting the research done!

That night he catches a glimmer of the entrenched mindsets which
will block the eyes and ears of Australians for years to come. Politics
in the Pub, it turns out, is just like most Australian lounge rooms. For
many on the left, refugees are an issue, but only insofar as they are
useful to attack the conservative government. For many on the right,
they represent a threat to social harmony and highlight the urgent
need for greater border protection. To successive governments, they
are easy targets to stampede voters. There is no sense of their individual welfare. Absolutely none.

Zachary Steel remembers his own awakening to the issue.

'It didn't engage me at first, and then slowly the evidence spoke to
me. I was as blind as the rest of us, but slowly I was aware something's
not fitting here and over time, it came to me.'

He began work in 1992 as a clinical research psychologist with
the Psychiatric Research and Teaching Unit at the University of New
South Wales. It was the same year mandatory detention was formal-
ised. At first, his research focus was solely helping those 8000–10 000
asylum seekers who had come to Australia with valid visas, and were
left in the community while their claims were processed.

At any one time Zachary Steel and the team could be running up to
25 research projects aimed at fine-tuning Australia's ability to absorb

and support these often traumatised asylum seekers. The team's clinical work was done through the New South Wales government's South Western Sydney Area Health Service.

'So I was quite upset even then about the way these asylum seekers who were living in the community were being treated. Little did I know they would be the lucky ones,' says Zachary Steel referring to the far worse fate awaiting asylum seekers who came by boat without valid visas and who were locked up.

Meanwhile those refugees selected from overseas camps by the government and formally resettled in Australia, the ones described by the government as 'real refugees', were not only given welfare support, but the programs available to help heal their often horrifying mental scars were among the best in the world. There were specialist torture and trauma centres in most capital cities.

In 1994 a colleague called Zachary about the state of asylum seekers being held in detention camps. Only then did Zachary realise Australia's policies also ranked among the worst in the world.

It was as if Australia had a split personality between how it treated those refugees selected from overseas camps and those who had made a run for it. For those who sought asylum in Australia, rather than waiting in vain for a government to choose them from an overseas camp, and that was only if they'd managed to make it to one, there were no programs to help or heal. Just months and sometimes years inside overwrought and overcrowded camps laced with razor wire. Even though most would eventually be found to be genuine refugees.

In fact, boat people had a higher rate of acceptance as refugees in Australia than those arriving with valid visas. For instance, between 1 July 1999 and 30 June 2003, 3125 asylum-seeking children arrived in Australia *with* a valid visa, and therefore were *not detained* on arrival. Only 25.4 percent of them were found to be refugees. In the same period, 2184 children arrived in Australia *without* a valid visa and applied for asylum. All these children were detained in immigration detention centres and an average of 92.8 percent of them were eventually recognised as refugees. Of the two biggest groups,

97.6 percent of the Iraqis and 95 percent of the Afghans, were found to be refugees.

Professor Patrick McGorry, an eminent psychiatrist from Melbourne University, was a world leader in the treatment of early psychosis. He told Zachary that he was astonished by the high levels of mental illness among the detainees he was treating inside Maribyrnong. It was more than the usual trauma associated with other refugees. There needed to be a proper study.

Pat McGorry sent Zachary early notes describing how the detainees were mainly Tamils who'd escaped Sri Lanka's savage civil war, only to fly headlong into Australia's mandatory detention net.

Zachary was transfixed by the material. This was an entirely new area of research in Australia; the sort that jump-starts an academic's adrenalin. It would be the first look inside the effects of a relatively new policy of mandatory detention. It would undoubtedly be of national importance and international significance.

But the adrenalin rush was tempered by a rising sense of dismay. Despite the Tamils' soaring stress levels, there were inadequate medical services. 'I was personally horrified at what I was seeing,' says Zachary. The rates were up to three times those of asylum seekers who were processed in the community. 'It just beggared belief. We had to know was there something about the detention environment or was it something else?'

Zachary Steel drew up protocols with Pat McGorry and others for a research program and wrote to the immigration department seeking permission including face-to-face interviews with detainees. It was to be the first of many forays into the Kafkaesque world of what was then called the Department of Immigration and Multicultural Affairs (DIMA).

DIMA said the research team could not have permission to interview detainees because of the detainees' need for privacy. They said the interviews would be too traumatic for the detainees. The department claimed the research could not be published. And on and on it went for years, first under the Labor government and then with even more hindrance under the new Howard Coalition government.

Zachary and his team would never be given permission to conduct formal research inside detention centres. Trying to co-operate with government had not worked. They would have to find another way.

But some people did get inside camps to assess detainees held under the Labor government. Paris Aristotle, the memorably named head of the Victorian Foundation for Survivors of Torture, had been asked along with other refugee service groups to assess 53 Cambodian detainees, and later 18 or so East Timorese asylum seekers.

'Everyone scored off the charts on depression,' Paris Aristotle says.

The assessments had a powerful impact on Paris Aristotle. He believed they contributed to the urgency of the then Labor government's efforts to find a solution for nearly 250 Cambodians.

While some of the worst affected were allowed to stay in Australia, most were repatriated to Cambodia on the understanding they could resettle in Australia after 12 months. Most did just that. The 18 East Timorese were all released into the community for processing in the wake of their assessments.

For Paris, it was a potent example of how working with government could achieve critical results.

Although the two men had never met, Zachary Steel and Paris Aristotle had followed similar paths. Both had started their careers as youth workers and ended up involved with refugee resettlement programs. Then they were inevitably drawn into dealing with the mandatory detention regime. Both found the regime repugnant and were battling to alleviate its impact.

But they chose quite different paths to try to make a difference during an often febrile political debate in which medical research had become a key battleground.

Paris was a sophisticated political networker whose soft, honeyed voice spoke the language of government: discreet, diplomatic and practical. Paris knew how to get the most out of the system for his clients. That often meant giving ministers and bureaucrats enough 'political space to find a solution', says Paris. Public lashings usually shut down options.

Zachary Steel was just as clear about his own role, 'We are really hardnosed researchers. We don't do anything without publishing. That's the stock of trade. I mean science has always been about advancing knowledge and now here's this interaction between science and human rights. So for us it is pivotal to publish. You know, the truth will set you free and all that.'

Zachary wanted to get his hands on the data gleaned from the assessments Paris had helped to undertake. But while the detainees could have access to their own assessments, the material belonged to DIMA. Another brick wall.

But by scrounging a variety of credible data, Zachary was able to publish a booklet with his boss, Professor Derrick Silove, in 1998 called 'The mental health and well-being of on-shore asylum seekers in Australia'.

The authors found that 'asylum seekers who have suffered the most severe persecution are being detained on arrival in Australia; and prima facie evidence that detention may be a powerful direct contributor to [the] severity of psychological distress in asylum seekers'.

The booklet and its clear message that Australia may be locking up the most persecuted refugees and that detention may be inflicting mental illness was sent out to scores of refugee, church and activist groups, journalists, bureaucrats and politicians. Zachary waited for a public outcry. There was none. No questions in parliament. No calls for further investigation. No media debate. The wire coiled tighter around the padlocked gates of Australia's detention camps.

Zachary Steel couldn't believe it. How could this policy be expanded under the Howard government if there was no proper analysis of its effects on people? How could there be informed public discussion of the worth of tough measures against potentially vulnerable people if the facts weren't being presented?

It seemed the fate of these 'rich illegal migrants', as the government continued to describe them, trying to elbow their way into Australia ahead of 'real' refugees was of little consequence. Zachary Steel's research proposal seemed hopelessly marooned.

But salvation was already on its way to Australia from Iraq.

Dr Aamer Sultan was a young medical graduate who preferred to steer clear of the deadly politics of Iraq's gruesome dictator, Saddam Hussein. His dream was to become a surgeon. But his family was Shia Muslim, meaning Aamer was identified with the majority population that had at various times rebelled against Saddam Hussein, who was a Sunni Muslim. Aamer was also treated suspiciously because his mother was Iranian and his father was a member of the Communist Party; both were frowned upon by the ruling regime.

By 1999, Aamer says, he was working at Karbala in southern Iraq, where unrest persisted against Saddam Hussein's regime. He agreed to secretly treat wounded anti-Hussein rebels. But the rebels were later arrested and soon after, Hussein's notorious secret police came looking for Dr Sultan.

Aamer managed to stay one step ahead. He hopped between family and friends before stuffing a bag with clothes and money and running for his life. He was 29. He thought he would never see his home, his family or his country again.

He joined a well-worn but terrifying refugee trail out of Iraq through the north, across a river into Kurdistan and then Turkey where he paid a people smuggler. He caught a plane first to Singapore and then on to Sydney, Australia, believing he would be safe and free at last.

Aamer Sultan was exhilarated about coming to Australia, because it was a western country, and he had long idealised western notions of liberty, democracy and justice. From the bowels of one of the Middle East's most brutal dictatorships, Aamer had been happily romanced by the idea that societies could aspire to a higher purpose without corruption or terror. He believed western rhetoric about the innate rights of all human beings.

So when his plane touched down at Sydney airport in May 1999, Aamer Sultan saw Camelot.

'I seek refuge,' he told an immigration officer. 'I am a refugee from the Iraq, from Saddam Hussein.'

He was taken into custody and locked up in Villawood detention centre. He would be there for more than three years.

It is July 2000. Two years after Zachary Steel's report concerning on-shore asylum seekers has sunk without a trace. Or so he thinks.

Aamer Sultan, whose English language is still developing, has read a copy.

At this point Zachary Steel has all but shelved his ambition to conduct research inside detention centres. Then he reads a letter from Aamer:

'Dear Sir ... I found the ... study as interesting and helpful to understand the overall mental status of the detainees and to help many of them ... it is impossible to achieve any further progress ... there is no sufficient researches ... I am writing this letter asking, thankfully, for your help and advice. Best regards while waiting for your kind response if possible, sincerely yours, AR Sultan (Qualified physician from IRAQ, detained since May 1999 for the refugee case proceedings purposes.)'

Zachary has never been to a detention centre because his many requests to DIMA have been refused. But when he rings Aamer Sultan, the doctor tells Zachary he can visit him inside Villawood any day, every day, during visiting hours. Zachary doesn't need special departmental permission.

It is a lightning-bolt of realisation. For years Zachary has lamented their inability to breach departmental restrictions blocking the research path into detention centres. In fact, there are none. Zachary seeks legal advice that confirms he is under no obligation to seek permission from the department to meet or interview Aamer Sultan, or anyone else for that matter. As long as he goes during visiting hours.

One Monday in September 2000, Zachary Steel and Aamer Sultan meet for the first time inside Villawood's caged visitors' yard.

Zachary is struck by how slowly all the detainees seem to move; as if they are wading through a sea of melancholy. But Aamer strides across the yard to shake his hand as if he is on fast-forward.

'He seemed to reach me in bounds. And it was obvious straight away he had a lot to say. He almost had pressure of speech.'

They are barely seated when Aamer overflows with observations and questions. He tells Zachary that he's chatted quite a bit to some medical officials inside the camp about how asylum seekers and their children seem to respond to indeterminate detention. Then how a visitor had smuggled in a copy of Zachary's booklet. It is fascinating, but is it complete? Shouldn't there be more research done?

Aamer barely draws breath. There seem to be a pattern of symptoms, he says. At first detainees become depressed and then angry. Some might self-harm or attempt suicide. Finally, they become lethargic, forgetful and confused. Some are virtually catatonic. It isn't just a minority. It is virtually everyone who spends a lengthy period in detention.

Children also exhibit bizarre behaviour: retarded speech, bedwetting even when ten years or older, aggression, bashing their heads against walls as well as other examples of self-harm and in some extreme cases, suicide attempts.

As he speaks, Aamer is pulling out bits of scribbled paper from every pocket of his jeans and jacket. He seems to have them everywhere, each one describing another shard of someone's shattered mental health.

'He was a bit like a mad hatter really,' says Zachary. 'Sort of pulling out pieces of paper everywhere. He'd been trying to tell everybody for months and had been writing to journalists and the AMA [Australian Medical Association] and the Royal Australian and New Zealand College of Psychiatrists. So I was just another person who might help at that time because he was tireless, pouring himself 100 percent into this.'

Zachary is overwhelmed. This whirlwind before him is the real deal. Aamer is making appropriate medical observations. He is not a trained psychologist although he had studied psychiatry as part of his medical training in Baghdad. He is not a trained clinical researcher, but his ability to record extensive amounts of relevant information is clear.

'What really gave me a lot of confidence was from my perspective, what he was describing was what I call, in research terms, appropriate participant observer language,' says Zachary. 'His English wasn't as good then but he was definitely clinically competent. I certainly didn't think he was fabricating. And his observations were backed up by two Villawood psychologists anyway.'

Aamer says he realised within just a few days of arriving in detention that many people were acting abnormally.

'They were clearly unusual even to a basic trained GP like I was,' says Aamer. 'I had liked psychiatry before arriving in Australia. I'd spent time at a Baghdad alcohol and mental health centre. I was only supposed to be there for a month but I dragged out three months because I really liked the work so much. When I met Zachary I just wanted to see whether what I'm thinking from a medical point of view is right.'

Zachary Steel is profoundly shaken by Aamer's description of widespread psychotic behaviour. It conforms to Professor McGorry's observations of the Tamils in detention in Melbourne. But it goes much further. Aamer is describing a systematic degradation of peoples' ability to function; a systematic loss of their ability to hope, even to retain their sense of self.

If this was the standard outcome for a system ordained not by a court as a punishment, but as a non-reviewable administrative procedure, Australia could be responsible for injuring thousands of people, including children, none of whom had been convicted of a crime.

Zachary realises his job is to work with Aamer, to guide him as he gathers information, to provide him with research protocols necessary to ensure his work is meaningful. It is not Zachary's preferred research methodology. But the story here is so terrible and the controlling authorities so obstructive, that he believes he has a duty to cobble together as many observations and record as many pieces of raw information as he can.

For the next year, Zachary and Aamer meet every week and talk on the phone every other day to give clinical form to what Aamer is seeing.

And Aamer sees it all. His medical expertise, fluency in English and unique reserves of energy among a debilitated population mean most asylum seekers come to him for help, especially those with children.

Aamer does his best to counsel other detainees, to let them talk their troubles through: parents agonising over the fate of their children, fathers tortured by their decision to uproot their families, mothers unable to care for their babies.

He'd seen, for example, Heman Baban punished for his role in helping organise the 2000 Villawood hunger strike. After which the man and his little son were banished to a solitary cell for 13 days in the Port Hedland detention centre.

There was the Al Abadey family from Iraq with four children, the eldest 17, the youngest just six years old. The parents had been charged over rioting and were in gaol in Western Australia. The children had been left to fend for themselves in Villawood.

Then there was the Badraie family from Iran. Their chronically ill child had stopped eating, sleeping and talking after seeing rioting and suicide attempts.

And the dejected Iraqi whose wife and children were left behind in Syria after he'd fled Iraq where he'd been horribly tortured and seen his eldest son killed in front of him. But the system couldn't handle his traumatised and erratic recounting of events so he'd been refused as a refugee. And now he'd heard another son had been killed and his wife lacked the money to bribe Syrian officials and was being forced back to Iraq. 'I've killed my family; I've killed my family,' he would say over and over and over.

Aamer is relentless in the face of this tidal wave of despair; helping detainees fill out endless forms demanded by DIMA for every step in the process to be granted asylum or to appeal a negative judgment, and then to appeal again; to help find lawyers and translate for them.

He also advocates within the centre; pushing for medication, more play equipment and for better conditions.

'They [the detention officers], even sometimes the doctors and nurses, were so freehanded the way they treated people,' says Aamer. 'I heard one of them telling an elderly man who was trying to remind them that he needed a blood test that "If you keep complaining we will send you back on the next boat." You realise they could get away with anything.'

Aamer's advocacy is a tricky role. His own case, his future, his life is in the hands of the same people he has to badger. But it never seems to slow him down.

'Aamer was one of the most remarkable characters in there,' says

Zachary. 'He told me that whenever any outside official was being taken on a tour by the centre manager, he would run up and introduce himself and just talk for ten minutes about what is happening, about the psychological impact on people. That's how he met the Ombudsman and various parliamentarians because the management used to try to steer them away from any detainees. But he kept a constant eye out for these people. Aamer wouldn't even give them the chance to talk, he'd just launch into it.

'One day he ran up and gave his spiel and then the manager said, "Sultan, I'd like you to meet the new gardener."'

Zachary suspects Aamer is able to maintain his own sanity because of this exhausting schedule of caring for others. It gives him purpose and distracts him from his own troubles. Aamer says the need is so huge and urgent that he has no choice.

'When I arrived I had one goal in mind and that was to be safe. So I was safe in detention but bit-by-bit you take in what's happening around you. I'm not exactly the kind of person who would help. I know myself very well before arriving at Villawood and probably I was quite selfish, quite self-obsessed, looking after number one. But when you're in a place like that your priorities change by necessity. There is nothing else. You are in there 24 hours with people of so many different nationalities. We don't know anything about our fate, but we are sharing the moment of trying to survive.'

When they first met, Zachary had been painfully aware that Aamer might want him to take on his case and help get him out of detention. But in all their months of working together Aamer never once raised his own case.

'It was a working relationship,' says Zachary. 'Every time I tried to ask Aamer anything about himself he wouldn't tell me. He said "I've got my lawyer. I won't trouble you with things like that." My admiration for him grew. It was in his interest to tell me, especially over time because I'd started doing psycho-legal assessments for other detainees. He knew I could have been useful but he never used me.'

In fact Aamer's case is looking like a lost cause. He's been rejected as a refugee and failed in all his appeals. The only reason he hasn't been deported is because Australia refuses to forcibly return people to Saddam Hussein's Iraq. So Aamer is left to rot in Villawood.

But he is determined not to be engulfed by the madness of despair he is documenting. His work with Zachary provides a critical focus.

Their research about what Aamer and his co-author Kevin O'Sullivan would dub 'Immigration Detention Stress Syndrome' is first published in the esteemed British medical journal *The Lancet* in May 2001, and then in the *Medical Journal of Australia* in more detail in December.

'Of the 36 detainees who have been held for over 12 months at Villawood detention centre, my observations suggest that 33 are experiencing clear evidence of severe depressive illness,' Aamer wrote in *The Lancet*. 'Six of the detainees have developed clear psychotic symptoms … Most of these people displayed little if any symptoms when first detained at Villawood. It is of great concern that the psychological state of asylum seekers deteriorates to such an extent while in detention.

'I and my fellow detainees came in search of freedom after suffering extreme persecution in our home countries. What has shocked us the most is that our human rights have been profoundly violated again, this time by a country that is supposed to respect the principles of human rights. If a western country can do this and get away with it, what hope do we have?'

In a commentary piece about the research, Zachary Steel acknowledges the limitations of Aamer's work in the *Medical Journal of Australia*: 'we acknowledge the limitations of our report. AS [Aamer Sultan] is faced with the same challenges that other detainees encounter and it might be claimed that he is motivated to advocate not only for others but also for himself. The only counterargument we can offer is our commitment to reporting our observations in what we consider to be as objective and truthful a manner as possible.'

This time, with the arrival of thousands of asylum seekers, the press takes notice. The research turns Aamer Sultan into a minor celebrity during 2001. He becomes one of Australia's best-known detainees. Journalists, human rights activists, lawyers, other medicos all want his time and insights.

The *Good Weekend* publishes a story on the friendship between Aamer and Zachary in a regular column called 'The two of us' in July 2001.

'I think of him the same way I think of some famous political prisoners who somehow manage to transcend the situations they're in,' Zachary is quoted as saying in the article. 'Aamer is in an environment that's soul-destroying and crushing, and yet he isn't bitter.'

'After Zachary came to visit me, I was so inspired and happy to know that someone in his field would have made the same observations that I had, because I was not quite sure that what I had been observing was correct ... I feel a big relief that someone like Zachary is there. He will always be a lifelong friend. I won't find many like him around – not even back in Iraq,' Aamer told the journalist.

Aamer is commended by the Australian Human Rights and Equal Opportunity Commission (HREOC) for his work on behalf of detained asylum seekers. It awards him a certificate inside Villawood after the immigration department refuses him permission to attend the official ceremony.

'That was pretty remarkable,' chuckles Zachary. 'Federal Labor MP Tanya Plibersek [now Minister for Housing and the Status of Women] came in to give him this award and she wanted a ceremony. So they put on this afternoon tea and some of his friends came, I was invited and some others and then all these people who loathed him had to come as well. There were ACM [Australasian Correctional Management] and [immigration department] officials and Tanya Plibersek says to them "Well, we must acknowledge what Aamer has done and I'm sure some of you would like to make a speech." So these guys had to get up and make speeches about, you know, this great award for Aamer and how "we don't always see eye to eye but we respect your representation on behalf of other detainees" etc. And then Aamer got up and made a short speech saying thank you and how detention made people sick and served no purpose and should be abandoned. It was quite a bizarre thing really.'

'I've still got it,' says Aamer of the commendation. 'It did mean a lot to me because it meant that there were people who recognise human rights were being abused in detention.'

Paris Aristotle watches the unfolding public controversy over

Zachary and Aamer's research with concern.

Not that Paris disputes the essential conclusion: that detention ruins people, especially children. And he acknowledges that Zachary and Aamer had no choice but to gather data informally because of the government's refusal to approve a research program. But their research 'made no impact on the government. None at all. It was too easy for the government to dismiss because it was identified as the work of activists rather than objective researchers.'

While Zachary and Aamer are working to publish their research on the damaging nature of indefinite mandatory detention, Paris has taken a different route. He's accepted an offer from Philip Ruddock to join a ten-person committee called the Immigration Detention Advisory Group (IDAG). This body, formed in February 2001, helps monitor detention centres.

It is chaired by former Liberal Party immigration minister, John Hodges, and also includes former Labor immigration minister Gerry Hand (who had introduced mandatory detention), Professor Harry Minas (associate professor, Department of Psychiatry at Melbourne University, where he heads the Centre for International Mental Health), and former Air Force chief, Air Marshall Ray Funnell.

'I knew I wanted to make some improvement in the policy,' says Paris. 'My staff and clients were distressed by what was going on in detention and I was personally and morally distressed. I'd had a lot of experience at working on policy with governments and departments. I couldn't have lived with myself had I not used that experience to try to improve the system and get people out.'

Paris's experience told him that his expertise working with the government would produce more effective results than public criticism. 'Mandatory detention was a longstanding bipartisan policy. Which party would let go while the boats were still coming and public anxiety was at fever pitch? What Zachary and the research advocates didn't get is that you had to address the politics also. By just opposing mandatory detention the government was able to dismiss them as naïve activists who would let everybody into Australia and who didn't want to combat people smuggling, which was in fact a real problem.

Some in the government and department believed they had 10 000 people in the pipeline. Now who knows if that was true?'

All the lightning-rod issues like children in detention and the treatment of mentally ill asylum seekers, Paris believes he can best address directly with the department or at times with the minister. 'Most of the times I went to Philip Ruddock about a case, I got a result,' Paris says. 'I've always had a good relationship with him in that I think he respects what we do and I was prepared to listen to him about what his concerns were and they were real concerns.'

But for Paris, the growing public conflict between the government and refugee advocates makes it more difficult for him to intercede. As the minister, his department and refugee advocates become 'stuck in trench warfare there was less room for compromise. It felt like the political contest became the issue more so than the asylum seekers themselves.'

To ensure he remains a meaningful player in government circles, Paris says he needs to maintain a degree of independence from high profile activists like Zachary Steel. 'If we were going to get results we had to be seen by the government as balanced and credible,' Paris says.

Their differing strategies clash when Paris Aristotle arrives at Villawood with four members of IDAG in mid-2001. They have come to review conditions and to hear from regular visitors to Villawood like Zachary Steel.

With hindsight, Zachary sees the meeting with IDAG as a missed opportunity for him and Paris to have synchronised strategies for their common cause. But at the time, he believes they found themselves across a seemingly unbridgeable divide. Zachary can't understand why Paris and Professor Harry Minas seem to reject his overview about catastrophic levels of mental illness. Especially since they all agree there are soaring rates of mental illness inside detention. Instead they seem focussed on the limitations of particular studies.

'I couldn't believe the resistance I was getting because I thought it was all so bleedingly obvious. And if you look at anything that Paris or Harry [Minas] have written there was absolute consensus between us that detention is harmful. I mean I was just exasperated and bewildered.'

Paris says Zachary loses the IDAG committee when he claims that 100 percent of the asylum seekers in detention are clinically depressed.

'That couldn't be backed up in a substantive way at that time,' says Paris. 'In fact we knew that the population in detention was a mixed one and we knew not all of them were clinically depressed. And the fact is that the government loved to paint statements like that as grandiose and exaggerated because then it could dismiss everything that's said. The message gets lost. One of the worst examples was when some psychiatrists compared detention to Nazi concentration camps. The comparison was simply unbelievable to the general public and again they could be written off as extreme and grandiose, and, as a consequence, any other meritorious points got lost in the process.'

Zachary doesn't remember saying 100 percent of the population was clinically depressed. But it would have been above 80 percent.

'It was just mutual shock, I think,' says Zachary. 'I wasn't going to back down. I'm a practicing scientist and I know how to draw appropriate inferences. We got locked in that impasse and we never got past it.'

Zachary says he understands it was a calculated strategy by Paris. 'From their point of view I guess they believed they couldn't do anything with our findings. They needed to identify an at risk population they could fight on behalf of, but if I'm saying the total population is at risk then the only option is to dismantle mandatory detention which they knew they would never get anywhere with. So the information I was providing wasn't strategically useful.'

Paris agrees he has to deal with an increasingly fanatical and bloody-minded political mindset in Canberra. This makes previous successes like those with the Cambodians and the East Timorese less likely in the future. Refugees have now become a key issue in John Howard's domestic political tussle over voters with Pauline Hanson's anti-refugee One Nation party.

'The government became locked into the mandatory detention model and the belief, which was wrong, that it was deterring other boat people,' says Paris. 'Detention centres made it look like the government was in control and was punishing illegal arrivals.

It became harder and harder to get them to move on cases. Every concession they saw as giving in to people smugglers or to advocates who wanted to unwind mandatory detention.'

Even when Paris tries to intercede on the plight of unaccompanied children left in detention centres, he is initially told that releasing them 'would simply encourage parents to send more children by themselves on boats'.

On another occasion a senior government advisor screams at him over the phone when Paris intercedes on behalf of a desperately mentally ill Afghan man.

'He's yelling at me that he didn't care [give a fuck] if this guy killed himself and that if he is let out then at least it will no longer be his [fucking] problem and he could spend the rest of his life in a psychiatric institution for all he cared,' says Paris. 'It was one of the sickest conversations I ever had. I had to keep telling myself not to react and after all the histrionics and abuse the visa was granted.

'The politics of the time had numbed their ability to respond in a reasonable manner,' Paris says. 'In the end they thought it was acceptable to have a system that relied on a degree of pain and suffering to deter others. That's why it was such a bad policy. And it didn't deter anyone by the way. The boats still came after mandatory detention was introduced and even after the government hardened the detention regime.'

Despite criticism that he is helping to prop up a toxic system by remaining on IDAG, Paris refuses to resign. 'The easiest thing for me to do would have been to spit the dummy and had my 15 minutes of fame in the press but I'm positive it would have changed nothing and it would have meant I lost any influence on the inside. By the end there were thousands of people outside protesting and not many of us inside. I could still get people out. But more importantly I could argue for more humane alternatives from the inside and create opportunities for constructive dialogue between government and non-government agencies. It was impossible to argue for that successfully from the outside only.'

'I'm not an insider,' says Zachary Steel. 'I'm no good at it. I think Paris believed it was better to work in the system, follow the rules and try to negotiate better deals for individuals through internal persuasion. And he has a long history of rescuing detainees, more than all of us combined were ever able to help. We needed Paris to do what he did. It took all of us in the end doing whatever we could. But I wanted to address the fundamental problems of detention through an aggressive research program.'

While Paris keeps his distance from Zachary's research, he and IDAG members support Harry Minas's proposal for a formal immigration research program as early as 2001. But they are blocked, year after year. He also complains bitterly that their advice about how to improve the system and increase psychiatric care and their pleas for alternative models to detention centres for women and children, families and seriously ill detainees are stonewalled year after year.

But Paris says it is still worth the effort. 'In spite of all the resistance we were getting, we were still managing to lay important groundwork for if and when the environment changed and a more compassionate view emerged.'

Philip Ruddock says he was aware that IDAG members were 'very anxious about what they saw and yes, some of them would have been prepared to walk away from mandatory detention. That could never be my position.'

The advocacy campaign 'needed both of us,' Paris and Zachary now say separately.

'It's a shame there were some tensions,' says Zachary. 'I actually think that Paris and Harry Minas and others served a critical role and that we wouldn't have got anywhere without them on IDAG. There needed to be an insider. In an ideal situation we probably could have worked in a more co-ordinated fashion. But you know I think in the end we probably were working together, we just didn't see it.'

Zachary Steel continues to document cases and take his concerns to any public forum he can find. He would go on to publish two more studies including the world's largest study of mental illness among asylum seekers who have been in detention.

But by early 2002, Aamer Sultan's burning endurance is starting to dim.

For years Aamer has watched other heavily-medicated detainees shuffle around the centre with vacant stares. Now he can feel himself slipping into the same agonising abyss. To the distress of his friends, after three years in detention, Aamer will join the statistics of chronically-depressed long-term detainees he has been documenting.

'I couldn't read or do anything. I couldn't meet many people anymore. What little energy I had I had to prioritise; first counselling for other detainees, second, representing detainees to management, then third, outside work with media. I kept that to a minimum just because I was trying to survive. But the word [about mental health inside detention centres] was out by then anyway,' Aamer says.

He finds himself in the queue with other detainees waiting for medication.

'I resorted to sleeping tablets. I was taking two a day. But not to sleep. It was to stop thinking. With the tablets, I think less. I was trying to do less damage to myself, to stop the degrading of my brain.'

Zachary tries to help, but some days Aamer can't even come out to see him. 'He really started to disintegrate,' says Zachary.

Aamer knows he is simply the victim of the length of time he has spent locked up in no man's land.

'That's why I worked so fast with Zachary. I knew I had to finish the work before it happened to me. I had seen it happen to everyone else. Why not me?'

And it does. Aamer starts to lose faith in ever rebuilding a future for himself.

'A man should not weep. But I have done this several times. On those occasions, Zachary really helped me,' Aamer says.

Aamer's actions help put conditions inside detention on centre stage. But neither he nor Zachary Steel or Paris Aristotle could have predicted how harsh the government was willing to become. The first to see it was Trish Highfield.

CHAPTER 3
The turning point

They arrive quietly, gliding into position on her front lawn and front porch. They knock loudly. Trish Highfield can't believe her eyes when she opens the door. A dozen or so immigration officers spill out across the driveway and onto the footpath.

'Are you Trish Highfield?'

'Yes.'

'We are from the immigration department. We have a warrant to search your house to look for escapees from the Villawood detention centre.'

'Escapees? What escapees?'

'There has been a breakout from Villawood and we're searching the houses of people who've visited detainees. We have your name as someone who regularly was in contact with one of them, an Iraqi man named Heman Baban.'

'I know nothing about any escape. I've heard nothing about any of this. But what about Mr Baban's son? Where is he?' she says, flabbergasted.

The official's tone becomes harsher. 'If you don't co-operate we'll call the police to enforce the search warrant.'

Over his shoulder, Trish notices some of the officers on the front lawn limbering up with martial arts maneuvers.

'I visit Heman Baban and his son as a refugee advocate,' she says. 'My work is on behalf of children in detention and it's known about by the minister's office. I find this all very intimidating.'

'I'm just a public servant doing my job,' he says with a shrug.

Trish can tell these compliance officers are unused to being challenged. She surveys the mob about to be unleashed on her home. She resolves not to be bullied.

'I'm not going to let you in until I check with my husband. He's on the radio now with the ABC, but he'll be off in a few minutes. He's a very well-known journalist. And I'm also going to check with [Minister] Philip Ruddock's office.'

Trish closes the door, her heart pounding. It is March 2001. She had just seen Heman and little Barwan a few days ago. Is this a trick? Have they deported Mr Baban and little Barwan? She has learned to be suspicious of the immigration department, but this seems ridiculous.

Trish rings the immigration minister's office and speaks to a senior staffer who confirms an escape including Heman Baban and his son. The staffer sounds sympathetic to Trish's shock at being raided: 'The minister will be most upset to think the home of an advocate has been searched.' The staffer asks to be put onto the immigration officer waiting at Trish's front door.

Within seconds, Trish notices the security officers stop their stretches and are backing away from her porch, except for the most senior one, who now looks a little pale.

Trish then rings her husband, John, who has just finished hosting *The World Today* news program. She is so anxious she momentarily forgets his name. 'Can I speak to ... ah ... my husband ... ah ... John ... John Highfield!'

John advises Trish to let only the senior officer into their home and to accompany him throughout the search to ensure nothing is damaged. He also observes that she's in the middle of a 'fantastic story! No one knows about this escape or these raids across Sydney. We can report it first!'

Trish Highfield is not so elated about her place in the day's news headlines. Neither is the lead immigration officer who by this time realises he might actually be the headline. His manner towards Trish transforms. He apologises to her and her husband: 'I'm sorry if I upset your wife.' He then conducts a perfunctory search on his own.

'I made him look under our bed,' says Trish.

The officer and his team retreat to their cars and depart.

Trish is left in her hallway, shaking and dazed.

She feels like she is in some other country, where an authoritarian government could reach into her world at will. She feels small and powerless, her trust in government pierced.

'It is curious that the houses of several other people in social justice work, whom I'd encouraged to visit the same young man and his son, were not subject to search,' she wrote angrily at the time in a 'Defence for Children International' newsletter. 'I conclude that this was a selective act of intimidation against an advocate who'd been very active in recent months putting children's causes before State and Federal authorities, politicians and others.

'And what of the 50 other homes across Sydney which were also searched? I know of one refugee family with young children which was raided in darkness. You can only speculate what memories of horror may have been revisited by people whose experience of the midnight knock on the door could mean disappearances or torture by agents of the State.'

Even John Highfield's renowned professional cool slips when interviewing the immigration minister, Philip Ruddock, the next day on his radio program.

JOHN HIGHFIELD: Well the Minister for Immigration and Multicultural Affairs, Philip Ruddock joins us on the line in Canberra now.

Mr Ruddock, I must declare a personal interest in this matter, a pecuniary interest in a sense.

PHILIP RUDDOCK: Oh I don't think it would be pecuniary, John.

JOHN: Yeah, well, my home was one of those visited yesterday as you know because of my wife's involvement in social justice issues and concern for children behind the razor wire.

I don't specifically want to talk about that as we were treated very courteously by the officers, but it does raise a broader issue and that is the sweeping powers which are now reaching out into the Australian community is surely something which Australians cannot be happy with. We don't want these sort of things happening.

PHILIP: You don't want what sort of things happening, John? Escapes from detention?

JOHN: No. Officers coming and knocking on Australian doors and saying we want to search your house because we're looking for asylum seekers.

PHILIP: Well, I mean, that's quite unlikely to happen unless there is good reason to believe that people may have some contact with those who are being visited.

JOHN: What do you define as contact though, Minister? Is this a concern, a social concern for people who have very young children behind the wire who are not getting an ordinary socialisation and that are living incarcerated in what in every sense is a gaol situation, are you saying that visitors with concern for the welfare of children such as my wife should not be visiting those centres?

PHILIP: Well what I am saying is that it's quite inappropriate to describe the centres as concentration camps ... I have been to the centre at Villawood. It's a centre that has schools, it has medical and counselling facilities. It has been the subject of a very substantial upgrade and while I'd never describe it as a holiday camp or a hostel I certainly wouldn't describe it as a gaol ...

JOHN: Why do you think that these refugees, these family people —

PHILIP: John, they are not refugees. Let me make it very clear. We do not hold refugees in detention.

JOHN: 97 percent of the people who are in detention centres in Australia today will go on to be given refugee status, Minister, those are the statistics.

PHILIP: No, that is wrong, John. It is a fact that amongst two classes of people – Afghans and Iraqis, which we're not dealing with here, the approval rates are high, but no refugee is held in detention.

There are people who are asylum seekers. In this case I can tell you, and I've examined all of the material in relation to each of them (the escapees), all of them have been assessed. They are found not to be a refugee ...

Because of a perceived conflict of interest, John Highfield agrees not to do any more interviews on refugee issues.

It is also a turning point for Trish, the childcare worker and mother whose self-effacing manner starts to give way to a ferocious campaigner. If this can happen to her, what is happening to the rights of the children of boat people in detention?

'I saw her change,' says her husband, John. 'Trish was always intensely devoted to children, but a very shy sort of person. Suddenly I could hear this person on the phone in our kitchen shouting at the most senior people in the immigration department.'

Trish is rocked by the news of Heman Baban's escape with his young son. 'Quite honestly I don't support escapes, because it's not in the best interests of a child to be on the run. I was so worried for them,' she says.

When she thinks back over her six months of visiting them, Trish realises that Heman Baban must have been planning the breakout for quite some time with quite a lot of help. Nine adults and five children managed to cut their way out through wire fencing on 26 March 2001, in what was then the largest escape from Villawood.

'He must have had a lot of people helping. Apparently they had cutters and other tools. I remember him saying to me once that if I could never get on to him in Villawood I should try a mobile number. I didn't think about it at the time but obviously it was a number to contact because he knew he would be escaping. I never called it. I didn't want to put them at even more risk,' she says.

Trish never hears from Heman Baban again. She often wonders what became of them. She's heard they might be somewhere in Canada. Happy and safe, she hopes. But she doesn't have much time to mourn.

Before he left, Heman had told Trish about the tireless efforts of Dr Aamer Sultan to support other detainees. She now turns to Aamer for advice about who else she can try to help in Villawood.

'She is unforgettable,' Aamer says of his first meeting with Trish. 'She is a woman who's very Australian in her late 40s, early 50s, coming with all that motherly compassion. It is so familiar from back home. You see this lady who doesn't have an agenda. She is coming because she feels for the child.'

Aamer puts Trish to work immediately. She's introduced to an abject 17-year-old Afghan boy named Ali who reminds her of her own 20-year-old son.

Ali is part of the ethnic Hazara tribe, an Afghan minority allegedly descended from Genghis Khan, with a long history as victims of massacres and enslavements. The fundamentalist Taliban regime was among the most savage persecutors, killing thousands of Hazaras, and rendering uninhabitable large areas of their traditional farm lands. Young Hazara boys are routinely rounded up and forced into military service as human mine sweepers.

Ali has a typical Hazara story: he says his family sold land to pay people smugglers so they could save at least one young son and send him to a better life. His older brother had already been killed by the Taliban.

Ali had been in Woomera before Trish finds him in Villawood. He is lost, confused, depressed and consumed by a sense of failure that his family's sacrifice has been for nothing.

'Sometimes all you can do is cry with them,' Trish says.

But as his detention drags on into its third year and depression overwhelms him, Ali eventually tells Trish, whom he calls his 'Australian Mum' to stop visiting him.

With tears running down his face, he tells her: 'Women's hearts are like glass, and I don't want to break your heart with the sorrow that is always in mine.'

'I just felt so strongly that some of these kids were on the verge of taking their own lives,' Trish says. She continues to visit Ali. Then toward the end of 2001 Ali is finally released. He comes to live with Trish and John for eight months. He now lives with friends and works a variety of jobs. They still stay in touch. But Trish is racked by guilt that 'we failed Ali' because she couldn't heal his mental scars after detention. 'He would pace the floor at night, he couldn't sleep or he'd want to go out late at night. We would try to talk to him. But poor Ali, I don't think we coped very well.'

Aamer also introduces Trish to two young Iraqi children aged six and ten years who are in Villawood with their older teenage brothers, but without their parents. Their mother and father are in gaol in Western Australia after being charged over rioting in the Port Hedland detention centre.

'My saddest day at Villawood was the day I met those two young Al Abadey children,' Trish says. 'As soon I saw them with their big heads and tiny bodies, that's what all the kids look like in detention because they don't develop properly because of the constant stress. And so pale, so frightened. Aamer brought them to me. I was very nervous. He brought the littlest one over, Afnan and said "She needs some warmth" and even though I was a stranger, she ended up cuddling me her need was so great.'

After three years in various detention centres including 15 days in isolation one of the teenage Al Abadey boys, 15-year-old Humam, would eventually cut himself, sew his lips together and threaten suicide. He would dig his own grave, lying in it facing north toward Mecca as the dead are placed.

He rings Trish late one night to say goodbye.

'I can no longer dream,' he tells her. 'I will take my chances over the razor wire.' She spends hours on the phone trying to talk him through his feelings. She contacts anyone else who might be able to help.

'The sense of urgency I had about all the children was intense,' says

Trish. 'I felt like each day they were at risk, both psychologically and physically. I was always panicking that I had to work, work, work as fast as I could to try to get them out.'

During another visit, little Afnan becomes rigid in Trish's arms, her eyes wide and glassy. Afnan is recalling an incident in Port Hedland, when her parents and older brothers were all in gaol and she was left with her 10-year-old brother. Guards dragged them both out of bed for a head count in the middle of the night.

'She said "They came in the night and they dragged me" and she demonstrated on me and it hurt and she said "they dragged me by my clothes and they threw me on the ground and they were shouting" and she was hyperventilating and her eyes were grey. You know she was somewhere else, right back there when it happened and her little body was so rigid. And then she just slumped, exhausted and all I could do was pat her and cuddle her. It took quite a long time for her to come back.'

Afnan's mother Nahtha, had rejoined the family by then and witnessed her little daughter's fit of trauma. 'I looked across at her mother,' says Trish, 'and I saw her tear-filled eyes and the powerlessness of a parent to protect their child and this was happening in my country!'

Each week Trish makes the long trip to Villawood, two hours on public transport, 90 minutes waiting in the visitors' queue. Each time she sees more acutely distressed children. Each day after work she spends hours trying to rally concern about children in detention.

'I kept ringing and ringing,' Trish says, 'every week, one, two, three times. If I couldn't get the person I wanted, I'd talk to their assistants or their receptionist. I'd say "You have to listen to this. You must understand what is happening to these children." Then I worked out you could often get people when their assistants went out for lunch so I'd call then.

'I guess I was almost hysterical at times, but I felt like it was up to someone like me without responsibility for young children, someone older, comfortable in life and basically un-embarrassable! You know I'm old, I'm angry and I'm not going away!'

She wants to tell every senior official and every politician what is happening. Maybe they don't know. She will make sure they do.

'I rang [the then health minister] Tony Abbott who's our local member. I'd tell him about the children I was seeing and I'd say "What will you do about this in Cabinet?" I would ask him how he could look his own children in the eyes knowing what his government was doing.'

John Highfield remembers answering their home phone one morning to be greeted by Tony Abbott's voice. 'I'm ringing in for my six monthly berating from Trish.'

Tony Abbott now says of Trish's advocacy '[it] was relentless, indefatigable, passionate and almost impossible to ignore, even if you didn't often agree with it. And it was quite effective. I found myself doing things that I otherwise wouldn't have done, although I've got to say I only did them because I thought "Yes, she's got a point. This is unfair and it is cruel and at least in this instance something needs to happen."'

Trish states that 'in a couple of instances he did help. But I'm not aware of anything else he did to try to change the policy. If he felt that it was cruel, why didn't he do more to change it? It might have saved so many children from so much suffering.'

Trish's dogged dialling gets her through to an array of staff in the offices of the immigration minister, Philip Ruddock, and Prime Minister John Howard.

'They listened while I described what was happening to every child I knew in detention. Sometimes I'd speak for about 45 minutes. They can never say they didn't know what was really going on because I told them. And they did nothing.'

She even confronts Philip Ruddock outside a public function. She holds out a bunch of yellow roses to him as he walks by media and protest placards. He moves towards her smiling, taking her hand and holding it to his chest as he accepts the flowers. She has him now!

'I want to offer you these roses, Mr Ruddock, as a sign of friendship and goodwill because you said the other day in the media that people like me who support asylum seekers have malicious intent. I am not of malicious intent, but I should let you know what is happening to children being held in detention,' and Trish is away.

Philip Ruddock probably really wants his hand back by now. But Trish is not budging. She speaks to him for nearly five minutes.

'I can't really remember what he said. I don't think he said much at all. But at one point he'd put his head down and that's when I used a terrible voice that suddenly came out of me, and I said to him "Look at me when I speak to you!" And he did and I thought he looked shaken, and for a moment I felt like an absolute bully.' The feeling passes quickly.

Mostly Trish feels bewildered by the lack of response from government, and the cautious response of traditional refugee advocacy groups. Though she understands many depend on government funding.

Her impassioned pleas for action are regularly blunted by lawyers and policy experts. These people make her feel as if only *they* know how to fix the bigger policy issues. *We must follow due process in the courts, lobby discreetly in parliament, or appeal to faraway international forums.* But the urgent reality she sees every week inside detention goes unacknowledged.

Until she hears Zachary Steel speak at a refugee conference. The clinical research psychologist is presenting his research on mental illness inside detention.

'I mean all the lawyers were good at talking about the refugee conventions, but Zachary just seemed to go to the heart of the actual human suffering,' Trish says. 'He was so fantastic, so compassionate.'

Trish nervously approaches him with some material she's compiled about how detention is affecting children.

'I was sitting in one section and he was sitting in another and I was so worried what he would think. You know in those days I was so worried about whether I was doing the right thing, whether what I thought about it all was right and whether I was really helping these children. I thought you had to understand the law in detail to be an advocate.

'But I looked across at Zachary and he was actually reading what I'd given him and then he looked across at me and he smiled and I was just so relieved because I felt, oh my God, he's taking this seriously.

'I'll never forget that. To get Zac's support at that stage was so important.'

It is the birth of a powerful advocacy partnership across a crowded conference room; both relentless campaigners, one with unswerving faith in the human heart, the other in the more pragmatic persuasion of science.

'I remember meeting Trish,' says Zachary. 'She was the most self-effacing person I had ever met, to the point where she almost didn't believe she had the right to talk to you!'

Zachary watches in awe as over time Trish's gentle demeanour becomes gripped by rage.

'I loved it!' Zachary says. 'I felt like I had to stay calm and rational all the time and speak only to the science. But sometimes I'd live vicariously through Trish when I'd hear she'd rung up a politician or a senior public servant. I'd be like "Tell me, Trish, tell me! What did they say? What did you say?" And then "I can't believe you said that!" She was great.'

Once the Immigration Detention Advisory Group was established, Trish also rang Paris Aristotle and Ray Funnell. 'Trish was really knocked about by this,' says Paris. 'But any decent person would be. She was really distressed and ... I think she did contribute to changes. It just didn't feel like it a lot of the time. She asked me at times to try to intervene in ways that I knew were just impossible.'

'I used to talk to Paris and he'd say they [the government] don't listen to us either,' says Trish. 'I had no doubt Paris did what he could, but I realised by then it didn't matter what professionals like him were saying. So I had a number of conversations with Ray Funnell and Paris, but after a while they didn't return my calls because I was ringing them all the time.'

Trish depended on Zachary Steel for professional advice when dealing with seriously disturbed children.

'Sometimes I'd ring him late at night,' says Trish, 'and he had young children so it wasn't very fair. I'd ring him about some young person threatening suicide and he'd go into Villawood at ten pm and deal with it. There was never any compromise with Zac. And I think he had a lot of respect among the people working there as well. I just can't say enough about him.'

Zachary was also noticing that Trish was not alone, but among the first of a new wave of refugee advocates finding their way into detention centres. By mid-2001, both he and Aamer had been observing the arrival of middle-class, middle-aged women in Villawood concerned about families.

There was something about them as a demographic; older, often with grown children, confident in their values and in those of the community they believed they'd nurtured, which seemed to render them fearless, bullet-proof.

Two of the boldest are a volunteer legal worker and ex-journalist named Jacquie Everitt, and her friend, a freelance travel writer named Ngareta Rossell. The two women have been friends since their daughters attended the same elite private Sydney girls' school, Ascham.

Jacquie had already worked with refugees in East Timor as an aid worker. After returning to Sydney, she started going out to Villawood with the government-funded legal group, the Refugee Advice and Casework Service. She was immediately struck by the number of ailing, detained children and decided to focus her attention on them. She asked Ngareta to come along as well.

They have been coming out to Villawood together for just a few weeks and meet Trish Highfield amid the plastic chairs in the visitors' enclosure. 'I remember her blazing, dark eyes,' says Ngareta. 'She told us she was a childcare worker. She didn't have to explain anything else. We all knew we were there for the same reason.'

They fall hungrily into intense relationships with each other. Their telephones burn late into each night.

'We would have these calls about midnight,' says Trish, 'and we'd just go through the same conversations round and round. "Who'll listen? No one will listen. No one cares. This is outrageous." The phone would ring at midnight and we'd always know it was Jacquie or I'd be ringing her or Ngareta.'

'We were all flying by the seat of our pants,' says Ngareta. 'We were working from gut instinct. We had no idea what we were doing back then. We just knew we had to do something.'

They are anxious, frustrated, disillusioned and angry, angry, angry.

'We would ask each other, "What else can we do?"' says Ngareta.

They find the answer when confronted by the appalling case of a six-year-old Iranian boy in Villawood. His name is Shayan Badraie.

Jacquie Everitt, a mother and step-mother of seven children, is introduced to the boy's family by Aamer Sultan. She'd contacted the Iraqi doctor after reading about him in the *Good Weekend* magazine's 'The two of us' column.

Before he got sick 'Aamer was the best advocate of all of us,' says Jacquie. 'Aamer engineered everything. He pushed me in a corner. He was not going to let anyone escape, and if it hadn't been me, it would have been someone else. He's very manipulative is Aamer. You know, he showed me the child. You can't walk away from a child.'

Jacquie remembers the bleak, rain-drenched afternoon when she first met the Badraie family.

It is July 2001. They huddle under the noisy tin roof in the visitors' enclosure.

The family appears depressed, they speak little English and have two children with them. One is a curly-haired toddler, but Jacquie's eyes fixate on the other child: a skinny six-year-old boy who hangs limp over his father's shoulder like a carcass.

'My God he looked dead,' says Jacquie. 'Like a puppet, his dangly legs sticking out of a track suit. I went around his father's back to look into his face but his eyes just stared. There was nothing in them. I took his hands and put them between mine. No reaction, there was no reaction the whole time, none.'

The parents and Aamer explain that the little boy, Shayan, had become disturbed after witnessing bloody rioting and slashed bodies both at Villawood and at the remote Simpson desert detention camp at Woomera in South Australia.

Woomera had become a notorious caged hell hole which the government will be eventually forced to shut because of endemic self-harm and violence. Little Shayan was locked up there for a year from March 2000. He'd seen a man climb a tree with broken glass screaming that he was going to kill himself. He saw another man he knew well with blood seeping through bandages around his throat and his wrists after attempting suicide. He saw hunger strikes and riots and was there when anti-riot squads unleashed tear gas and water cannons.

The family was transferred to Villawood in March 2001 in a bid to improve Shayan's mental state. But there he saw a man who had collapsed after slashing his wrists.

Shayan became progressively worse with each violent episode. At first he suffered nightmares, bed-wetting and insomnia. But then became mute and finally he refused to eat. He now appears to be catatonic. The technical diagnosis is post-traumatic stress disorder.

Jacquie is horrified. Why isn't Shayan being treated in a hospital? Aamer describes how Villawood management sends the lifeless boy under guard to hospital for emergency care. He's then brought back to detention. This happens nine times.

Every expert medical opinion, as well as some Australasian Correctional Management health staff, advise the immigration department that Shayan and his family must be taken out of detention if he is to recover. Every expert is ignored.

The rain pounds on the tin roof above them. Jacquie stares in disbelief at this family sitting quietly before her, nursing their broken child. *Why are you so passive?* she thinks. *Have you given up on him? On yourselves?*

Their asylum case is also a mess. Amid the stress of their son's debilitating physical decline, they fail to appeal within the 28-day time limit. The Badraies have been notified they are to be deported back to Iran. The father, Saeed, who is not a Muslim, claims that he faces persecution because he'd protested against the ruling theocracy.

The family slowly, sadly gets up to leave. Jacquie jumps up and throws her arms around the mother, Zahra. 'I promise I'll get you out of here,' Jacquie says. 'We're going to be friends. You'll be my friend and I'll be your friend and your children will go to school and it'll be alright.'

As the family disappears back into the locked compound, Jacquie bursts into tears. 'Why did I say that? How can I keep a promise like that?' she exclaims to Aamer.

'It's okay,' Aamer says.

'I'm just so ashamed, Aamer. I'm so ashamed.'

Jacquie, who had also worked as a journalist, believes she must make Shayan's story public to force the government to save him.

'I knew as soon as I saw Shayan that he was dying. There was no question,' says Jacquie.

Four weeks later, Jacquie and Ngareta are back in line at Villawood waiting to clear security to see Aamer Sultan. Jacquie is wearing a stylish Italian overcoat and a clutch of heavy silver necklaces. She and Ngareta stand out from the mostly poor, ethnic women also in line many wrapped in Muslim garb, their arms sagging with plastic shopping bags full of food.

'Get back from the desk!' a guard is yelling at those toward the front of the queue. 'Youse won't get in if youse don't get back from the desk!'

Jacquie strides forward when it is her turn. 'Hello there. How are you today?' she says confidently to a guard. The alarm is set off. 'Oh dear,' she says handing over her keys. It goes off again. 'Do you think it's my necklaces?' she smiles sweetly, moving to take them off. The guard smiles back. 'Yeah, nah, that's it. Don't worry. Just go through.'

The guards return to painstakingly searching the myriad plastic shopping bags. Doors and gates click open for Jacquie and Ngareta who quickly find Aamer Sultan. They try to remain calm as they surreptitiously hand him the video camera hidden under Jacquie's coat.

'I was scared,' says Jacquie. 'I thought I might be breaking the law so I was mainly scared for the embarrassment for my children if I was arrested. Of course, I realised later I was only breaking a stupid regulation!'

Aamer slides back to his room where he hides the camera in piles of discarded toilet paper packets and other refuse just outside his door. It has been provided by the award-winning investigative *Four Corners* program on ABC TV. Reporter Debbie Whitmont and her partner and producer, Peter McEvoy, had already contacted Aamer to ask if he would agree to film inside Villawood, if they could find someone to smuggle in their camera. They want to show people for the first time what is really happening in detention centres. But it all depends on whether Aamer can do enough filming without getting caught.

Aamer knows what he is about to do could bring the full force of the immigration department down on his head. Troublemakers are routinely transferred to Woomera, that blast furnace of a detention centre in the South Australian desert. This is far from his support network in Sydney. But he believes a direct appeal to the Australian public is his last resort.

'What was there to lose? For Shayan's parents their boy is so ill and they are about to be deported. I had to speak out. The child was so sick. Even today he is still shattered. We had to try to get him out,' Aamer says.

But with no previous camera experience, his first attempts fail. In another tense visit to Villawood, producer Peter McEvoy smuggles in a new tape and provides more detailed advice for Aamer to try again.

Between musters when guards count off each detainee, Aamer secretly films his own testimonial and that of the Badraie family about life inside Villawood.

'When you have got nothing but to watch yourselves and the others around falling apart little by little,' Aamer says to the camera. 'Trying to help them, trying to reach them, trying to give them as much as you can. I feel as though I couldn't cope with the number [of sick detainees] any more. The number is getting more and more.'

Then he turns a slightly wobbly camera on Saeed Badraie who describes the agony of his son's fading life.

'Our child won't drink water, he won't eat. And he doesn't move for four or five days at a time … He just sits in a corner not speaking. We go to the medical services two or three times a day. Then after four or five days they take him to the hospital. Sometimes they tell us the child can survive for four or five days meaning that only when he is about to totally collapse will they take him to hospital.'

Just over a week later, on 13 August 2001, the grainy images of a flaccid child escape from behind the razor wire onto national television. For the first time, the boat people have a human face; a pale, tormented child's face. The *Four Corners* audience is stunned. The program's website is overloaded as 5000 people, twice the previous program record, register their anger and shock that Australia allows such misery. It galvanises widespread public protest.

Sydney businesswoman and mother, Junie Ong, is so outraged she sits up all night compiling a list of everyone she can think of to start calling at seven the next morning. 'We have to do something!' she tells family, friends and colleagues. Before long she and her husband, Tom, start a Sydney-based group called ChilOut. The group campaigns for the release of more than 800 children in detention. It will eventually boast a support base of up to 4000 people, and co-ordinate visits for volunteers to support Villawood detainees.

One of Australia's leading child psychiatrists and the national spokesperson for the Royal Australian and New Zealand College of Psychiatrists, Dr Louise Newman, had also watched *Four Corners* in disbelief. She had just spent two days reading through mountainous files about the deteriorating mental state of detainee families. These were sent to her in ever heavier envelopes by Ngareta Rossell, who hunted her down with frantic determination.

'I found [reading the files] incredibly difficult,' says Louise. 'There were terrible stories. I had no idea how accurate they might be, but they rang true. Because I'd worked in abuse for so many years they were very typical descriptions of how disturbed children might behave. They were authentic descriptions.'

Dr Newman had planned to first master the detail of refugee policy before pursuing a formal response through the College of Psychiatrists. Until she saw Shayan Badraie on *Four Corners*.

'I thought this is much worse than I thought and it wasn't possible to wait for endless policy construction. It was fairly clear what needed to happen, just from a clinical point of view because the child is being damaged as a result of the absolutely toxic environment in detention. It was just so striking.'

Dr Newman composes an audacious strategy that would see for

the first time, every single medical college of specialists as well as the Australian Medical Association representing GPs join together to oppose government policy. That is the entire Australian medical profession.

Efforts by the immigration minister, Philip Ruddock, to stem the public outcry initially backfire. In one interview the minister refers three times to Shayan as 'it' including 'I understand it receives food and receives liquids.' Mr Ruddock also implies on the 7.30 *Report* that Shayan's condition may be due to the fact that Zahra is his step-mother, not his biological mother:

PHILIP RUDDOCK: A lot of the psychiatric conditions arise because you have a predisposition to them. You don't know to what extent it may be related to the family's situation and I don't wish to go into that. Some people might think it was prejudicial if I introduced those elements. You don't know –

KERRY O'BRIEN: But in effect you are introducing it. You appear to be implying something without actually being prepared to say it.

PHILIP RUDDOCK: Well I'll simply say that the child is not the natural child of the mother – it's a step-child.

It was an ugly first shot in a government campaign to try to counter-act the power of the *Four Corners* program. In the weeks that followed some media reports stated that Saeed Badraie had stolen Shayan from his biological mother. Others claimed that Saeed and his wife were coaching Shayan not to eat and teaching him how to draw psycho-logically-disturbed pictures.

'We love our children,' Saeed said. 'How could a human being possibly prevent his own child from eating?'

Reporter Debbie Whitmont says none of her other stories had ever been subjected to such a systematic attack.

'I was surprised,' she says. 'I always felt that if as a journalist you can prove that something very wrong is happening, then people will want to change it. But there was a campaign by the minister [Philip Ruddock] which let out a lot of personal information about the people in our story and which was targeted to certain journalists who wrote, I think, quite shocking pieces.'

'The ABC produced a real tear-jerker of a program about a young Iranian child seemingly trapped in an Australian refugee detention centre,' wrote Piers Akerman, a columnist with the *Sunday Telegraph*. 'Audiences were only given one side of the story ... Is it not possible that Shayan Badraie was neglected or rejected by his step-mother (not his mother, as the documentary claimed) after the birth of her own child shortly after the group arrived in March, 2000? Perhaps he pines for his natural mother. Perhaps something happened on the boat that brought him here.

'Or has his whole tender life been massively disrupted by the decision to drag him illegally to Australia? We don't know, because his father speaks for him.

'What we do know is that his health improves as soon as he is in hospital.

'And we know the Badraies are still in detention – although their case was decided last September – because Iran refuses to accept those who are returned involuntarily.

'Shayan Badraie would not be in detention if his father agreed to take him home.'

The immigration department continues its propaganda that detention centres are nice places even for children. In a 25-page media kit responding to the *Four Corners* program, it claims that up to 80 people play tennis each week. 'Unfortunately there is no tennis court in Villawood,' says the program's producer Peter McEvoy.

Peter McEvoy also points out that the government has 'been very effective in keeping the media out of detention centres and keeping the reality behind the razor wire under wraps. Apart from departmental guided tours the media has no access to detention centres or detainees.'

The minister does not release the reports of medical specialists blaming Shayan's continued traumatised condition on his incarceration. Nor does he release the multiple recommendations for the child and his family to be let out. Among those reports is one marked 'Truly

Urgent' from Paris Aristotle and Harry Minas of IDAG warning of long-term damage to Shayan. Philip Ruddock writes the word 'Bucklies' (that is, Buckley's) in the margin of a summary report, which includes yet another medical expert recommending the family be released.

Shayan is released from detention and placed in foster care without either his father or step-mother, against medical advice, on 23 August 2001. This is ten days after the story on *Four Corners*. He is eventually joined by his step-mother and sister five months later in January. He waits for a year before he can again live with his father, who is eventually released in August 2002.

Shayan Badraie will go on to become the first child in Australia to be formally recognised as having his rights breached under the United Nations' *Convention on the Rights of the Child* as determined by the Human Rights and Equal Opportunity Commission. It recommends the government apologise and provide compensation. The government rejects the findings, but years later agrees to an out-of-court settlement for $400 000.

Now a 'gentle and quiet' teenager, 'Shayan's self-confidence is returning and his parents believe his spirit will reignite,' says Jacquie Everitt.

Instead of facing a scandal over the treatment of Shayan Badraie, the government shifts the debate to blame asylum seekers for a national security crisis. At the time, Prime Minister John Howard is facing a tough election beset by volatile polls. His voting base is threatened by Pauline Hanson's One Nation party. This is a potentially damaging right-wing movement, which finds traction railing against boat people. John Howard has vowed to the party room that he will get all the One Nation voters back.

And then out to sea, a small overcrowded boat, the *Palapa*, stops dead in the water. For days over 400 mostly Afghan men, women and children are adrift and gripped by despair. Finally a cargo ship, the Norwegian tanker the *Tampa*, is spotted heading towards them. 'There was nothing left for us in this world if the ship goes past,' says Khodadad Sarwari, one of the passengers.

The *Tampa* rescues them on 28 August 2001, requests permission from Australian authorities to disembark the shipwrecked asylum seekers who are filthy, exhausted and ill. But Prime Minister John Howard personally orders that the ship not be permitted to enter Australian waters. He vows that the rescued asylum seekers will never set foot on Australian soil. When the ship's stunned captain, Arne Rinnan, defies John Howard's order, SAS troops are sent to board the *Tampa* and stand over the men, women and children huddled on its deck. The asylum seekers are eventually removed to an Australian naval vessel, and sent to the remote Pacific island nation of Nauru.

The secrecy around the operation to repel boat people is so stifling that it is described on 13 October 2001 by the *Daily Telegraph's* chief political correspondent, Malcolm Farr, as 'a deliberate program of censorship on a scale which would not be out of a place in a war'.

There is no war: just 433 mostly Afghan men, women and children. But there is an election and the government's ruthless response wins the day. Polls show 77 percent of Australians support John Howard.

The Labor Opposition meekly falls into line supporting new laws that vastly shrink Australia's immigration zone and backing the use of the navy to turn boats around which try to breach that zone. Any asylum seekers who make it through are to be taken to Nauru for processing. The Pacific Solution is born. Along with mainland detention, it's been estimated that the government's tough response will cost more than a billion dollars; a price tag usually reserved for an actual war. But what political purchase power! It becomes seared into government mythology that John Howard's stand against the *Tampa* wins many backbenchers their parliamentary seats, and neuters the Labor Party for years to come.

And yet even as most workplaces, pubs and dinner tables clamour in support of John Howard's actions, individual dissenters continue to step forward. For many, it becomes an unexpectedly life-changing, often traumatic and sometimes frightening decision.

In Melbourne, one of the nation's most formidable lawyers, Julian Burnside QC, is briefed in a case against the government over the *Tampa*. He loses on appeal. But the impetus that transforms this lifelong Liberal voter into a refugee advocate happens shortly after when he represents a detained family whose 11-year-old daughter hangs herself with bed sheets. Although the child is cut down in time, her treatment by immigration officials enrages Burnside. They also ignore medical advice for her and her family to be transferred from Woomera to metropolitan detention, so she can receive adequate clinical care. When they finally relent and the family is transferred to Maribyrnong, officials fail to arrange psychiatric care until after she hangs herself. The shocking episode stirs Burnside to become the advocacy movement's unofficial orator. For the first time in his 30-year career, he receives death threats.

Julian Burnside initially believes his involvement would last maybe 12 months. Four years later he is still going. 'Whenever I got tired, I just brought to mind the image of that 11-year-old child hanging herself in a lonely cell and, I tell you, that galvanises you.'

The *Tampa* also unleashes artist Kate Durham, Julian Burnside's wife, who starts a national organisation called Spare Rooms for Refugees. The couple open their art-adorned villa in Hawthorn to recently-released refugees and collect a database of another 1000 people prepared to do the same. Kate also begins a support network of people prepared to write to the 1232 asylum seekers ultimately banished to Nauru. Once the driving force behind the Melbourne Fashion Week, she will fly to Nauru and secretly film interviews with detainees. These are subsequently used in a BBC documentary called 'Australia's Pacific Solution'.

'I just couldn't imagine anybody thinking we needed to rub salt in the face of a refugee who had already suffered. I was scared of the consequences. And I thought if most of them end up in our community having children, then we don't want people who've had awful experiences at our hands or are resentful or afraid of us,' says Kate Durham.

'Which is another way of saying that enlightened self-interest points in the same direction as basic humanitarian decency,' says Julian Burnside.

In the conservative bucolic southern highlands of New South Wales, three middle-aged women are so enraged by the treatment of the *Tampa* refugees, they form the optimistically named Rural Australians for Refugees (RAR). Despite the media cliché of country rednecks, RAR will ultimately boast 100 groups around Australia with 15 000 devotees, the largest and most influential of the refugee groups. Members write to and ring detainees, raise money and lobby politicians for visas, so refugees can work in country towns.

Anne Coombs, one of RAR's founders, says when they first set up their weekend stall in the main street of Bowral, New South Wales, they were often abused and people would cross the street.

'When people eventually took the time to listen or if they spent time with some refugees, their attitudes changed,' says Coombs. 'And bit by bit people would get involved with them teaching them English or how to drive. In rural Australia that idea of a fair go is really strong still. They'd find that they were good young men who lived clean, worked hard and when they got to know them better, they heard how sad their stories were. They thought *bang on, these blokes deserve a chance.'*

The powerful bonds with asylum seekers that Trish Highfield, Jacquie Everitt and Ngareta Rossell have felt are soon replicated across Australia. Hundreds become 'Australian Mums' to young detainees without any family. Jews and Christians find their lives devoted to advocating for the release of devout Muslims. Country folk extend their already meager resources to skinny young men from the other side of the world. Psychiatrists find themselves speaking through megaphones at protest rallies. And law-abiding citizens become part of an underground for escapees.

It is a disparate, grass-roots movement bulging with middle-class activists. They are ablaze with passionate certainty that they can change policies, convert public antipathy and get asylum seekers out of detention hell holes. Even though both major political parties and all the opinion polls are arrayed against them.

'I thought, unlike Aboriginal issues, there was no history, this could be unravelled quickly,' says Kate Durham. 'I honestly thought this was a mistake and with the right press it would go back to how it was [when we treated refugees more humanely].'

If only the rest of Australia knew the truth, they thought. *That it wasn't the asylum seekers trying to con us: it was the government! For goodness sake, this government campaigned for votes by falsely claiming that asylum seekers threw their children overboard!*

And then in faraway Manhattan, two jets fly into the twin towers of the United States' World Trade Centre. The terrorist explosions of 9/11 fill the ears of most of the electorate in Australia, leaving them deaf to every refugee prayer.

CHAPTER 4

Direct action

Fleeing over dusty red sand through the cold desert night air, two escapees from Woomera detention centre follow a refugee activist. They're desperately trying to find a hiding place, far from the melee of police and protestors behind them.

They are moving fast, breathing hard. Little is said. They all know they could end up in gaol for up to ten years if they're caught. But after three hours on the run over low scrub and rocks, the desert refuses to yield a sanctuary. They move through the shadows of the undulating terrain under a brilliantly moonlit night. But the escapees are flagging. By morning the three men will be treacherously exposed. 'Toby', a research scientist and refugee activist, urges them on.

'These guys were getting pretty tired and didn't have much left. I decided to try to get them to the railway line south of Woomera and hide them in a culvert somewhere. But even that was a bit of a stretch, since it was getting late and these guys were just not able to keep up a pace I would have liked. A couple of years in detention puts a physical strain on a person, as well as a psychological one,' says Toby.

The two escapees, 'Mohsen', an Iranian in his late 20s, and 'Hassan', an Afghan in his early 20s, had been in Woomera for more than two years. Even though he was the youngest, Hassan was especially strung out by the experience with scars from self-mutilation zig-zagging up his arms and his body still weak from a hunger strike. He was struggling to keep up with the others.

They'd had three close calls. After sauntering brazenly through the bright lights of a police cordon pretending they needed to pee, the three men had dropped quickly into a combat crawl and disappeared into the darkness as an alert sounded belatedly behind them.

Police four-wheel drives roared out over the sand to chase them down. But the men stayed low, crawling for several hundred metres across plant spikes and rock shrapnel that shredded their hands and knees. When police headlights approached, they stopped dead.

'We had to rely on the darkness for concealment since there was no vegetation to hide behind. But it is actually hard to make out a shape in the dark, especially if it lays low and still in a large landscape. Human vision, particularly peripheral vision, is more attuned to motion than it is to shapes, so we had that going for us,' says the activist.

Toby was just the right activist in the right place to help the escapees. Most of the 1000 other protestors at Woomera that crazy Easter weekend in 2002 had turned up with food, shelter and a few colourful banners. None of them had expected to breach the fences of the detention centre and help more than 50 detainees escape, however briefly. Toby hadn't expected a mass escape either. But he always liked to be prepared. He had acquired topographical maps, researched communication nodes and packed a Global Positioning System (GPS) navigation device.

Even more important were skills he'd not used in more than a decade. Toby had once been a bow and arrow hunting enthusiast; a sport requiring great stealth, navigation and vigilance. Now a vegetarian, he'd never expected to again draw on his days in the bush killing feral animals. But those pig-hunting skills were coming in handy tonight.

On two occasions police vehicles pass within ten metres of the men who lie motionless and unseen. Another time Toby realises he and the two escapees will pass briefly out of the shadows as they cross a ridge so he tells the men to drop, sensing a trap. They wait and watch. Sure enough, after ten minutes, a car engine rumbles to life and headlights pierce the night. Police had been lying in wait at what was an obvious crossing.

'We lay low again until the police went by. I wasn't really concerned. We had at all times been against a dark background in dark clothes with no reflective patches. In a hunter versus hunted situation, it's all about who sees who first. I knew it was next to impossible to spot us,' says Toby.

But now it isn't the police worrying Toby. It is how much further Hassan and Mohsen can go. Finally they get lucky. Trekking down into a wide depression, they come across a giant spread of dry reeds about 200 square metres wide and about one metre high; tall and dense enough to provide cover if you lay down.

Toby marks the position on his GPS. The two men are given one day's supply of food and water and extra warm clothes. Then Toby leaves. 'I will come back tomorrow night,' he says before darting off.

Mohsen and Hassan are suddenly alone in an eerie stillness. But the shouting chaos of Woomera still pounds in their heads. After tunnelling in among the thick bed of reeds, they rest. They can just make out stars overhead. Have they made the right choice?

Neither man expected to be here tonight. There had been no grand breakout plan. Just fortuitous circumstance and a broken fence. After more than two years in detention, the men had seen the gap and flown through it, running across the emptiness around Woomera with a hysterical mob of more than 1000 young Australian protesters chanting 'Freedom!' It had been joyous, if surreal. Now it felt dangerous.

They had put their lives into the hands of a stranger, a young professional who lived and worked in a big city in a rich democracy. What did he know about surviving on the run, about life underground, about how to find them again in a desert? What if this guy gets scared or arrested and never comes back?

Almost as soon as Toby leaves, Hassan begins to fret about the venom-infested vastness of their new prison, the discomfort of staying prone among the reeds and the likelihood of the activist ever coming back.

As each hour passes, Hassan's resolve deteriorates. In the morning, he is ready to bolt and make his own way to Adelaide when they hear a police helicopter overhead. Mohsen persuades Hassan to crawl back under the reeds. He tells Hassan that Toby will come with more food and water tonight, that he will get them out of here.

Toby returns that night with more supplies, using the same techniques to avoid detection. But there is bad news. He does not yet have an escape plan. The two men will have to hide among the reeds for another day. The police search is just too intense.

Toby tells them the news that more than 50 people escaped from the detention centre during the Easter Friday protest. He tries to lift their spirits by telling them that the protestors and detainees 'whipped the arse' of the immigration minister, Philip Ruddock. The men don't understand the expression so Toby jumps up, bends over and pretends to whip his own backside by way of visual explanation. Mohsen and Hassan burst out laughing and also jump up to imitate the 'arse whipping' of Philip Ruddock. 'We must have been a really strange sight,' says Toby. 'Three grown men in the middle of the desert laughing and pretending to whip their own butts!'

Toby also tells them that only 11 of the 50 remain free. Some of the escapees handed themselves back after doing media interviews, content simply to have had their stories heard. The rest were picked up at the protestors' camp and at roadblocks. One man, he warns Hassan, trekked through the desert to a road and flagged down a van to take him to Adelaide. It was full of off-duty policemen.

Toby promises to return again the next night with a plan to get them out. He hopes Mohsen's steady personality will help calm Hassan's obvious jitters.

On the way back to camp, Toby flattens as he sees three men walking along a road carrying shopping bags. He quickly realises they are also escapees. When they hear a car, they dive onto the side of the road. Toby wants to help them. But he stops himself. He is concerned that he and his four friends are already stretched thin looking after Mohsen and Hassan. Yet he knows these three men are unlikely to make it without his help. He is horribly torn, but he must focus on saving the two men in the reed bed who are relying on him. He remains silently hidden as the three escapees walk by.

For the third night in a row, Toby treks the exhausting three-hour 20 kilometre round trip to the reed bed, this time carrying an achingly heavy backpack full of long-term supplies.

'My pack was so heavy with water that the rocks slipped and sparked beneath my feet,' he says.

He also brings an escape plan, although it is not what Mohsen and Hassan are hoping for.

There is no way to get them out at the moment, Toby tells them. Every road, every town is red hot with police. They will have to stay out here. For a week.

'The whole essence of our plan was that it was such an outrageous proposition that people could hold up in this barren open landscape for a week, that nobody would ever consider the possibility hopefully,' says Toby.

Mohsen and Hassan gasp. They hadn't considered such a possibility either! But they have little choice.

Toby tells them he has to go back to his job interstate for the week, but that he will come back for them next Saturday at midnight. Toby had learnt a few words in Farsi, spoken by Iranians and which most Afghans can also understand. 'Shenbeh,' Toby says. Saturday. 'Shenbeh.' By then the roadblocks will have been lifted and they can all drive safely to Adelaide where they will be farmed out into rapidly forming sanctuary networks.

Toby gives Mohsen an anonymous mobile phone, meaning it was purchased with fake ID and cannot be traced to a real person or address. He tells Mohsen to turn it on each day at midday when Toby will ring to check on them and confirm the pick-up. He also gives them $400 collected from other protestors in case the plan goes wrong and they are left to fend for themselves.

This time when Toby leaves, even Mohsen wonders whether Hassan is right and they should strike out for Adelaide themselves. How can they stay here among the reeds for another week? It is an unbearable sauna during the day and a fridge at night.

By the next morning, Hassan has had enough. He takes some money and sets off across the desert towards Adelaide. He hopes. He is arrested the next day. He is crestfallen when he hears what eventually happens to Mohsen.

Mohsen decides to hang on. *This man Toby has mobile phones and GPS devices and wily bushcraft when so many others have been arrested. He has always come back when he promised. If he is crazy enough to bring me here, he is probably crazy enough to get me out!*

Mohsen closes his eyes against the singeing glare of the sun. He doesn't want to risk going back to Woomera where he's seen Iranians persistently rejected as refugees even though Tehran's ruling theocracy is routinely reviled by Western governments. He's already been rejected once, and is awaiting an appeal against his deportation. He'd fled Iran after being beaten by religious police for talking to girls. It wasn't his only transgression. Mohsen was always bucking the fundamentalist regime choking his country.

To go back to Iran would mean being marked for life and probably imprisonment and more beatings. To go back to Woomera means he will surely lose his sense of self, his dignity, his sanity. Mental illness engulfs everyone there sooner or later. There is no life in Iran or Woomera. Better to have a life, even if it is on the run.

The nights are worst as he waits to be rescued from the reed bed. There is no one to talk with to ease his anxieties and Mohsen can't see what's around him. He jumps at every rustle: *Is it a snake, a scorpion? Or the police?* His fears are heightened when the battery dies in the mobile phone. Lost and incommunicado, Mohsen doubts he can last.

Toby also has trouble sleeping that week, monitoring every bulletin for any news of arrests of escapees, his heart racing as he sneaks out of his office to call Mohsen who tells him Hassan has gone. When Mohsen's phone battery fails on Thursday, Toby can only hope he survives until Saturday night, despite his deteriorating physical and mental state. He is tormented thinking about the two men. Had he done the right thing?

None of the activists had expected to be involved in such clandestine planning when they converged on Woomera over the Easter weekend.

More than 1000 people came expecting to create theatre in the desert with banners and kites, to oppose the treatment of asylum seekers. Not to spark a mass breakout.

'We were totally unprepared for what happened both logistically and mentally,' says Toby.

'I was really angry afterwards that we had not prepared better,' says a protest organiser, Damien Lawson. 'We should have had a plan in case anyone did get out. We just hadn't prepared for that possibility. It was irresponsible on our part, because it meant so many people were recaptured.'

Toby, who had been involved in student politics but who now held a job as a research scientist in a major laboratory, arrived Easter Friday after lunch with a small group of about five people, half of whom had only recently become involved in refugee activism. They were excited by the vast tent city stretching out before them, a colourful force of humanity which had been named the 'Woomera 2002 Festival of Freedoms'.

It was an impressive turnout because the Woomera detention centre is nearly 500 kilometres north of Adelaide in South Australia's rugged outback. It is located on the Commonwealth's historic Woomera rocket range about five kilometres outside a small township.

It is also the most notorious of the government's detention camps.

Woomera had been described as a 'hell hole' even by one of the government's own advisers, Paris Aristotle, who had recommended it be shut down after his first visit in 2001. When he returned in January 2002, the camp was even worse. That's partly why so many protestors had come so far this weekend ... because of what Paris and his colleagues told the media about Woomera earlier that year.

As a member of the Immigration Detention Advisory Group (IDAG), Paris Aristotle had been asked to help end a mass hunger strike and protest among 300 mainly Afghan detainees in January 2002.

The dramatic scale of the protest prompted international media scrutiny of Australia's harsh detention regime.

'Australia has traditionally been relatively generous to recognised refugees ... But when it comes to the treatment of asylum seekers arriving illegally, Australia is one of the toughest countries in the world,' reported the BBC.

By now Paris was finding the chaos and despair in most detention centres overwhelming. 'It always took me a while to recover from a visit to a detention centre,' he says.

His hopes of persuading the government to adopt a less rigid form of mandatory detention seemed to fall on deaf ears in Canberra. He was battling a bureaucratic and ministerial mindset, which dismissed the psychological deterioration of detainees and the increasing number of protests as manipulative and deceitful.

The Woomera hunger strike was no different. The government expressed revulsion at the news that up to 70 of the hunger strikers had sewn their lips together and of a mass suicide attempt by swallowing shampoo and detergent. Hassan, the young Hazara escapee who had been recaptured, had been one of them.

This was 'alien' and 'offensive' to Australian culture, the immigration minister, Philip Ruddock declared. 'It's something that offends the sensitivities of Australians.'

Some of the protestors had even forced children to suture their mouths, he claimed. The government would not be blackmailed or manipulated into giving visas to such people. If these people didn't like Woomera, they should 'go home'.

Prime Minister John Howard claimed the hunger strikers were acting like bullies. They were trying to 'morally intimidate' decent Australians, he says. 'I don't make any apology for [our detention policy].'

Many Australian commentators and newspaper editorials agree. Lip sewing 'reinforced the majority [of Australians] against [the detainees]. The test is simple: who wants as neighbours people who have stitched shut the mouths of their children?' wrote Malcolm Farr in the *Daily Telegraph*.

Paris Aristotle and other members of IDAG arrive at Woomera on Tuesday 22 January, a day when the air is burning at 42 degrees. In summer it regularly tops 50 degrees. Yet as Paris squints through the flashing glare of successive fences, he can see hundreds of hunger strikers outside in the blazing sun, a field of mattresses, as one ACM worker calls it, with detainees lying or writhing under blankets. They had been outside and without food for nearly a week. Today a constant stream of stretchers move back and forth to the camp's medical centre as people collapse. ACM staff try to tend to the ailing protestors.

GUARD: Do you need any water, food?

DETAINEE: Freedom.

GUARD: Freedom. I cannot grant you that. I can give you food, water and medical assistance if you require it.

DETAINEE: Visa.

GUARD: I cannot give you a visa. That is out of my power. What about medical assistance? Do you need any medical assistance?

DETAINEE: No.

It is a piteous sight. While some hunger strikers are willing to die here, most are agitated. There is danger in the air.

'It was the most terrifying thing I had ever seen. I'll never forget it,' Paris says. 'I asked one of the detention managers how close did they think the situation was to exploding and he said "Oh look it's been bad but it's ok, I think we've got it under control." I mean, we got out into the compound and it was a powder keg. But you know hunger striking and self-harming had become so commonplace it was the norm to them and had distorted their sense of perspective. It was just bizarre!'

It takes Paris and his group a short time to realise the protestors have genuine grievances. And that while some children have tried to stitch their lips, none have been coerced despite government claims. The adults who have sewn their lips do it to symbolise that they feel they have no voice. It is not a cultural statement. Inmates of Soviet labour camps had taken similar action.

Most of the hunger strikers are Hazara Afghans, a historically-persecuted minority, especially under the Taliban government which has been accused of ethnic cleansing. But the Australian government has suspended finalising asylum applications because US forces ousted the Taliban in retaliation for hosting Osama Bin Laden's Al Qaeda. This terrorist group claims responsibility for the 9/11 attacks in 2001.

The suspension was implemented with unseemly haste on 23 November 2001. Barely two weeks after the fall of Kabul and the federal election. Australian election ballots were still warm, while the bullets in Afghanistan were red hot.

The newly re-elected Howard government recognises the role that its tough anti-boat people stance has played in helping to increase its majority. Now voters will see tangible results: some of the 'illegals' will be sent home.

The hunger strike begins when the Hazaras are informed of the freeze on their asylum claims and told to consider returning to Afghanistan. The fact that the Taliban has not been finally crushed, and still dominates sections of Afghanistan, or that other territorial strife persists between various warlords is dismissed by Philip Ruddock.

'[People all over the world face] a whole range of physical risks ... mines ... wanton acts of lawlessness ... drought ... but it doesn't mitigate against people being able to go home and start rebuilding lives,' he says.

On 22 January 2002 Paris Aristotle and other IDAG members spend 18 hours straight with the hunger strikers and others. They continue to meet over the next week, trying to find a solution as the men fade before their eyes.

'We'd be sitting across the table talking to [hunger strike leader] Mahzar Ali and the stitching in his lip would stretch a bit when he opened his mouth and then when he closed his mouth it would sort of hang loosely around his lips. And then on the first night when we were talking things through with some of the other protesters [not the Afghans] several others in the compound started drinking shampoo. It was insane, off the air and yet in Canberra we had departmental people telling us we were overreacting, even though they had not been to Woomera to see it for themselves!' says Paris.

Paris again tells senior bureaucrats they should close Woomera, because a toxic culture of self-harm and mental illness is now entrenched within it. 'It was endemic and had reached a quite staggering degree. And I spoke to this one senior official and said "Someone's going to die, you have to come out and say it will close." But she just shouted down the phone at me that they weren't going to close it, that they would say nothing of the sort. You know, they had convinced themselves they were right no matter what the facts. When you create an apparatus to support a system like this [for mandatory detention] it finds ways to justify itself.'

The close working relationship Paris had with many government advisors gives him a unique insight into their thinking.

'They had developed the mentality that any concessions to a detainee [were] more of a concession to people smugglers ... [and] that everyone in detention was going to become psychotic so they could get out and that this would get back to people smugglers. Smugglers would then instruct their clients to all behave that way so they would get out ... It's obscene to have a system that is punitive and causes suffering in order to deliver a message of deterrence to someone else they don't even know or in the case of smugglers, who don't even care. From my point of view it was we as a nation who self-harmed with this policy.'

Paris and the IDAG members fly to Canberra to brief Philip Ruddock. They are blunt. The Afghans are not pretending to hunger strike. There could be mass fatalities. It's lucky no one is already dead. The Hazaras most certainly do not want to go home to another civil war between tribal factions, including vicious remnants of the Taliban. They do not share the minister's optimism that Afghanistan is safe for them.

It is a bizarre meeting. All of Ruddock's senior departmental advisors are in the room, but the minister forbids them to interrupt. IDAG members speak and then leave. Paris Aristotle has no idea if Ruddock thinks he has been poorly advised by his own bureaucrats or if he is frightened by the political fallout if there really is a fatality.

'Philip was very disturbed by what we said and he took the advice seriously,' says Paris. 'The stakes were high. He knew there was no one willing to stand behind him if someone died. The rhetoric out of Canberra chilled.'

But as the hunger strike looks like dragging on into its third week, escalating tensions threaten to erupt inside Woomera over the Australia Day weekend. There are media reports about mass suicide pacts including children. Philip Ruddock warns that anyone attempting to hang themselves will be taking 'inappropriate action'. In a desperate attempt to defuse the madness now engulfing some hunger strikers, one of their leaders, Mahzar Ali, takes matters into his own hands.

'He was a very calm, very intelligent young man who spoke with great sincerity with us,' says Paris. 'He was very anxious that several people were talking about committing suicide. So the only thing he felt he could do, the only sense of control he had, was to say to people "Don't you do anything, I will do something."'

On Sunday, Australia Day 2002, Mahzar Ali, stripped to the waist, climbs to the top of one of Woomera's fences, raises his arm as if calling for all Australia to see, and then plunges into coils of razor wire. He is taken to Woomera township hospital where he needs 100 stitches. The shocking incident is captured by a distant camera and replayed on TV news, which Paris watches in disbelief.

'He was so close to slicing his jugular vein. He was a mess. But certainly my view and the view of my colleagues at the time was that if a group had suicided that weekend the situation at the centre was so fragile that it was likely to explode. So in a strange sort of way that action by Mahzar Ali actually allowed us to resolve it peacefully. I'm not trying to paint him as a hero, but he was in a situation where he believed that's all he could do to prevent disaster.'

The IDAG team win agreement that the department would look at restarting the processing of asylum applications if 'people genuinely felt they could still face problems going back [even though the Taliban were gone],' says Paris.

It is a significant backflip by the government, although Philip Ruddock tries to paint it as a 'misunderstanding' on the part of the

Afghans. 'If they have more information they want to put forward about their situation [for their asylum applications] we are happy to look at it,' Philip Ruddock says.

IDAG members choke up when the hunger strikers, one of whom is so weak he has to be held up, finally agree to end their 16-day protest.

At a press conference outside Woomera later, IDAG member and the former head of the air force, Air Marshall Ray Funnell's eyes well with tears. 'We did not ask them to end the hunger strike. They of their own volition did so,' he says emotionally.

Paris says, 'I told him later "You know mate, out of everything we just said, that's the only clip that's going to be on the news." And there it was all over the country. There's Ray choking up in front of the cameras. But in all sincerity, Ray's leadership was amazing, and I shudder to think what may have happened without him.'

The protest and IDAG's involvement is a turning point for public awareness of detention centres. Paris and other members of the IDAG team are widely quoted in the media. For the first time, detainees are described with respect. Not just by refugee activists, but by IDAG members, who are all handpicked government advisers like Paris Aristotle, and Ray Funnell.

According to them the hunger strikers are not manipulative monsters sewing up their own children's lips, but 'calm and courteous ... humane and caring'. Their grievances are real and 'there was evidence' that Afghanistan remains unsafe for them. The protest shows the extent to which 'they have lost all hope and any real control over their lives'.

Under a banner headline 'Woomera: The truth', the IDAG team write an article in the *Sydney Morning Herald* and *The Age* warning 'of a tragedy of unknowable proportions inside Woomera'.

But their efforts to depict sensitively the detainees' grievances is a short-lived glimmer of empathy from those associated with the government. The door shuts loudly behind Paris and IDAG members as they leave Woomera. Further restrictions are announced on media access when an exclusion zone around the detention centre is increased to almost a kilometre. An ABC journalist is arrested after questioning why the media should move back.

Mahzar Ali's dramatic jump highlights the seemingly arbitrary and heartless nature of the system. It publicises the plight of his sister, Roqia Bakhtiyari. She was in Woomera with five children even though her husband, Ali Bakhtiyari, had been recognised as a refugee and had been living in Sydney for a year. Roqia had come to Australia after her husband, but her refugee claim was rejected. They found each other in Australia only by chance through another Afghan released from Woomera. What happens to the Bakhtiyaris will become one of the most contentious episodes in Australia's treatment of refugees.

In the meantime IDAG's intercession sees most of the hunger strikers released within months. Paris Aristotle, who had come close to resigning, redoubles his efforts to argue inside government for more humane alternatives.

'The system the government put in place was inhumane and so was the rigidity in the way it was administered,' says Paris. 'It was counterproductive for the government because it created serious psychological deterioration which affected [detainees'] ability to make rational decisions. It created more resistance as each group "dug in". As a result it became a lightning-rod for protestors concerned about human rights.'

Two months later over the 2002 Easter weekend the protestors come in their hundreds. 'We wanted to break through all the secrecy around detention centres,' says one of the protest organisers, Damien Lawson. 'The government had the media thrown out when it was trying to report on the hunger strike. That was a big deal for us.'

'We had to go to Woomera and take more direct action. It felt like no one could negotiate or reason with the government,' says Toby.

Protest organisers are promising brazenly not only to march into the exclusion zone on Easter Saturday, but to pull down the fences and dismantle the detention centre.

'There was a lot of bravado I think,' says Damien Lawson. 'We had made an enormous theatrical pair of wire cutters and we were all going to wear orange and let off red flares to signify what an emergency it was inside the camp.'

Lawson's group, No-One Is Illegal, from Melbourne is in close contact with activists like Ian Rintoul and the Refugee Action Collective in Sydney. Ian doesn't make it to Woomera.

Damien Lawson also believes in direct action and civil disobedience as a catalyst for public awareness and change. But the group he is involved with prefers protest action that is 'creative, fun and artistic'. No One Is Illegal had already climbed on to the roof of the Maribyrnong detention centre in Melbourne, holding banners calling for its closure as well as flying kites and kicking soccer balls over its fences.

'We were the first to say if you get close enough you should try to pull down a fence at Woomera,' Damien Lawson says. 'But we thought we'd never even get anywhere near the perimeter fence, that the police would stop us and hit us over the head or arrest us or whatever, but that would still be ok because we'd created such a big media event.'

The breakout turns out to be more akin to an unpredictable prank on ABC TV's *Chaser* program, than a premeditated operation.

'I'm embarrassed to admit that at one meeting someone actually said "What happens if we get to the fence?" Everyone was like "Nah, we're not going to get near the fence!"' says Damien Lawson.

Activists have been in close contact with various detainees to discuss the protest using smuggled-in mobile phones. At the time mobile phones are not allowed, but the rules have since changed. For many advocates, getting a mobile phone into the nation's various detention centres was often their first defining act of civil disobedience. There were sundry methods: from simply throwing one over a fence, to wrapping one in foil and stuffing it into a cooked chicken, or hollowing out and reconstructing a can of Coca Cola.

'My best one was using a Coles bread cake,' says Ngareta Rossell. 'You could cut it in half, take out the centre, put in a phone or charger wrapped in glad wrap, put the top back on and wrap it all up in glad wrap so the guards could see what it was.' It was 'nerve-racking' going through the checks but 'the trick was to smile and present a face of calm. We felt like we were in the [World War II French] Resistance.

We had to learn to be devious.'

It also meant at least some detainees could let activists know what was happening in detention centres and liaise regarding protests like at Woomera during Easter, 2002. 'They wanted us to be there,' says Lawson of the detainees. He says more than 20 asylum seekers signed a letter urging the protestors to come. It is these detainees who now urge protest leaders to hold an initial march late Easter Friday afternoon. So they set out, unsure how far they can get.

To their surprise the protestors clamber easily over the first low, wire fence. They head towards a taller fence topped by razor wire marking the exclusion zone. They are also surprised that there are no police. So they begin pushing and pulling the fence and within minutes, it collapses. 'Fucking hell!' says Damien Lawson. The way is clear into the exclusion zone.

Protestors hop over the prostrate barbed wire loops, their clothes, feet and legs occasionally catching painfully. Only later would they realise they could have walked easily around the fence.

Chanting and singing, hundreds flood towards the camp's outer steel fence. Hundreds more stay behind, hesitating at what they assume is the legal limit of their protest march.

Meanwhile dozens of detainees are climbing over the camp's inner-most fence and down into the small buffer zone stuffed with rolls of razor wire. There is now only one fence left between them and the approaching protestors. Detainees thrust bloody hands over the jagged blades of wire, and through the last set of steel bars keeping the two groups apart.

Still there are no police. But now the festive mood of the demonstrators darkens as they come face to face with the anguish caged inside Woomera.

'We are not animals! We are human beings!' tearful detainees cry out.

'I am here because I have problems in my country. It is a place of slaughter. Otherwise I would not come here!'

'Thank you! Thank you for coming! Viva Australia! Please, I am not a terrorist!'

'We are dying in here. Please help us!'

For the protestors who make it this far, the emotion is overwhelming. Some protestors weep. Others chant 'Freedom!' which is echoed by the detainees' 'Azardi!' the Farsi word for freedom. 'Freedom!' 'Azardi!'

'If they leaned over as far as they could and you squeezed your arm and shoulder through the outer steel pickets you could just touch each other,' says Toby. 'And with each human contact I knew we were defying the physical barrier as well as those the government had created in our minds.'

'When you are confronted like that with the face of another person and a fence between you and this person and that fence is determining whether they're an animal or a human, of course what is going to happen?' says Damien Lawson.

Not all protestors have come this far just to chant. Wire cutters are passed through to the detainees. Others start kicking the steel bars which form the $1 million outer palisade fence, which is supposed to be 'escape proof' according to the former head of operations at Woomera, Allan Clifton. 'That's what they told us when they installed it. But the palisade rails could also be twisted apart quite easily once some leverage was applied.'

A small, brave band of outnumbered police begin to move along the fence.

'I would have hated to have been one of them,' says Toby.

'Please,' a South Australian police officer pleads, 'if you could move to the other side of the road, we would really appreciate it. We don't want any upset.'

But the demonstrators form a thick, impenetrable hive blocking police. By now the detainees are using a steel bar to prise the fence apart. Suddenly a gap appears. They fly out.

Some land on protestors like it is a mosh pit. Others jump down whooping with joy before sprinting madly away. It is a moment of breathtaking euphoria for protestors and detainees. Then chaos descends.

Police reach out to grab as many detainees as they can. Protestors jump on police to try to free the detainees. Women are screaming. A little girl is pushed through the gap, sobbing wildly. Where are her parents?

Most escapees make it back across the exclusion zone to the protest camp. But no one knows what to do next. They hide escapees in tents and cars. But everyone believes a big, violent police raid will come any minute. Some protestors stuff their car full of escapees and drive off. One escapee is smuggled out successfully in a large empty tool box. But few others make it through.

In Sydney, Ian Rintoul receives a high-pitched phone call from one frantic driver: 'Ian, we're in the car with people who've escaped, but we're coming to a roadblock with police. What do we do? Should I turn around? Should I drive through?'

'Slow down, pull over,' says Ian quickly. 'It's over.'

As night descends, police make some forays into the vast crowded campsite. Protestors run decoy actions linking arms around tents as if escapees are inside, then dissolve before police reach them. But a full-blooded raid never happens. 'I think they were even more confused and surprised than we were,' says Toby. Instead spotlights are erected and police encircle the protestors. It will be a long night.

The camp vibrates with emotion. Some protestors are rushing around aimlessly, others are crying, still others hold what turns into a perpetual meeting or 'spokes council' passing motions about what to do next. Damien and others head off a suggestion that a report is given on the whereabouts of all escapees. 'That's not such a good idea,' he says.

Some activists end up with virtually no clothes. Toby comes across a friend wearing only desert boots and green jocks after he had stripped down to help escapees change out of their distinctive garb.

One especially adrenalised group of activists are still marching and chanting up and down the road next to the camp at three am. 'What should we do now?' they ask Damien. 'What about you try going to sleep?' he advises.

During the evening, Toby's group notices Mohsen and Hassan standing around conspicuously trying to look inconspicuous. After talking to them, Toby and his friends decide to try to get them out.

There is only one option, Toby believes.

'Someone had to walk them out of there. I also understood that among our group I had the best equipment, navigational abilities and hiking experience. It was pretty clear I was their best chance so I volunteered,' says Toby.

As he's collecting his gear and mapping out a plan, Toby turns to a friend: 'Fuuuck! I could go to prison for this!'

But he believes he has no choice. 'To do this thing was scary, but to not do it would be to betray not only these two desperate men, but my own values. To not do it would be to put my own comfort ahead of the freedom and welfare of another human being. There's no way I wanted to be someone like that.'

Now more than a week later, Toby is heading back to the reed bed to try to find Mohsen. This time he has the support of a large activist network that has paid for his airfare and car hire and provided two drivers.

Unlike the makeshift escape, the activists have tried to think through every detail: working out when the roadblocks were lifted, finding drivers who had not attended the protest to take the escapees out of South Australia, medical care, clothes, a cover story if they are stopped, food, money and a series of safe houses on the east coast.

'I don't think that Australia has the same tradition of an underground as they do in Europe,' says Damien Lawson. 'We had to learn how to do that. But it was quite informal and unorganised. Friends of friends; pass the parcel.'

By midnight Saturday, Toby's GPS is telling him he is close to where he had pre-arranged to meet Mohsen. Suddenly a figure emerges from the darkness his arms stretched wide. 'Toby, Toby, I dooon't believe it, I dooon't believe it!'

Neither can Toby. The Iranian asylum seeker is exactly where Toby told him to be. The two men embrace with great relief. After eight nights in the desert, Mohsen's food supply is exhausted, and his water is running low. Toby gives him a sports drink and a chocolate bar to consume on the spot. Then they clear away any evidence of their presence and leave the reed bed behind, trekking for about 20 minutes to the road to meet the getaway car.

They reach Adelaide the next morning where Mohsen and Toby say goodbye to each other. Toby flies home and back to his job. Mohsen settles down to sleep under a blanket on the back seat of a car heading toward Melbourne.

They never meet again. Toby hears that Mohsen is taken in by various people over the next couple of years until he decides to give himself up to try to become legal. He goes back into detention, but is eventually released. He is now an Australian citizen and does not regret escaping. It was better than enduring years of madness inside Woomera.

Hassan ends up back in Woomera, where he is astonished to hear that Mohsen got away safely. A few months later, when a group of disorganised activists drive their cars up to Woomera, Hassan and more than 30 others escape again. Most are caught within hours – one even falls off the back of the car as it speeds away – but not Hassan. He makes it into the sanctuary network before being picked up in a raid looking for illegal workers. He also finally becomes legal and now has a partner and a child.

Toby settles back into his job although his reputation precedes him; he will be called upon again to help when two older middle-class women arrange to break out a detainee from Port Hedland, only to panic when the escape plan works. 'Yeah, they kind of freaked out,' says Toby. 'They'd never done anything like this before. I had to go up there and stay with the [asylum seeker] in the bush for a while. It worked out. He got over to the underground in the eastern states ok.'

But many in the refugee movement are increasingly upset by violent or illegal behaviour, which they believe is counterproductive. Long-time refugee advocate and migration agent, Marion Le, is scathing about those who facilitate escapes, because it dramatically delays the chance of an asylum seeker's legal release. An escape conviction rules out a refugee's ability to get a permanent protection visa for four years.

'The advocates didn't have to suffer the consequences,' says Marion

Le. 'Where were they when those young men who escaped had to go and stand in court and have a sentence passed against them? They didn't take responsibility for what they did. They got people out and then left them, that's what they did. There was no one there to support the refugee in court.'

There were 373 escapes from immigration detention between January 1999 and July 2008. According to departmental figures, only two were gaoled, 183 were recaptured and deported, and 13 left Australia voluntarily. Seventy-six now live legally in the community and 94 remain unresolved.

The emerging refugee movement has become a gangly, amorphous group numbering, by some counts, at least 15 000. It includes top medical specialists, middle-class housewives, rural workers, leading lawyers and radical students.

Not surprisingly, tensions soon erupt over what is the most effective strategy.

CHAPTER 5

Lost in the argument

Ian Rintoul received the news from Melbourne late at night. His heart sank.

'We've been told federal police could swoop anytime,' he was told. 'We are taking the boys to the British consulate tomorrow to seek asylum there.'

What lunacy, thought Ian. *The British will never go for it. The boys should stay underground.* But those now controlling their fate could not be dissuaded.

The boys were two young Hazara brothers named Alamdar and Muntazer Bakhtiyari, aged 13 and 11. They'd escaped from Woomera during a second mass breakout in June 2002, leaving behind their mother and three younger sisters. Their family was in a bizarre, but not unique situation. Their father, Ali Bakhtiyari, had already been accepted as an Afghan refugee and was living in Sydney. But his wife, Roqia, and their five children, including Alamdar and Muntazer, who'd arrived in Australia 15 months after Ali in January 2001, had their refugee claims rejected and were marked for deportation.

Their wrenching plight was dramatically publicised by Roqia's brother, Mahzar Ali, one of the hunger strike leaders who had plunged into Woomera's razor wire on Australia Day 2002.

It was the first of many vivid acts of desperation that would turn the Bakhtiyaris into the best-known and most controversial asylum seekers in Australia. Because of their high profile, this Hazara family would attract the full chaotic force of the budding refugee movement, eager to claim a human story to stir public sympathy. But the iron fist of a government also slammed down on them, determined to make an example. The ensuing clash would scar all who joined the battle; none more so than the Bakhtiyaris and their children.

It would also expose asylum seekers' often complicated stories. Many were not simple Hollywood scripted tales of imminent death, flight and refuge. Hazaras, with their distinctive Mongolian-like features, had rolled back and forth across Pakistan and Iran to find opportunities denied them at home, where they were treated like 'untouchables', their history pitted with massacres.

They had all been further uprooted because on one side, Afghanistan's fundamentalist Taliban regime was operating with virtual impunity in northwest Pakistan. On the other, the Iranian government began turning away or locking up hundreds of thousands of refugees.

But the Australian government had ruled that living in another country continuously for seven days meant you were not eligible for permanent refugee status. A lifetime wandering between countries, marooned as an underclass in the black market, afraid of ethnic or religious persecution, and unable to secure a future, was not enough if you'd stopped over somewhere else first.

Public donations allowed Ali to finally travel nearly 2000 kilometres to Woomera in March 2002 to reunite briefly with his family. This was more than a year after they had arrived in Australia. And nearly three years since he and Roqia had last seen each other. That was when he had told her to follow him to Germany, where he thought the people smuggler was taking him.

But after an arduous and dangerous journey with five children had ended at Woomera in outback Australia, Roqia had been shattered when her refugee claim was rejected. She had now spent more than a year in detention. She was not coping well. Sometimes she was found in her room curled into a fetal position.

The children were also suffering especially Ali Bakhtiyari's youngest daughter, Amina, now five years old, who had a glazed look 'like her eyes were dead', Ali said later. 'The doctor says she cannot concentrate on anything.'

Meanwhile his sons, Alamdar and Muntazer, whose singular ambition had been to educate themselves once they reached the west, had instead succumbed to Woomera's viral madness of hunger strikes, riots, lip-sewing, tear gas, water cannon, self-mutilation, suicide attempts and violent security crackdowns. Their once bright, curious personalities, as noted by a welfare worker, had become dark, misshapen temperaments. They had slashed themselves, stitched their lips together and threatened suicide. The eldest, Alamdar, had carved the word 'freedom' into his right arm.

'Please this is not a camp,' 13-year-old Alamdar tells a reporter early in 2002. 'This is an oven. We are burning here.'

◎

On a Sunday evening late in June 2002, just three months after the mass Easter breakout, five or so battered, painted cars with a group of alternative environmental protestors popularly dubbed 'fezzes', short for 'desert ferals', breach the exclusion zone and drive up to Woomera's outer fence with their horns blaring. The young activists, many of whom had driven from Melbourne, had meant to arrive a week earlier on World Refugee Day, but had 'dawdled' along the way and 'stopped for a few too many sunsets', according to Ian Rintoul.

'They were not refugee activists as such. But they wanted to show support to the refugees,' he says.

They bring musical instruments and loud speakers to entertain detainees; most are marked for deportation and many are on a hunger strike. Dozens of asylum seekers have pressed in between the two outer fences to talk to the activists. One of the activists begins filming interviews.

'I am *not* like Saddam Hussein! I am opposite to Saddam Hussein!' an Iraqi man cries out to the woman holding the camera.

'What is bad about Woomera?' she asks.

Another man shouts, 'Even animals not live in this detention! We are not animals! We are human!'

Suddenly plans to play the bongos seem pretty lame. Some detainees say they can prise the fence apart if the activists can drive them out of there. 'OK! Come on! Let's get them out!' Just like the Easter breakout three months before, the palisade fence is prised apart and with just a handful of inexperienced guards looking on, about 35 detainees, almost all Afghans, including 'Hassan' who was awaiting trial for his first breakout at Easter with 'Mohsen', take flight.

Alamdar and Muntazer Bakhtiyari rush to their mother. 'We're going too! We're going with them!' they tell her. Two weeks earlier the boys claimed to have been assaulted by ACM guards who grabbed them by the throats and slapped them as they chanted 'We want freedom!' They stand before their mother. Alamdar has no shoes on. Roqia gives him her slippers.

The two boys make it into the back of a mini-van with another seven or eight adult escapees. The crazy flotilla of getaway vehicles jerk away from the camp and career into the night.

For such a successful mass breakout, it was really a dangerous muddle.

Alamdar's and Muntazer's getaway driver stops the mini-van in the desert and tells the detainees this is as far as he can take them. 'The main roads aren't safe,' he says, 'and the van can't travel much further cross country with such a heavy load.' They must walk across the desert or got back to Woomera.

The detainees are horrified. They refuse to walk into the desert with children and they refuse to go back. The driver eventually agrees to drive north to a protest encampment to try to work out what to do next. When they arrive, they find another escapee has also made his way there; his hair already braided by the 'fezzes'.

Various other groups of escaped detainees are dropped off along remote highways and into bushland as police roadblocks loom. Some are told to wait for help. No one comes back. Others flee into the darkness near the mining town of Coober Pedy, across land pitted with unmarked mining shafts.

Within a few days, 25 of the escapees have been caught. They include two men who give themselves up after trying to survive sub-zero temperatures in the desert without enough food, water or clothes.

At the protest camp, more reliable vehicles are organised and the Bakhtiyari boys are whisked away before police arrive. Within a week, Alamdar and Muntazer as well as others, including Hassan, are driving through Melbourne, their first Australian city, where they are hidden by the refugee 'underground'.

'It was kind of an open secret that the boys were somewhere in Melbourne. There was a really big buzz about it,' says refugee activist and Woomera Easter protest organiser, Damien Lawson.

But what loomed intriguingly in the media as an extensive sanctuary movement actually comprised a flurry of frightened phone calls, frantic seat-of-the-pants decisions, and luck.

'Oh God, we had no idea what we were doing. We were pretty crappy,' says a middle-aged mother, 'Anna', who helped to find accommodation for escapees including Alamdar and Muntazer.

'It was about calling friends who would call their friends and so on until we found someone we thought we could trust.'

Anna became involved with refugees when church contacts asked her to help recently released detainees. Some young Afghan men had been left at a 'sleazy motel' and a busload of Iraqi families had been dropped at a suburban childcare centre.

'The families had endured a 19-hour bus ride from Woomera with only a bottle of water and a cheese sandwich each,' Anna says.

'These people were sitting there when we arrived. They were happy. They were high on freedom. But the rest of us and the local council were running around trying to find a place for them to stay, a bed for the night. They had nothing. I went home and raided my cupboards for crockery, plates, anything I could lay my hands on.'

Anna's outrage was entrenched when she began visiting detainees in the Maribyrnong detention centre. 'In those days you had to smuggle in paper and pen. Imagine! This is the great Australian democracy where people can't even write something down!' Even though Anna never participated in a break-out, she never turned down a request to help an escapee.

Ian Rintoul, who says he had too high a profile to risk hiding people, boasted he had 200 names of people in Sydney who would. 'Many were older people. I mean the number of people who remembered experiences from Word War II, people whose parents were refugees for instance. I don't think they were the sort of people to come to a protest rally. They were often more quiet types. In some ways they were the people you would least expect to rise to this occasion, especially given the degree of vilification in the media and the increased penalties the government introduced.'

The government had increased the maximum penalty for escaping from detention to five years' gaol, and for harbouring escapees to ten years' gaol. And there were some arrests. Five people, including an Irish backpacker, were arrested after the Bakhtiyari boys escaped. Most were given small fines and suspended sentences.

A middle-aged, middle-class teacher, 'Nicholas', who agreed to hide an African escapee for two months, says he was contacted by a friend of a friend.

'I never hesitated. I wasn't involved in the refugee movement, but I was opposed to what the government was doing. I just thought I have to be willing to do something to help out if I could. I rang my partner and she agreed straight away as well.'

Housing an escapee created anxious times for two people, who were otherwise average, law-abiding citizens. They chose not to disguise the identity of their temporary house guest when trusted friends came for dinner. But a nosy neighbour almost gave the game away.

'He came to the front door to ask us to a BBQ and he kept peering over my shoulder at [the escapee] who had come downstairs and he was saying "That's one of those people who've escaped from the refugee camps, isn't it? He's escaped, hasn't he?" And I couldn't think what to say, so I just yelled at him "Shut up!" and slammed the door in his face. It was awful.

'When we went to his BBQ, he started up again, but this time in front of everyone saying "I know who that bloke is staying with you. He's an escaped refugee. I'm right, aren't I?" I took him aside and said "Look, you have to stop talking about this! You know me and my partner could get into a lot of trouble." And thankfully he did. He never called the police.'

Some escapees were so mentally damaged that their 'underground' hosts couldn't cope. A leading psychiatrist was contacted late one night by a group of terrified young advocates. They were driving around Sydney as an asylum seeker was increasingly convulsed by hallucinations.

'They asked me if they could bring him to me and I could inject him with something. But I told them it had gone way beyond that, and the man needed to go to a proper psychiatric hospital. They were really scared so I told them where to go and what to say, but I heard later they took this guy into the waiting area, pinned a note on him and then ran out!'

◎

For nearly two weeks Alamdar and Muntazer are shunted around various Melbourne homes along with two other Afghan escapees. But the boys are so 'hot' that their Australian carers are especially anxious for them not to be seen. They go out only occasionally to the shopping mall and to a swimming pool.

'They were kids for heaven's sake! They had to go out! But we were very nervous,' says Anna, the middle-aged mother who ferries them between 'safe' houses.

'We tried to be very careful. We were told by some lawyers who were trying to help us not to discuss anything on the phone, but especially mobile phones and whenever we met to always take the battery out of our mobile phones. Apparently you can be traced that way,' Anna says.

She believes the boys cope well with the stress of life on the run. They become most upset at the thought of going back to Woomera.

'They spoke of their mistreatment there, how much they hated it, how much they didn't want to go back.'

But the agonisingly urgent question for all involved is what to do now? It is untenable to maintain two children in such a clandestine and nomadic lifestyle. 'We were adamant that they had to be reunited with at least one parent as soon as possible,' says Anna.

But her network is equally determined that the boys not be handed back to the immigration department. 'It would have been like putting them into the arms of their abuser,' says Anna.

Some radical activists wonder if they can smuggle the boys and their father out of Australia. They have done so before; sending more than a dozen escaped asylum seekers to New Zealand and Canada. A much smaller number of hard-core people are involved in this operation. 'It required a much higher level of commitment and risk,' observes one activist. Federal police would raid a number of homes in Sydney and Brisbane claiming to find evidence of document forgery including passports, but all charges were eventually dropped.

Anna's small group of 'four or five' is in contact with some sympathetic lawyers who suggest they think about applying for asylum for the boys in other countries. They could argue that Australia is breaching its obligations under the United Nations' *Convention on the Rights of the Child* by incarcerating the boys. The group discusses driving Alamdar and Muntazer to Canberra to meet their father, Ali, and taking them all to one of the Scandinavian embassies like Norway. Media coverage of such an event will also highlight conditions inside detention and embarrass the government.

Anna is unclear why that plan suddenly changes, except that they are contacted by one of the lawyers who warns them that federal police are about to descend in force on Melbourne to look for the boys.

'We were told there was no time to waste, that the police could set up roadblocks outside Canberra and that we should take them into the British consulate in Melbourne,' says Anna.

On 18 July 2002, Anna picks up the boys at 8.30 am and drives them into the city where they are met by a Catholic nun. This sister has agreed to escort the two nervous boys, Alamdar and Muntazer, into the consulate. 'Despite what everyone thinks, the nuns did not hide the boys!' says Anna.

Soon dozens of refugee protestors and a crush of media arrive. Walking up the street towards them is Melbourne solicitor Eric Vadarlis, who had run a high profile case against the government over the *Tampa* refugees, which he'd lost on appeal. He was called this morning and asked to represent the boys in their claim for asylum.

As he approaches the office tower housing the British consulate in downtown Melbourne, Eric Vadarlis knows the chance of success is small.

'Looking back on the day, I thought the boys had at best a 40 percent chance,' Vadarlis says. 'But I also thought what else could they do? Stay on the run on their own, or worse, suffer a police raid? Imagine the trauma. This was not an ideal situation; it was probably the least objectionable course of action. And I thought, well, they are in the consulate, they would get a fair hearing from the Brits, they are big on process and as I walked up, I genuinely thought the Brits would go through a proper process for children claiming asylum.'

Eric Vadarlis, who is with another solicitor, Peter Burt, join the two boys inside the consulate. Ominously about 15 federal police arrive soon after, locking down the seventeenth floor where the consulate is situated. They take up positions outside the glass door entrance.

'What are they here for?' Muntazer asks Eric Vadarlis as they both watch through the glass doors.

'Don't worry about them. Just ignore them. They're not allowed to touch you,' Vadarlis reassures the boys.

'If they catch me they'll put me back inside Woomera,' Muntazer says.

'Don't worry,' Vadarlis says.

The lawyers and the boys make their case to the British officials citing the international children's convention as well as medical reports of the boys' mental health problems inside Woomera. Eric Vadarlis also arranges for a legal team to be put on stand-by in London.

And then the waiting game begins. It drags on for more than eight hours.

Alamdar and Muntazer draw, play soccer in the kitchen, watch television and try to sleep. An official takes the children down to a street-side cafe for a snack before a more senior diplomat realises that means the boys had left sovereign British territory and could be arrested. He rushes downstairs and herds them quickly back into the consulate.

As dusk falls, preparations are in place to bring in camp beds for the boys. It could be a long night, they're told. The boys are allowed to call their mother in Woomera. They talk for an hour. The youngest boy, Muntazer, cries.

Eric Vadarlis is suspicious. He wants to know why a decision is taking so long. Or has one already been taken and they're being strung along? He later discovers that a decision had been reached by four pm by the then United Kingdom foreign secretary, Jack Straw, who was flying en route to Hong Kong. But the British diplomats in Australia had delayed telling them. He speculates they wanted to avoid the evening news and any possible further legal action.

Finally just after six pm, the boys and the two lawyers are called into a vast, scenic office. The deputy high commissioner, Robert Court, who happens to be in Melbourne, tells them the British government will not allow the boys to make an application for asylum. 'There are no grounds to hear an application for asylum. Both the Australian and British governments are signatories to the 1951 Refugee Convention and Britain is not at liberty to even consider an application.' This was because there had already been an application for asylum in Australia.

Eric Vadarlis demands more time so they can mount a legal challenge in London. The deputy high commissioner, Robert Court, is brusque. They are out of time. The two boys must now walk out the front door and into police custody.

Muntazer bursts into tears and pleads. 'You can't let us go back there. It's not fair. Don't send me back to gaol. I don't want to go back to Woomera. Don't send me back there.' Alamdar is slumped in his chair, resigned, exhausted.

Eric Vadarlis refuses to accept the meeting is over. He remains seated. 'We tried to keep talking. I wanted more time, more time. To this day I wonder if we should have staged a sit-in.' While this is going on, Peter Burt phones the lawyers in London. But there is a tube strike, London is gridlocked and the British lawyers can't get to court fast enough to lodge a challenge.

Robert Court will not countenance more delays. There are only two choices now, he says. The boys must hand themselves over to the police, or he will invite the police into the consulate to arrest them.

The boys look to Vadarlis. 'What should we do?' Eric Vadarlis has no choice. He rises from his chair and walks slowly to the front doors of the consulate. The boys follow, Muntazer still weeping.

Vadarlis, who has children about the same age as the two boys, can't bring himself to say goodbye. As the glass doors open, the police reach out and grab the boys' arms. 'I don't want to go. I don't want to go,' Muntazer sobs. Vadarlis gets into the lift unable to look back. The boys are taken out separately through a back entrance and pushed into a car between Australian officials. They are taken straight to Maribyrnong detention centre.

'It haunts me to this day,' Vadarlis says. 'Did I do the right thing on the day? Could I have handled it differently? Did I exhaust all avenues? Many have said to me since that there was a better way. If only they were there. Hindsight is beautiful thing. There is no doubt in my mind that the claim for asylum was appropriate. It gave the boys opportunities that they would not have otherwise had to publicise their plight.'

Pictures are taken of Muntazer's devastated, tear-stained face in the back of the car as he and his brother are being taken back to detention. These flash onto TV screens and front pages around Australia and the world.

Anna and her group are distraught. What had they done? The boys they had just spent two weeks protecting were being dragged back to detention. It had completely backfired.

'We were just gutted. We had failed those boys, we had failed that family. [Going to the British consulate] was the stupidest thing I've ever done in my life. I deeply regret it,' says Anna.

The attempted asylum bid is widely dismissed, even within refugee activist circles as a cockamamie stunt. 'It made the movement look like it didn't know what it was doing,' says Ian Rintoul, 'and it put the government on the front foot.'

'You know looking back,' says another lawyer, who tried to help the Bakhtiyaris later that year, 'that was the turning point for that family. It was all down hill with the government after that. Ruddock and Howard would not stand for that kind of public embarrassment, and the fact that it would be used to try to defeat their system of mandatory detention.'

'If all this hurt the boys then I am sorry. By the same token, by the time I became involved, they were in the consulate. My job was to help them on the day. But for the record, I think they never had any chance of freedom with the Howard government anyway,' says Eric Vadarlis.

Ian Rintoul had been watching the disaster unfold in the media throughout the day from Sydney. He had been in close contact with the boys' father, Ali Bakhtiyari, ever since Alamdar and Muntazer escaped from Woomera. Ian had offered to run a public campaign against the continued detention and deportation of Ali's family. The Refugee Action Collective had also been helping to financially support Ali. Ian had passed on messages from the underground that his boys were okay while they were on the run, although they wouldn't let Ali speak to his sons.

'We were so worried that Ali's phone was bugged and we'd been told he was being watched. We were afraid that if we made direct contact they would find the boys,' Anna says.

Ian Rintoul and other activists agree that Ali Bakhtiyari should now go to Melbourne to see his sons, whose futures now hang in the balance.

Ian knows a campaign photo opportunity when he sees one. Despite the debacle at the consulate, many advocates hope the children have given refugee detention a compelling and tragic public face. One that will force the government to find a more humane outcome for the Bakhtiyari family, maybe for all families. The sight of Ali Bakhtiyari trudging into a detention centre to visit his boys would add another gut-wrenching dimension to the terrible saga. Ian Rintoul makes sure the media know about the father's imminent reunion with his sons.

He contacts Pamela Curr, a non-parliamentary spokesperson for

the Greens on refugee issues, who has visited Maribyrnong detention centre. They ask her to meet Ali and an interpreter at Melbourne
airport in the morning, and to escort him out to see Alamdar and
Muntazer.

Pamela Curr, who will later help expose the wrongful detention of
the mentally ill Australian, Cornelia Rau, meets Ali at the airport. A
frenzy of cameras and reporters greet them.

'I want to see my family,' Ali says. 'I want to stay with my family
and I don't want to be separated.'

At some point an activist rushes up, squeezes through the crowd,
and whispers a message. She says Pamela should take Ali to the
German consulate to try for asylum. A note with the consulate address
is slipped into Pamela's pocket.

Pamela barely registers what is being said before getting Ali into
a taxi to go to Maribyrnong detention centre. The media pack is hot
on their heels. Her phone rings. The government has already flown
both boys out of Melbourne. Alamdar and Muntazer are on their way
back to Woomera.

Pamela Curr can barely speak. Through an interpreter, she tells
Ali what has happened: that the government has taken his boys. Ali
Bakhtiyari puts his hands to his face and weeps. 'My heart is broken,
my family is broken.'

When asked why they took the boys before their father could
see them, government officials state it was more important to reunite
the boys with their mother, who remains in Woomera, as quickly as
possible.

Flustered and upset, Pamela pulls out the note about the German
consulate. She redirects the taxi there, the media posse following
close behind. But it is another pointless exercise. The Germans turn
them away.

'I mean, why did we go there? I don't know,' says Pamela Curr. 'I
thought we were going to meet somebody there, but the person who
gave me the message forgot to give me the name of the person to ask
for. So when we turned up, they didn't want to know us. Ali said to me
"These people do not want us here. We will leave." So we did.'

By now they are flailing players in a farce. Outside the German consulate, they can't find a taxi and are left stranded on the footpath: a distraught Ali Bakhtiyari, who again has no family, and two activists with no transport, no plan, nowhere to go and a media pack heading towards them.

'Look at them,' Ali says. 'We are a plate of fruit and they are feasting on us.'

Eventually Ali goes back to the airport where he waits forlornly for his flight to Sydney. A 'rough looking older Australian man' claps Ali Bakhtiyari on the back: 'Really sorry for you mate.' Ali couldn't have guessed how much worse it was about to get.

In South Australia, the Woomera nightmare Alamdar and Muntazer fled nearly three weeks earlier now looms out of the desert once more.

Leading psychiatrists and others warn the government that such long-term incarceration is devastating for children; that the boys, who have already been locked up for 18 months, have exhibited serious psychological injury with suicide attempts and self-mutilation; and that it is irresponsible to return them to the very environment causing such severe mental health damage.

Philip Ruddock's staff assure journalists that a doctor could find nothing *physically* wrong with the boys. They are locked up again by that evening.

'We have been sent back to Woomera hell,' Alamdar tells journalists by phone.

But the federal government senses growing public discomfort with its actions. A child welfare report concludes the boys are continuing to suffer emotional and social harm inside Woomera. This prompts the South Australian premier, Mike Rann, to ask for the release of the Bakhtiyaris.

'These children have been in detention for 18 months; that is the kind of sentence handed out to adults convicted of very serious criminal acts – it is not the way we should be treating innocent children,' Mr Rann says.

The immigration minister, Philip Ruddock responds swiftly to the gathering storm. The day after the boys visit the British consulate he declares that Ali Bakhtiyari and his family are actually Pakistanis. He says the government is in the process of revoking Ali's temporary visa, and that the whole family will then be marked for deportation.

'We believe his visa was granted inappropriately, in other words the claims that were put were false claims,' says Ruddock.

It emerges later the department was relying partly on an anonymous dob-in claiming Ali was actually a plumber from the northern Pakistani city of Quetta.

And it is not a one-off case. The government announces there could be up to 700 cases of Pakistanis posing as Afghan refugees. The widespread fraud will be investigated and visas revoked, Mr Ruddock warns. Ultimately the government revokes just 27 visas. But the public smear does its job. The Bakhtiyaris and other detainees are cast once again as undeserving and untrustworthy boat people trying to manipulate decent Australians.

'We always underestimated how far the government was willing to go,' says Pamela Curr.

For the next two and a half years the advocacy movement fights to save Ali, Roqia and their five children. But there are as many different strategies as there are strands in the burgeoning, but disparate refugee movement.

The days of lonely protests outside Villawood have gone. Diverse new groups have now flocked to the barricades, and they don't always agree with each other.

Lawyers want to find a clever way to unwind the government's policy in court. Doctors want to end it on mental health grounds with ever more shocking research. Radicals want to smash it with mass protests. Advocates want to overturn it through heart-breaking stories. The Bakhtiyaris are their lightning-rod.

Ian Rintoul believes the only way forward is to continue an aggressive public campaign. Just four days after Alamdar and Muntazer are returned to Woomera, Rintoul arranges for a gaunt-looking Ali Bakhtiyari to address a protest rally at Circular Quay holding up photos of his children.

'They are saying I am not Afghan. What I have to say [is that] I am proud to be Afghan,' Ali tells the 100-strong crowd.

Philip Ruddock retaliates mano-a-mano. 'I know in relation to Bakhtiyari's case what he has been seeking to do is run the arguments through the media. I wouldn't be talking about this case but for the fact that they have sought to use the media to put pressure on me to give outcomes to which they are not entitled,' Philip Ruddock says. At the time, besides his own personal press secretary and staff, the immigration minister can also call on a department, which includes specialist media staff.

But while Ian Rintoul is hard-wired for this kind of political combat, does Ali Bakhtiyari understand the implications of such a confrontation with the immigration minister? 'I don't think he understood that much about the law or the motivations of the government. He was a lovely guy, a very simple guy and it was difficult because he didn't have English,' Ian Rintoul admits. 'But we always consulted him and he always told me to keep going. He said he had nothing to lose.'

But on some days Ali sits alone in a park rather than go home to his Auburn flat. He's avoiding the waiting media pack. By now he has been largely ostracised by other Afghans, who fear their refugee and family reunion claims will suffer if they are identified with the Bakhtiyaris. So he has few friends. 'The guy was destroyed,' says one of the myriad lawyers involved.

Ali's lawyers advise him to stop speaking out and withdraw from the battlefield. 'They thought it was better not to upset the government – as if that was going to make a difference,' says Rintoul. 'The Bakhtiyari family's situation exposed every facet of the government's refugee policies. The government lies, the leaked information, the withholding of information. But the lawyers gave Ali no choice and that was the end of it. The end of the public campaign meant that family was doomed.' Or did it?

Whether to run a public campaign for an individual asylum seeker or work quietly through legal and government channels is one of the most enduring sources of friction in the movement.

'There was a lot of tension about whether to go to the press or not,' says Ngareta Rossell. She had helped publicise cases such as the trauma afflicting a three-year-old, Naomi Leong, who had spent her whole life in detention. The Malaysian toddler was released in 2005, but only after widespread media coverage describing how Naomi was banging her head against the detention centre's walls. 'I've got a lot of flak from people, but I couldn't ever believe that it was not a good idea to go to the press.'

'I now know that going to the media is dealing your last card,' says Pamela Curr, 'and you've only got five or six in your hand anyway. If you go to the media it's the last resort and you're either going to win or lose. I felt mostly we lost. And after the Bakhtiyaris, many detainees didn't want to touch the media.'

Jacquie Everitt now wonders whether she would again smuggle in a camera to expose the horrific decline of six-year-old Shayan Badraie in Villawood. 'You know I think it marked that family and the minister then set about punishing them. Maybe I just should have gone to see him and promised to look after the family and they would have gotten out much sooner,' she says.

Two of the movement's newest high-powered players bemoan what they see as the political ineptitude of many advocates. Anne and Gerard Henderson, of the Sydney Institute, a privately funded current affairs forum, had become involved with individual cases through Anne's friends. Anne Henderson became a regular visitor to Villawood, and combined with her husband, who had been a chief of staff to John Howard when he was Opposition leader, they were quietly involved in helping up to 40 asylum seekers get out of detention. This was a remarkable record admired throughout the movement.

But 'quietly' was the name of the game. If the movement wanted results, the torrent of public criticism of the government's refugee policies had to stop, they said.

The Bakhtiyaris 'probably would have got their visas' if they hadn't been turned into a high profile test case, says Anne Henderson. Most of the advocates 'didn't understand Philip Ruddock and they didn't understand the Liberal government. And anyway, if you're going to get something from someone you don't spit in their face.'

Some of the most outspoken advocates 'opposed John Howard on everything whereas Anne and I supported him on some things like the war in Iraq,' says Gerard Henderson. 'So [government ministers] are more likely to listen to us. You can't call John Howard a fascist at morning tea and ask him to get someone out of detention that afternoon.'

'I knew Howard very well and the worst thing you could do is to publicly yell at him. He is very stubborn. You'll get nothing. A senior member of government essentially told me that if everyone had backed off the Bakhtiyaris they would have got their visas.'

The notion that the government would only consider granting visas to the meekly compliant seems a scarily petulant way of determining people's fate. But there's no doubt that the Hendersons forged a formidable pathway into government circles on behalf of asylum seekers, some of whom faced imminent deportation.

Anne Henderson, with the support of her husband, focussed her efforts on polite, lengthy and powerfully argued letters to successive immigration ministers which requested cases be reviewed according to whatever new research they could unearth from conservative institutions like the US State Department. 'We didn't use [information from the international human rights group] Amnesty International, for example, because the government would just say "Oh, Amnesty would say that",' says Gerard.

'I mean I think we started the trend because by the time Amanda Vanstone came in [as immigration minister in October 2003] she was flooded with similar letters because we succeeded,' Gerard says.

Gerard took their case for reform directly to the prime minister in December 2004 after John Howard's thumping election victory. 'Howard believed in the policy, he wasn't just doing it for votes. But you could always talk to him, it's not easy, but if you want to you can,' says Gerard. 'I went through it all, the problems with the department and the policy and I said it is far too tough. I said "Look, some of these people are not particularly truthful, but they've come here for the benefit of their family, they've sold up all their property, maybe they've made a mistake in life doing it, but now they're here and they're basically good people, so we've got to resolve it. I'm not saying they're saints, but in these circumstances you or I may have done the same thing."'

While John Howard was careful to point out he could not resolve individual cases, he allowed Gerard Henderson to ring the immigration minister's office and advise that the prime minister would like four cases raised by the Hendersons, including two imminent deportations, reconsidered.

Six months later Anne and Gerard welcomed John Howard to a speech he was to give at the Sydney Institute.

'As he got out the car he said "Those matters you raised with me, I understand there's been some progress," and I said "yeah they're ok, they're good. In fact most of them are here tonight, do you want to meet them?"' says Gerard. 'And he did and he was perfectly courteous and polite as you'd expect. I don't know if he'd ever really met asylum seekers before.'

'He as good as admitted to us that night that he was a prisoner of his own conservative upbringing,' says Anne Henderson.

But the Hendersons' links to the governing elite were not available to everyone.

Trish Highfield remembers Gerard Henderson advising her to stop yelling at politicians. Gerard was 'very nice and he and Anne did so much but he would say "oh you can do it quietly, you can get people out the backdoor". Well three might come out that way, what about the other 500? I still don't hold with that and anyway it was wrong. The policy was wrong and when something is so evil it has to be blown apart,' Trish says.

The cliff's edge urgency of a campaign dealing daily with people's survival inevitably fractured groups and advocates as strategies diverged.

Ian Rintoul believed the strategies of some middle-class groups – like ChilOut and Rural Australians for Refugees – were fatally flawed. Generally because they called for incremental reform, like getting children out of detention, which was the focus of ChilOut. Many conservative advocates were appalled by radical activism that included disruptive protests and the Woomera escapes. Some new advocates were incensed by the haughty reserve of well-established groups like the Refugee Council of Australia. Whereas Margaret Piper, former head of the Refugee Council, was at times horrified by the dangerous naïvety of the new wave crashing into refugee advocacy. For example, when they revealed personal details about asylum seekers in open email lists.

There was a brave, but ill-fated attempt, to bring all the groups together under one giant umbrella called 'A Just Australia'. This was backed by such heavy hitters as former prime minister Malcolm Fraser, former Australian Council of Trade Unions leader Bill Kelty, broadcaster and writer Phillip Adams, Baptist minister Reverend Tim Costello and cricketing legend Ian Chappell.

But the sheer range of strategic differences, personality clashes, public rivalry, the odd dummy spit and intense exhaustion meant there never really was one all-encompassing refugee movement. Instead a series of collaborations and alliances rose and fell around friendships, individual detainees and political events. In other words, everyone pretty much did their own thing. There was no central command.

There wasn't time for much else. This was a protest movement driven by a sense of perpetual crisis, like running in front of an avalanche. This was not about saving a tree for the next generation. This was about saving the Bakhtiyari family and other asylum seekers today.

Six months after Alamdar and Muntazer are taken back to Woomera, their father, Ali Bakhtiyari, has his visa cancelled and, after nearly three years of freedom, is put back in detention in December 2002. A few months later, the boys' beloved uncle Mazhar Ali, who had been with them on the trip to Australia, who had impressed Paris Aristotle and other IDAG members as a leader of the Afghan hunger strike and who had jumped into the razor wire for the Bakhtiyari children, is deported. The government declares he is really from Pakistan.

Mahzar Ali immediately leaves Pakistan to travel to Afghanistan where, like other Afghan citizens, he is given a voting card. He sets about gathering documents to try to prove his sister and her family are also Afghans.

Meanwhile the federal government uses a Swedish language analysis company to prove the Bakhtiyari family speaks with Pakistani accents. The government spends more than $2 million applying the test to hundreds of asylum seekers it suspects of fraud, even though the test is criticised in Sweden in 1998 for producing dramatically flawed results; for example, eight people are deported to the wrong countries! In 2003, a group of Australian linguists analyse 58 Australian cases involving Hazara refugee applicants from Afghanistan. These people's applications have been refused and language analysis has been used in each case. On appeal, all but one of the original decisions is reversed. 'Examination of the information about language analysis provided in each case showed that the methods used were very crude, sometimes painfully so,' says Tim McNamara, professor of applied linguistics at Melbourne University.

The Bakhtiyaris' lawyers have to produce two of their own experts who say Ali Bakhtiyari speaks like an Afghan. The government counters that it has tip-offs that Ali is really a plumber from Quetta. His lawyers produce two Hazaras who claim they know Ali from Afghanistan. The government also produces what it claims are Pakistani identity documents for Ali Bakhtiyari. His lawyers produce Afghan identity documents.

'Look, I think there was a credibility problem with the initial story the Bakhtiyaris gave when they got here,' says Marion Le, who was involved in other Afghan cases accused of being Pakistanis.

It was Roqia's apparent inability to identify Afghan currency or describe her escape route that crashed her asylum application. There were also some critical differences between her story and that of her husband about how much time they had spent in Pakistan. Journalists who travelled to war-torn Afghanistan reported they could not find anyone who knew the Bakhtiyaris.

Alamdar would later admit that his father had lived and worked in both Pakistan and Iran just like many other Hazara men trying to provide for their families.

Marion Le says many Afghan asylum seekers were coached by people smugglers to tell a simple story of persecution by the Taliban.

She commonly dealt with similar credibility gaps in other cases which were eventually awarded refugee status. Telling some lies doesn't mean an asylum seeker is not a genuine refugee, she says.

'Ali Bakhtiyari was a very nice person actually,' she says. 'What he said to me about it all was "I am a peasant. I came here to give my family protection, to have an education, for them never to have to roam from place to place, but to have a safe home. And what has happened is that instead of everyone getting to know the name Bakhtiyari because my sons became doctors or teachers or lawyers, now they all only think the name Bakhtiyari means liars."'

'You often saw truly tragic interactions between the asylum seekers and the refugee decision makers,' says psychologist, Zachary Steel. 'The very first interview with immigration officials would happen within hours or days of arrival, when many detainees were still suffering from exposure, exhaustion and illness. No lawyer was present. The interviews were taped and they would form the foundation of all future decision making. The applicants never had access to these interviews. Some of the detainees I have spoken to barely even remembered having had the interview, let alone what they had said. Many asylum seekers, to their own peril, tried to guess what the officials wanted to hear; to say whatever it would take. Even sadder were those asylum seekers who, because of the severity of their pre-migration torture and trauma experiences, could no longer tell a coherent story; their life stories had become a series of disconnected images of horror and terror. While we know this is a common outcome in survivors of severe trauma, the refugee decision makers didn't, instead the refugee applications, just like all of the others, were assessed on the basis of consistency and credibility.'

The Refugee Review Tribunal's own guidelines have now changed to state that 'the lack of credibility of a person's account, because it is unreliable, does not necessarily imply that the person is dishonest.'

Because of disagreements with some of the lawyers handling the family's cases, Marion Le acted only briefly for the Bakhtiyaris. But she did take up six or seven other cases of Afghans accused of being Pakistanis. Like the journalists, she decided to go to Afghanistan herself to help prove their identity.

'I was bloody terrified actually,' says the mother of nine who donned the burqa. 'When I got back, having got all the identity documents for these people, I went to see Philip Ruddock and he said to me "What was your feeling when you were standing in [one of the asylum seeker's] village?" I said "You want to know what my feeling was Philip? I was so angry with you because I was sitting in that bloody village with everyone terrified of being bombed by the Taliban and Al Qaeda that if you'd been there I would've hit you!"'

Her clients were all eventually given visas. 'I absolutely know the Bakhtiyaris were Afghan Hazaras because they had the same documents as the ones I got for my clients. They should have been given visas too. There's scarcely a day goes by that I don't think of that family,' says Marion.

Lawyers from three different states would run 20 cases costing more than $500 000 to try to prove that the Bakhtiyaris were Afghans and that the family, or at least the children, should be released from detention. Mostly they lost.

But one surprising legal ploy works; at least long enough for the five children to finally shake off the red dirt, batons and razor wire of detention and discover friends, school, the beach, the movies, shopping and Saturday morning sport.

In June 2003 the Family Court delivers a landmark ruling that the Bakhtiyari children should be released. It is hailed by advocates as the death knell for mandatory detention. The government quickly lodges an appeal.

After weeks of more legal argument, on a Monday morning in August 2003, Dale West from the Catholic welfare agency, Centacare, dashes from Adelaide to collect the five children from outside the new Baxter detention centre near Port Augusta.

He finds a little group of bemused children with no parents waiting for him quietly as an equally small group of local advocates release red balloons to celebrate their freedom.

The children have to leave their father behind alone in Baxter detention centre. Their mother, who would soon give birth to her sixth child, a boy named after her brother Mazhar, had been moved away from her husband and children to live under 24-hour guard in a motel in Adelaide closer to a hospital.

With a media convoy in hot pursuit, Dale West and a colleague drive the children to see their mother for the first time in weeks. The youngest, Amina, rushes into her arms. Although unwell, Roqia cooks her children dinner. She tells their new guardians to 'take them to the beach, to the movies' as if knowing it might not last.

The five children are not allowed to stay with their mother so they drive to another house three kilometres away where they choose rooms and unpack. Suddenly Dale West realises one of the boys is missing.

'I thought "Oh no! I've lost one already. He's done a runner!"' But when he looks outside to the large, grassy, brightly lit backyard Dale West sees Alamdar standing with his arms stretched up looking up at the night sky. 'He was breathing in freedom,' says Dale West.

So began a new phase for the Bakhtiyari children. For the next nine months they are free to attend school each day, catch the bus, go to movies and play sport. The girls struggle to adjust the most, especially the youngest, Amina, who 'showed evidence of severe trauma after being locked up so long. Her carers said she would curl up into a ball of rage and scream uncontrollably,' says Dale West.

But over the next 16 months, Alamdar and Muntazer bloom, proudly dressing each day in their uniforms and finding their own way to Adelaide's leading Jesuit secondary school, St Ignatius College. They both received full scholarships to attend. After being classed as unruly and wild in detention, the most trouble they find at St Ignatius is wearing hair gel against the rules.

At sport on Saturday mornings, St Ignatius parents barrack as one for the Bakhtiyari boys. 'It was great Monty [Muntazer] was quite good at cricket and soccer. I remember everyone cheering when he belted his first four. One Saturday Alamdar scored three soccer goals. Yeah, it was great,' says Dale West.

The then St Ignatius principal, Father (now Bishop) Greg O'Kelly, says the boys were embraced by the school community. Monty was more out-going; Alamdar more thoughtful and artistic. 'They turned up every day and they excelled,' he says.

'They were very popular,' says Bishop O'Kelly. 'I saw a lovely scene where their mother came with the new baby to school and Alamdar walked around holding the baby out in front of him just looking at him. The girls came from all directions and were all around him. It was a very touching scene especially also to see his mother smiling.

'Alamdar told a beautiful story at a dinner I had with them once. He said "Oh Father, there is a mirror in the centre of our hearts and the Lord looks down at it and the angels look down and see the face of God in the heart of man. But as time goes on, dirt and litter falls on our hearts because of the things we do and the image of God becomes clouded and the angels can no longer see the heart of man clearly. The only thing that can clean the mirror is love."'

By the end of the year, Alamdar amazes his teachers by reaching a Pass level and winning the school prize for English as a second language. He is given the go ahead to do his HSC. 'Alamdar did so well,' says Dale West. 'Both boys really did very well given they'd never really been to school properly before. Their father had drummed into them that they had to take every opportunity to learn.'

But the boys' dreams of high school graduation are dealt a blow when the government wins its appeal in the High Court. The court rules that the Family Court has no jurisdiction over immigration detainees. The children are to be re-detained. The government also makes it plain it is still determined to deport the family. All requests for special ministerial intervention are rejected. With all legal options exhausted, time runs out for the Bakhtiyari family.

At 7 am on Saturday 18 December 2004, about 20 immigration officials and detention guards arrive at their Adelaide house unannounced. They push aside the beach bags ready for a seaside trip planned for that day. They tell the mother, who is now living with her children, to get her family into three waiting cars which will take them back to Baxter detention centre.

'No time to dress properly, no time to pack, no food, no access to toilet, no explanation,' wrote Dale West at the time. 'Sixteen months of integration into schools, social networks, and building trust destroyed in three frantic minutes. No nappy change for a baby boy snatched from his cot by a stranger to cry all the way to Port Augusta. No bottle for him either. No time to change the clothes of the youngest girl who wet her pants as a fear reaction to being awoken by strangers. Simply forced to sit in the wet until arrival' at Baxter detention centre.

'I walked down to their house and the gates were padlocked,' says the family's most loyal Australian friend and supporter, Marilyn Shepherd. 'I just stood outside the gates. I was bawling my eyes out. They were whisked away like animals. That was the last time I ever saw them.'

Supporters desperately try to negotiate with the new immigration minister Amanda Vanstone for the family to stay. 'I have no doubt Minister Vanstone would have let Roqia and the children stay if Ali had agreed to leave them. But the family didn't want to split up,' says a supporter.

Senator Vanstone declares that the family should go to Pakistan. It is 'beyond doubt' they are Pakistani nationals, she says.

A few friends visit them in Baxter detention centre. 'We know the next three hours may be the last three hours we spend with them,' says Pauline Frick, who worked with Dale West and whose son went to St Ignatius College with Alamdar.

On 30 December 2004 in the middle of the night the guards finally come for them. With no more legal, political or public strategies left, Ali Bakhtiyari, his wife Roqia, and their six children are driven to nearby Port Augusta airport. At three am they're herded onto a private charter plane to be deported to Pakistan.

Looking out one of the windows before take-off, Alamdar is photographed looking hapless and dejected, his dream of high school graduation shattered. He had first arrived in Australia as an eager 12-year-old. Now a young man of 16, he has lost four years of his life to a convulsing saga that almost destroyed his family. What does he recall as the plane lifts him out of the Australian outback for the last time? Woomera's riots, tear gas and self-mutilation, the mad escape with desert ferals and life in the underground, the disastrous visit to the British consulate or his friends at St Ignatius College and their parents cheering his soccer goals?

And then he and his family are gone. The Bakhtiyari saga is over.

Within three weeks of being deported, the Bakhtiyaris have gone back to Kabul in Afghanistan. At last check, they remain in Afghanistan today.

There will be a heavy price to pay for the Australian advocates.

CHAPTER 6
The cost

Julian Burnside, QC, can't pinpoint when he first realised it was happening.

For nearly 20 years he had shared barristers' chambers on the same floor with colleagues who numbered among the most brilliant commercial barristers in Melbourne. Some have since become judges, and many Julian Burnside admired and counted as friends. Then one day he realised he was no longer welcome on his own floor.

'I became aware of it progressively,' says Julian Burnside, 'that I was the odd one out. There was some awkwardness, at times some hostility. It was their silence more than anything.'

Burnside was, after all, an upper-class, private school, Liberal Party voter, who worked among the aristocracy of the Melbourne bar.

But he had embraced high profile advocacy for asylum seekers, which included a succession of test cases against the government, regular media interviews in which he would accuse immigration ministers of 'crimes against humanity', and about four weekly public speaking engagements.

'I thought, I'll just convert Australia one by one. Didn't work,' Julian Burnside laughs. Although he did help to convert one federal member of parliament (MP).

National Party MP and government parliamentary whip, John Forrest, clashed with Julian Burnside during a bruising debate in Kerang in northern Victoria. After clarifying that asylum seekers had a legal right to apply for sanctuary in other countries, Julian Burnside questioned how John Forrest, 'as a practising Christian, can justify mistreating innocent people in order to deter others?'

'Listen Mr QC, this is not a court room, I am not a witness and I won't be treated like one. How I pray is my own business!' John Forrest retorts.

But Forrest, who was already uncomfortable with the policies towards asylum seekers, admits it was a turning point. 'Yeah I remember that meeting. I began working behind the scenes after that to help as many people as I could.'

'To be honest,' says Julian Burnside, 'I reckon I did more good on that day than in all other endeavours put together! Which goes to show you never give up, you never miss a chance because you don't know which is going to be the lucky shot!'

But Burnside's public eloquence was met with pursed lips back in chambers. Barristers are unaccustomed to playing a prominent role in the public spotlight, many regarding it as rank self-promotion. So his colleagues in chambers shunned his work with asylum seekers. For four years 'no one said a word' when he won even a small legal victory in the uphill battle against the government's policies.

'It was as if I ceased to exist for them. For four years I was simply tolerated around chambers, but conversation was limited to mundane practicalities like how to share the cost of the photocopier,' Burnside says.

Burnside was admonished at a social function by the wife of an elite member of Victoria's legal fraternity. She asked 'Do you think it is appropriate that a member of the bar should comment publicly on matters like this?'

'Do you think it is appropriate to know about things like this and remain silent?' Burnside replied.

Julian Burnside eventually had enough. In early 2005, he was invited to join other chambers and decided to move. He was heartened when some of his old colleagues invited him to a farewell. But when he arrived, he realised the cake, flowers and speeches were all for his secretary, 'a wonderful person and assistant'. Nothing was said about Burnside's two decades on the floor or his departure.

'I almost laughed it was such a pointed snub,' he says. 'At least I knew I'd made the right decision.'

For Julian Burnside, the personal costs of four years of refugee advocacy were stark. As well as losing friends and colleagues, he lost 'the big end of town' as clients worried he was upsetting the Howard government. He gave up about 'a third' of his income doing pro bono cases, which he almost never won. As government members and other commentators counter-punched hard accusing him of exploiting refugees for money and fame, he lost his anonymity. And he was deprived of sleep as he and his wife, the artist, Kate Durham, worked late into each night following up on their visits to detainees and corresponding with those on Nauru as well as advocates and, at times, hate-filled critics.

Of course, he doesn't regret any of it and would do it all again.

'It was a very surprising experience to be involved in something where doing it was what mattered. It's one of the few occasions in my life where I did not think I could win, but I knew I had to try. And knowing that you have to do this or else you can't live with yourself is surprisingly liberating,' he says. 'I'm stressed and overworked and all that but I feel happier.'

And Julian Burnside is sanguine about his shunning. 'There were friends who dumped us for sure. And to be candid, looking back, I'm not surprised. I had never been a political person. I didn't like politics. But I became a different person and they liked the previous me. I can understand why they gave me the flick. I was an uncomfortable needle in their conscience.'

It wasn't just starchy barristers ducking behind office plants as the Burnsides appeared. Kate Durham says she lost just as many friends, some of whom were artists or from the fashion industry. Kate had been an instrumental campaigner in setting up the now internationally recognised Melbourne Fashion Week, and was also an acclaimed jewellery designer and artist.

'We've made efforts to patch things up,' she says, 'but I guess I can't ever feel the same way about them. There's something gone.'

'In times of difficulty,' says Burnside, 'what you notice is not the taunts of your enemies, but the silence of your friends.'

'But [Burnside and I] are not looking for pity because we met so many people [through the refugee movement] who are so fantastic,' Kate says.

'So many other artists and actors and writers did get involved. It was marvellous. And lawyers as well who put themselves on the line running cases pro bono. A few friends dropped off, but we've more than replaced them,' says Burnside.

Between them, Kate and Julian started writing letters to detainees on Nauru, ran weekend training sessions for lawyers who wanted to become involved in refugee cases, established a network of refugee lawyers, held fundraisers for advocacy causes and gathered together artists, musicians and actors who wanted to make a contribution. And more if they could fit it in.

The experience has transformed Julian Burnside into one of Australia's most outspoken human rights' advocates. 'Those whose rights and interests most need protection are almost always the voiceless, the powerless, the marginal,' he wrote. 'Their interests can only be protected by those who have a voice.'

At the peak of their refugee activity, Kate Durham lost her will to make art. 'I couldn't do artwork or anything like that while this was going on,' she says.

When she is finally able to resume in 2004 she produces a profoundly wrenching, hypnotic swirl called SIEV X, comprising nearly 350 painted panels of hauntingly placid, drowning faces. They represent the 353 men, women and children who died at sea. She has ensured they will never be forgotten. A permanent memorial has also been created in Canberra.

As Kate and Julian are speaking, three Afghan refugees join their dinner table. They are now part of the Burnside extended family: a young married couple who have since had their first baby, and a teenage boy the Burnsides are putting through school. After living in the house with them for the past three years, separate residential quarters for the married couple have been built at the back of the house.

What happened to Julian Burnside and Kate Durham is replicated in varying degrees across the refugee advocacy movement. Just about everyone says they lost at least some close friends over the issue.

But then it's hard hanging out with zealots.

Kate Durham admits to trying in vain to curb her obsession when she was with friends who were indifferent to the issue. 'I tried to talk about the things they were interested in, but my attention wasn't there. They would have sensed I was faking it.'

Ngareta Rossell remembers a friend visiting to talk about new curtains. 'I was just flabbergasted! I could not believe that she thought I would waste time talking to her about curtains when she knew what I was involved with. I just thought how selfish she was. In fact I thought that a lot of the time about most people. How selfish they were not to care!'

Even Ngareta's daughter, who was sympathetic to refugees, grew weary of her mother's fixation. 'Oh she [my daughter] would tell me to stop talking about it for a few hours or she'd leave! She accused me of becoming a zealot! I didn't realise it at the time, but of course she was right.'

That's what it took to make the difference, though. An absolute commitment by an activist core. This would ensure the movement was not an inconsequential wisp, but one with a racing pulse. No one realised it would devour them. What started out as a few piles of heartrending cases multiplied into towering stacks. Papers and folders spread like a contagion across advocates' dining tables and into their lounge rooms. And ultimately through just about every minute of their lives.

Ngareta wrote in a diary about how it affected her: 'The reality is that those of us who went behind the wire are not the same people we were before. We, like the boat people in detention, have changed. Like them we have walked on the dark side. Like them we have the scars of detention embedded in our souls.

'So do not talk to us about the violent movie you saw last night. Because tomorrow we will speak with a man whose family was blown to bits in Baghdad. And do not be surprised if your child's first day of school goes un-remarked by me. The children I meet stare at the wall and bang their heads on the floor.'

Like the Burnsides, volunteers around the country took time away from earning income or spent their own money to help those in detention as well as refugees released into the community. Unlike Julian Burnside, many did this without the financial safety net afforded a successful commercial silk. It would often add up to thousands of dollars invested by individual advocates in travel, food, lawyers, accommodation and donations, telephone and computer bills, phone cards for detainees, clothes, shoes, petrol and household items.

The dual pressures of time and money generated enormous resentment in many advocates' families.

Jacquie Everitt joked that her entire family, including her seven children, were going to divorce her. 'I was absent without leave and they got sick of it. Yeah, they hated the refugees or how the issue affected them anyway. I remember after one of those big escapes from detention I heard my youngest (who was then 14) at the foot of the stairs to the attic calling out "It's all right refugees! I'm just coming up to get a book, don't worry!" Of course there weren't any up there but she was convinced we had them all up in the attic!'

After being banned from visiting detention centres for smuggling in another camera, this time into Port Hedland, Jacquie says 'it gave me the excuse I needed' to pull back from the exhaustion of intense daily advocacy. 'Julian Burnside said to me "Let's challenge your ban in court" and I said, "No, I'm too tired."' Instead she focussed on helping the Badraie family recover and adjust to life in Australia, as well as pursuing their compensation case. 'You pass the baton on to someone else and then pick it up again when it's your turn,' she says.

Some women totally submerged themselves in the lives of the asylum seekers they were helping, says migration agent, Marion Le. 'Especially when the Hazara boys would ask them to be their Australian mums. These women reacted in a very human way and so many of them would say "This is my son." People would ring me and say "I'm worried about my son," and I'd say "Where's your son?" and they'd say

"In Baxter detention centre." Some of them became so emotionally involved that they thought it really was their son stuck there, and it really was their grandchildren in Afghanistan.'

'One night he said "I love you like my mother",' recalled one rural advocate of her phone calls to a young Afghan detainee. 'I got really upset and said "We love you too, like you're our son."' From then on, they ended every conversation with 'I love you.'

It was intense and unchartered emotional terrain. There were even some affairs with detainees, generally involving female staff or advocates, and some marriages. Then there was the difficulty of redefining relationships once an asylum seeker was freed.

'You've got a relationship in detention when asylum seekers say they needed these people to come in, but once they got out they don't necessarily need the same support. It's different,' says Marion Le.

It was literally a killer for some marriages. 'I know a lot of marriages that came under a big strain because the wife was no longer available to cook dinner and look after everyone,' says Ngareta Rossell. 'There were lots of resentful husbands and children. It worked best when they were all involved.'

'There's been a lot of people who've collapsed and burned out in the refugee movement,' says Julian Burnside. 'I could not have survived this without Kate. If we hadn't both been in it, it would have been impossible.'

'He was always the optimist,' Kate Durham says. 'Always saying we'll try this or try that, we'll find a way. I would just sort of melt into grief and be terribly pessimistic. I would say to him he's got some toolbox to help him cope.'

But occasionally even Kate and Julian found themselves at odds. Once they were invited to a fundraising dinner for the arts, only to find out after arriving that John Howard was to speak.

'I was thinking "Oh no. Oh God, what are we going to do?"' says Kate.

She and her husband, whom she refers to simply as Burnside, were seated at the front of the room close to the stage, so when John Howard got up to speak she was confident the prime minister could see her. Kate Durham decided to copy an Aboriginal protest she'd seen directed at John Howard.

'I turned my chair around so my back was to him and I faced the other direction through his entire speech!'

Julian Burnside, however, faced the front as he listened to the prime minister. 'Oh Burnside was mortified. He said "Well now I'm going to have to go and shake his hand!" Which he did!' Kate says.

It is not an altogether surprising difference in approach given their backgrounds. Kate Durham had had a left-wing bent for as long as Julian Burnside had voted Liberal. They met on election night in 1996 when John Howard first became prime minister. For hours Kate 'ranted' to Burnside about the catastrophe that was about to befall the country. Julian Burnside listened intently.

'I was so depressed about it,' says Kate, 'and [Burnside] seemed as though he was too. I don't think now he really was. He was just going "Mmmm" while I was ranting and I assumed it was assent. I think he just knew I wouldn't have gone out with anyone who voted Liberal!'

'I had no such idea,' says Julian Burnside. 'The election result was a matter of complete indifference to me. I was not sure why she was going on about it.'

Romantic frisson triumphed over the ballot box. They were married two years later.

But they would both suffer from another kind of heartbreak endured by many advocates. A searing disenchantment with government and a deep, wounding grief over Australia; the country that some felt had betrayed them.

'I will never recover the love I had for my country,' Kate Durham says.

Ian Rintoul watched the painful journey of many middle-class advocates from bright-eyed citizen crusaders to dark disillusion.

'At first when they saw how our country was treating people,' says Rintoul, 'they believed it was a mistake that could be easily fixed. You know, if only the government really knew what was happening sort of thing. So they took up individual cases and visited local MPs and took cases to the immigration department and they couldn't believe it when doors were slammed in their faces and refugees were thrown out. So then they found out it wasn't a mistake; that it was a cold-blooded, deliberate government policy.'

Even more disconcerting was that for a long time, most other Australians supported what the government was doing to refugee families. Julian Burnside remains confident they didn't really know. 'I still think Australia's pretty good. I think mostly people who went along with it didn't really understand the facts.'

'How could they not have known?' says Ngareta Rossell in a tirade typical of some other advocates. 'Of course they knew! I don't believe people now when they say they didn't know. They chose to ignore it. They voted for Howard and his policies. They allowed this to happen. I will never understand it.'

While some advocates were losing old friends, Ian Rintoul lost an entire political party. In 2003 he resigns from the International Socialist Organisation (ISO) he'd co-founded 27 years earlier. There had been growing acrimony over whether building campaigns such as the Refugee Action Coalition was taking too much energy away from building the ISO. Not surprisingly, members of ChilOut and Rural Australians for Refugees were not proving a fertile ground for socialist converts.

'Yeah, it was very hard,' says Ian. 'These were people I'd campaigned with for many years, who I thought shared the same approach as me. But we couldn't work it out. I lost quite a few close friends and stalwarts over that. But if you have a socialist ideal, you have to be able to respond to what's needed, what's hurting people here and now, or your ideal is meaningless.'

But Ian Rintoul found it most difficult to keep going when his long-term partner, Denise Bopf, died suddenly from a brain aneurism the same year. He may have felt isolated or marginalised politically, but never personally. 'Nothing I did would have been possible without Denise. She supported the refugees and she supported me in everything, including all the time I was spending on the campaign.'

There's a look that settles heavily on the faces of many advocates: it deepens lines, drags down flesh, blots out hope. It's a cursed look, that seems to have come through the ages, that belongs to those forced to witness great tragedies.

'Oh my daughter would say "Mum stop it! You're getting that look! It's that look again!"' says Ngareta Rossell.

You see it when they tell you about the people they tried to help and lost; about the people who ended up in psychiatric institutions; or the children who drew birds in razor wire cages or pictures of spurting blood and baton-wielding guards. You see it when they talk about the children who stopped eating or tried to hang themselves. As they speak their eyes stare hard somewhere beyond you into a soulless abyss.

'You and I have spent the last five years in a state of grief,' Julian Burnside says to his wife, Kate Durham.

'Whole crowds of people who were sent away,' Kate agrees. 'I remember all those gorgeous Nepalese boys. Deported, deported. Afghan women with kids. Deported, deported. All the time we were saying goodbye.'

The pair visited up to ten people at Maribyrnong detention centre every week for nearly three years. Kate also regularly corresponded with many of the detainees on Nauru, the desolate island detention centre where more than 1200 detainees were processed, including the *Tampa* refugees.

'The most terrible emotional element of all this,' says Burnside, 'is that it's like watching an awful car accident in slow motion over the course of about six years.'

'You can see it happening,' says Kate.

'You just see the [psychological] damage [to detainees] piling up and you are powerless to do anything about it. Basically you watch an awful human tragedy unfold. It's horrible,' says Burnside.

On Nauru, no one can hear you scream. Asylum seekers were not only denied the embrace of advocates and support groups, but also many basic legal rights available to people processed in Australia. There was no legal supervision or right of appeal. Julian Burnside was at Melbourne international airport, ready to fly to Nauru to run a constitutional challenge to its Australian-funded detention regime. At the last minute he was told his visa had been cancelled.

'To be quite candid, I think the Nauruan government realises that the legality of detaining asylum seekers in Nauru is fundamentally flawed, and what they don't want is for us to get there to make the argument,' he said in a radio interview. 'I expect that [my clients will] be pretty upset ... they've been there for two and a half years, sitting locked up behind wire, in topside camp, at the top end of rubbish dump road Nauru, wondering what on earth the world is doing to them.'

Julian Burnside tells the story of a tape recorded interview of an unaccompanied minor (a child travelling alone) on Nauru. This Hazara boy from Afghanistan was being told the Taliban had been removed and that he could receive $2000 (from the Australian government) if he went back to Afghanistan voluntarily. And the difficulty with the tape was that 'you scarcely hear what the official was saying because the boy was sobbing so loudly'.

This unrelenting bleakness was relieved only occasionally when Julian Burnside squeezed out a small dollop of justice in the courts. Like for the Pakistani man who had been in detention for more than four years. He'd been told he couldn't take his sketch book into the visitors' area anymore because he hadn't applied for permission in advance. There was an argument. He was on crutches and used one of them to crack a pane of glass in frustration. He was charged with criminal damage and dragged into a solitary cell by six guards injuring his back, wrist and leg.

'The [Magistrate's] court was a little surprised to see me rock up for this guy's trial,' smiles Burnside. 'But I got to cross examine the woman who had ruled he couldn't take in his sketch pad and who'd ordered he be taken to solitary.'

'Why didn't you let him take it in?' Burnside asks the woman.

'Because there's a rule about it,' the officer replies.

'Is there? Here's the rule book. Show me the rule.'

The officer looks through the rule book, at length.

'Oh, there isn't a rule,' she says finally.

'There was no rule,' Burnside says. 'She was just being a shit which everyone knew. The Magistrate tossed it out and got a costs order against them. It was fantastic.'

Another time, Burnside was ordered to leave the detention centre because lawyers could only see detainees between nine am and five pm even though he was there socially.

'That's the rule,' says the guard.

'Can I see the rule?' Burnside asks.

'No.'

'Why not?'

'It's secret.'

'Well can I fill in another form to see one of these people socially?'

'No.'

'Why not?'

'There's a rule. You can only have one form.'

'It really struck me,' says Burnside, 'that if they're prepared to jerk me around knowing I'm a poncy silk, what are they doing to them [the detainees]?'

Philip Ruddock railed against lawyers and judges spending so much time on asylum seekers. He attacked lawyers for draining the public purse by dragging out cases unnecessarily, accusing some of being vexatious. The lawyers were to blame for prolonging incarceration, he said. Ruddock also claimed courts were trying to overturn the will of the parliament by ruling some of his laws invalid. He warned that refugees were getting inordinate priority 'and most Australians with court cases pending would not think that was fair'.

At the same time, the government rushed to contest any challenge to its absolute authority over detention centres. This included trying to stop chronically ill detainees from receiving independent psychiatric treatment, and countering efforts by the Family Court to release children from detention.

Philip Ruddock even passed laws to shut down virtually all appeal avenues for asylum seekers in 2003, until they were effectively overturned by the High Court in 2005 (although appeals remained strictly limited). But most of the key challenges to immigration law were lost, leaving a trail of powers more akin to a third-world dictatorship.

'In 2004 the High Court decided three very important cases,' says

Julian Burnside. 'In one, they held that it was constitutionally valid to hold any asylum seeker in detention for life, if it was not possible to remove the person from Australia (for example, if the person is stateless). This is so even though the person has not broken any law, and is not a risk to the community. In another, they held that no matter how harsh or inhumane the conditions in detention, it was still constitutionally valid. In the third, they held that it makes no difference if the detainee is a child.'

One case in particular indelibly imprinted on Julian Burnside the human wreckage of the system. On the eve of a case to defend an Afghan Hazara against escape charges, Burnside interviewed his 24-year-old client for the first time in the court house cells. The man had been locked up for five years.

'We had a great defence for this bloke because he stepped through a hole in the fence [at Woomera] made by protestors straight into the arms of police. He never got within a bull's roar of the edge of the gazetted immigration detention centre. But it was important that he be able to recount accurately what happened.

'The problem was he couldn't seem to remember anything. So I asked his mother's name. He couldn't remember. I asked his brother's name. He couldn't remember. After a few questions about his childhood, it was obvious he couldn't remember anything at all. His past had completely disappeared. He just stared into the distance saying "It's too long ago now." No past. No future. He had become nothing. It's one of the most devastating things I've experienced.'

Vicarious trauma was a real and present danger for many advocates. Hearing intensely traumatic stories over and over inside detention centres and during late night phone calls, bonding with detainees only to watch them disintegrate, believing you are their only saviour and yet feeling utterly powerless and suddenly adrift from the rest of society. For some it was all too much.

Psychologist and researcher Zachary Steel tried to warn advocates to take mental breaks, to debrief, to form support networks, to watch out for symptoms of depression like the loss of enjoyment and interest in life, poor appetite and sleep disturbance.

'For me personally, I couldn't have done it without him,' says Trish Highfield. 'I was on the phone to him non-stop getting his advice and he was so wise. I think back and think, *my God how did he cope?* I was ringing all terrible hours in the day.'

Trish Highfield admits that her unrelenting exertions took a heavy physical toll. Stricken with a genetic back complaint, at times she was so bent over after months of stress and sleeplessness that she looked like she was actually carrying the burden of all the families she was helping in detention.

The detention regime worked like a poison, provoking varying degrees of reaction, depending on a person's emotional immunity and how much of it they had to absorb. If traumatised asylum seeker families were especially vulnerable, so were some of the inadequately trained guards who stood over them. Many detention centre guards and other staff have now also been diagnosed with trauma-related illnesses.

The former operations manager at Woomera, Allan Clifton, suffers from depression and post traumatic stress disorder. 'I continually have flashbacks of incidents I was involved in. My wife says my legs are thrashing around even when I sleep. You relive it, you see faces again, you hear things, you smell things. You never forget the smell of (tear) gas.'

Allan's illness has seen him admitted to hospital twice. He says the lack of support from ACM head office, despite the dreadful reality of Woomera, stressed him the most. A senior manager would tell him, 'You've gotta think about the shareholders.' It was 'all about the bottom line,' Allan says. 'They believed staff and detainees were dispensable. That manager would say of guards who couldn't cope, "If we lose them, Mr Clifton, we can always replace them."'

Allan Clifton knows of many other former guards also struggling with psychological trauma following their time at Woomera. There was a 'happy-go-lucky lady in her early forties who ended up in a mental institution in Perth, thrown in the same area as Vietnam vets. She had been involved in a couple of violent incidents in Woomera and at Perth. It sent her over the top,' Allan Clifton says.

Inadequate resources and planning, meant guards as well as detainees, could be exposed to brutal confrontations that scarred them all.

And the trauma wasn't confined to those inside detention centres. Paris Aristotle knows 'several very good people in the department [in Canberra who] were personally crushed by this. They still suffer I think to this day. Apart from having to implement policy that they felt very uncomfortable with, they were always under siege. Departmental officers would go out with their friends and the policy would be discussed. Then there would be arguments and terrible stuff in the press, with some advocates describing them as being like the Gestapo, or having iced water in their veins. It was pretty awful, and in my view largely unfair and unhelpful.

'You know, one way of assessing whether a social policy is good,' says Paris Aristotle, 'is to look at how it affects all of the people it touches. In the case of mandatory detention policy it was absolutely terrible for asylum seekers, it caused distress to health professionals working in the centres and for many of the guards also. Advocates and activists were frantic and distressed and departmental staff often struggled to cope. There's a litany of people who have been damaged by it. Anyone who was touched by this policy was worse off as a result.'

Zachary Steel says he should have seen it coming. His workload had become stupendous. He was responsible for a rapidly multiplying number of psycho-legal reports. These were vital to determine the weight accorded a detainee's mental health in court cases. Each one took two to three weeks to compose and that was on top of his other research projects, clinical counselling, public speaking and media interviews and constant support for detainees and advocates as well as his own young children.

'I just gave myself entirely to it all. I knew I should have put boundaries, but it was all-consuming. It was as if someone gave you the end of a rope and then jumped off a cliff. You felt like you couldn't let go,' Zachary says.

Then one day he had to let go.

He was visiting clients in Villawood in early 2003, four men whom he'd assessed 18 months earlier. None of them had any hope of being released soon, although experience with similar cases indicated they could be released eventually. Perhaps that knowledge is why Zachary found it so hard that day as one by one the men tried to describe to him their frightening mental health spiral.

'They were all worse than the last time I'd seen them and I'd already recommended their immediate release the previous year, because they were so sick. And they were all coming up to me saying "Doctor, Doctor, can I talk to you?" and then they would try to talk to me. They were all middle-aged men, strong men, and each of them after about five or ten minutes couldn't keep talking, you know, they just started sobbing.'

They tried to stop. They couldn't. So they left. One after the other.

'Literally they got to a point where they started sobbing and they had to go away because they couldn't talk anymore. And by the time I got to the fourth person, I could barely contain myself. I'd reached my personal breaking point. It was just horrifying. I'd already known how broken they were and they were more broken still.'

Soon the only person left in Villawood's visitors' compound, bent over in anguish as if infected by the same poisonous despair as his patients, was Zachary himself.

He went out to the carpark, but was too debilitated to get into his car.

'I knew I was breaking inside. I threw up. I physically and mentally collapsed.'

That's how it started. It would take Zachary Steel another year before he realised he had to pull back from the cliff's edge.

'I just suddenly woke up and thought "I don't have the internal resources inside anymore." I had tried to keep going, there were so many cases coming at me all the time each one with a horrendous story,' he says.

'I wasn't processing the horror that I was seeing and it had just built up as trauma often does. And then one day you realise the trauma has actually taken you over because you can never undo what you have seen. You try to deny it, try to push it away, but you can't escape it. I was too busy fighting battles and it just took me by surprise. It was the human suffering and the powerlessness I felt about it. You know that was a shock for so many [advocates]. As Australians we're not used to being so powerless.'

He sought help from friends who were trauma experts including his boss, Professor Derrick Silove, who had fled the brutal injustice of South African apartheid. 'I remember something that Derrick told me. He kept saying "Don't worry Zac, this system will eventually collapse. It's built on lies." And he said "We all gave up on apartheid. We thought it would never end. But the lies that it has to manufacture to keep going, it just collapses under its own weight as time goes on."'

It took Zachary three years to fully recuperate from his depression as he implemented his own advice to other advocates. Take breaks, sleep, debrief. 'I had to stop and help myself first,' he says.

And when he'd recovered, he threw himself back into the same work, more focussed than ever on the intersection between medicine and human rights. He has since completed the world's largest study on the rates of mental illness among asylum seekers who have been in detention. His work is now used as a reference by the immigration department.

'I've really learnt from my own experience. So much of the anger and the depression and the breaking down of asylum seekers was because of injustice. That was the most intolerable thing I think. I mean certainly being caged with the threat of going back to torture didn't help. But worse than that was the betrayal of an injustice the whole society denies.

'I had so many of them say to me "Yeah I was beaten, I was tortured, I was gassed, I was raped, I saw my family killed in front of me, but I survived all of that. But then I got here and they broke me. They broke me because I expected better." You know they had idealised the west, all its talk of human rights. It was the ultimate betrayal. And injustice is the hardest thing to heal from. Because you have to just swallow it and go on and that's so difficult. Most people can't do it and that's why I think it was so damaging.'

He also learnt the very real difference a helping hand can make. At one of his lowest points, there was a knock at Zachary's front door. It was his former research partner from Villawood, the Iraqi asylum seeker Aamer Sultan.

Aamer had been finally released from Villawood in mid-2002 and had taken off on a cycling trip down the Pacific Highway. He was in search of his sanity and for Australia's common humanity, far from detention bureaucrats and security guards. He found both and after a year or so, he began retraining as a doctor in Brisbane. Aamer and Zachary had remained close, Zachary helping his friend make the difficult transition.

'Aamer, what are you doing here? I told you I was okay,' says Zachary.

Aamer had called from Brisbane the night before.

'I thought there was something wrong in your voice,' says Aamer. 'I flew down this morning. I thought you might need a friend.'

CHAPTER 7

Hitting back

The woman sounds normal enough.

'I've been given your number by someone. Look my son has just come home from school traumatised. He was sitting next to a little boy in class today who was taken away by immigration officials and that little boy was his best friend. Can they do this? Just come in and take kids out during class at a primary school?'

Even Ngareta Rossell is taken aback. She has heard lots of ugly stories about the cowboy behaviour increasingly associated with immigration department compliance officers. But barging into a primary school during class?

'Where was this?' she asks the woman.

'Stanmore Primary School.' In Sydney's inner-western suburbs. 'They took the little boy and his younger sister. They took them both away. Lots of their friends saw this and are really upset.'

Just a few years earlier, Ngareta would have been unsure about her next move. But now, three years into the movement, she springs to action.

'Do you want to know how the immigration officers took those children?' says Ngareta. 'They came to the school, they walked around the playground and saw the staff were having afternoon tea through a window. So they knocked on the window holding up an immigration badge against the glass saying "Let us in."

'The deputy principal came out and they said "We want these two children" and the deputy principal said "I can't just give you two children" and she's told "You have to. Immigration overrides education." So the principal is called in and she makes some calls and eventually she tells her staff "I've been told by the education department that there is nothing we can do. We have to give the children over.'"

Frightened and bewildered, the children are taken out of class and handed over to the immigration officers.

'It's the stuff of nightmares that this happens in a primary school,' says Sandra Robinson, a parent at Stanmore Primary. 'You've got little children here from kindergarten to year six and you've got unknown men coming and taking them away in the back of a car.'

Within an hour Ngareta has found out the two children are part of a Korean family, scheduled to be deported that night.

And she knows exactly who to ring: an unassuming, modestly dressed, softly spoken Campsie solicitor and migration agent named Michaela Byers.

Michaela is the kind of no-frills lawyer that highly paid counsel working for the immigration department often dismiss when they arrive at court. One of them even used to wink at her. She enjoys this because she beats them so often. Over the years, the winks disappear and Michaela Byers is even offered their jobs, which she refuses.

The idea that children could be hauled out of a school (which the eldest had been attending for seven years) and put almost immediately on an international flight without any legal recourse offends Michaela's sense of fair play. She tells Ngareta to get copies of the children's birth certificates and she books a hearing at the Federal Court.

'There was absolutely no need for such a heavy-handed display, walking into a school like that. Why didn't they wait until after school?' says Michaela Byers.

With only hours left before the Korean Airlines jet is due to take off, Ngareta is wondering how to mobilise further action when Ian Rintoul calls her.

'Ngareta, I'm here at the airport. Where do you want the placards?' he asks.

Ian and a small protest group have gathered at the international terminal. 'We used to wonder how he knew when to turn up!' says Ngareta.

'Yeah, we had pretty good contacts by then,' says Ian. 'We had leafleted airport workers, you know, clerical workers, baggage handlers, check-in staff. We were telling them they could take a stand against deportations that breached human rights so, yeah, there were people we could ring to find out what was going on.'

The Hwang family, a mother and her two children aged 11 and six, are being held in Villawood, in preparation for their deportation to South Korea. Their immigration status is a mess. The father has already been deported after being convicted of fraud. His wife has also been deported once without her children. They then live with their aunt in Sydney. But the mother has now re-entered Australia on a different passport. The two children, who have lived in Australia for eight years, the youngest child born there, are both in Australia legally.

Just before four pm, the Federal Court grants an injunction against the deportation. It turns out that the little girl, Janey Hwang, has an outstanding application to be declared an Australian citizen.

But the deadline is nail-bitingly near. While Michaela Byers tries to alert the appropriate immigration officials in Canberra and Sydney of the Federal Court's decision, one of her colleagues faxes the injunction out to Korean Airlines.

'Michaela said to me "If they put that family on that flight I will make that plane turn around and come back!" She was pretty determined,' says Ngareta.

This time it's a win for the advocates. The deportation is aborted.

The Hwangs are held in Villawood for four months before being released back into the community. It is discovered their visas have been technically valid all along, and that they have been wrongfully detained. In other words, the two children had a perfect legal right to remain in their primary school classrooms that afternoon.

Instead they are both seriously traumatised during their four-month incarceration in Villawood, after witnessing another detainee try to commit suicide by drinking bleach. The eldest, Ian Hwang, who turns

12 in Villawood, is particularly affected. He calls his aunt in Sydney to tell her that he too is contemplating suicide.

'He's just a 12-year-old boy and he told me he wanted to commit suicide. My heart broke in that time,' says his aunt, Jane Hwang.

The mother and children have now been granted permanent visas and are suing for compensation. The father is still waiting in Korea. Their case is but one indication that not all is well inside the immigration department.

Advocates have been trying to tell journalists that the department is out of control. Some compliance officers have developed a 'mean and inflexible attitude' says Michaela Byers. It is as if they have a mission to clean out what they believe are all the liars and cheats, trying to sneak into Australia. It started with boat people, and now they will round up all the 'illegals' in the community as well.

'Some immigration officers just wouldn't listen when people tried to explain their situation. Consequently a lot of their rash actions had to be undone in court,' Michaela says.

In another case, a restaurateur is pinned against a wall in front of customers, as immigration officers accuse him of being illegal. The man, a native Macedonian, tries to explain he is now an Australian citizen, and has a passport to prove it at home. When the officers take him to his home, the man is made to sit downstairs with his shocked wife, children and elderly mother-in-law, while the officers search his bedroom. Eventually he is called up to locate his passport, which is then dismissed as 'probably forged' and he is taken off to detention.

As they leave the house, one of the officers informs his family they might not see the man again, because he will most probably be deported. The mother-in-law collapses and is taken to a hospital by ambulance. Two days later the man is released when his Australian citizenship is verified. He is now suing for compensation.

Later investigations into the immigration department will uncover nearly 250 cases of wrongful detention. The most notorious is the mentally ill Australian resident, Cornelia Rau, who is held for ten months. One government-appointed investigator, a former senior police officer, who looks into the Rau scandal, says he is 'shocked at how so serious a step as depriving someone of their liberty was regularly done by junior immigration officers, without adequate training or any of the checks and balances we had in the police force'. Compensation for 116 of the cases is still being negotiated with the federal government.

Advocates are no longer surprised by the department's blinkered excesses. But they have learnt to more effectively combat them. Sometimes, with inside help from disaffected staff.

For instance, an Australasian Correctional Management (ACM) staffer, alerts Ngareta Rossell about the plight of a Chinese woman picked up by immigration officers. When Ngareta rushes out to Villawood she sees a young man bring in a fractious, malnourished five-month-old baby. A young Chinese woman sits crying while her baby tries to suckle from her painfully engorged breasts.

The young mother had been picked up at a chicken factory two days earlier. She was taken straight into detention, leaving her breast-fed baby dehydrated with her distraught husband. She gives Ngareta the telephone numbers of the compliance officers who arrested her.

Ngareta Rossell berates the senior immigration officer on duty at Villawood. He's put both the mother and child at risk! She demands the woman's immediate release. 'We can do this the easy way or the hard way,' Ngareta says.

Then she calls Trish Highfield who has long since abandoned all her polite caution. Trish now gives new meaning to Ian Rintoul's left-wing philosophy of 'direct action'. Forget protest placards outside Villawood; she demands to speak to the Villawood manager.

'Do you want to have a dead baby on your hands? Then you'd better act really, really fast!' she says.

'Oh I'll get the woman's case officer to ring you,' the manager replies.

'When?! The baby's dehydrating as we speak!'

'Oh, in the near future.'

'When! In an hour, a week or a month?'

'Within the hour.'

'Well they'd better ring within the hour, otherwise I'll be ringing [the senior detention official] in Canberra.'

'Don't do that. We can handle this locally.'

Trish then rings the mobile phone numbers of the two compliance officers who picked up the woman. Both officers are female. She gets through to one of them.

'How can you do this to another woman?' Trish yells at her. 'This woman has a five-month-old baby who is now dehydrating because she can't breastfeed!'

'I didn't know there was a baby,' the officer pleads.

'It was your job to know that there was a baby! This is unforgivable. I can't believe you did this!'

Trish waits for one hour and ten minutes, but does not hear from the case officer as promised. So she rings the senior Canberra official.

'I just put the case to him very calmly and [the official] knew me and knew that I meant business and I repeated that he could have a dead baby on his hands unless something was done immediately,' says Trish.

She and Ngareta also make out a report to the New South Wales child protection authorities and begin planning a media assault.

'And then I got a call from a very nice ACM guard who said quietly "There's a lot of action out here today, Trish" and he said "She's going to be released at 4.30 pm today!" And I said "Thank you very much." We were so relieved. But really, what a dreadful thing!'

The amateur activists have hit their stride. They have built up their own political arsenal, combining inside information, high level contact lists, tenacity and extensive networks.

'I would never have imagined that I would end up ... having so much to do with someone like Ian Rintoul!' laughs Ngareta Rossell.

And they have sheer brazenness.

One advocate knocks on Philip Ruddock's front door on a Saturday morning. He delivers the news that the Federal Court has granted a last minute injunction against the deportation of an Algerian man. Philip Ruddock comes to the front door in his tennis outfit and socks. The deportation is stopped.

When another advocate witnesses a mentally ill Baxter detainee being bundled into a van by guards, she whips out a camera, takes some photos and then follows the van to Port Augusta airport. Realising the detainee is being flown to Sydney for deportation, the advocate, Kylie, a mother of three, immediately books herself a ticket to Sydney, ringing ahead to alert the advocacy network.

Kylie had been visiting the young Iranian detainee for four months. This is after her mother, Helen, who had been fired up by the local priest, had first taken her to Baxter.

When Kylie arrives in Sydney, she discovers her friend has been taken to Banks House, the locked psychiatric ward of Bankstown Hospital, after he spiralled into a nervous collapse. Before flying back to her children in South Australia, Kylie calls Trish Highfield.

Trish moves quickly. She and her husband John Highfield hope to bluff their way into the psychiatric ward. Luckily, the ACM guards have popped out for a smoke, so the Highfields stride down a corridor and into a room where 'this young man was all hunched up in a profound state of psychological distress'.

Trish gets down onto the floor to look up into his face, to let him know they know his friends and are here to help, but he is too frightened to respond.

'I've never actually seen anyone as bad as he was,' says Trish Highfield. 'I didn't know what to do. And then suddenly, I couldn't help it, but tears were just rolling down my face. I felt terrible losing it like that. And then he turned and looked at me, and when he saw me crying, he then put his hand on my hand,' says Trish. 'That was one of the saddest days, poor boy.'

Trish rings bureaucratic and ministerial phones off the hook to try to stop the deportation. Most importantly, she also rings some doctors who are increasingly providing the advocates with heavy-duty back-up. After five years in detention, the young man is finally released. He now has a permanent visa, lives in Melbourne where he has recovered enough psychologically to work two jobs, and is engaged to be married.

By now a formidable new force has entered the public fray. One which will see some of the nation's top medical specialists finger drill the government over the disastrous effects of detention.

Dr Louise Newman, one of Australia's leading children's psychiatrists, and a councillor of the Royal Australian and New Zealand College of Psychiatrists, orchestrates virtually the entire medical profession to support a joint submission to the Human Rights and Equal Opportunity Commission.

This is no small feat. For the first time in its history the profession has been united as a single political voice. The Medical Alliance, as it becomes known, includes the Australian Medical Association (AMA), representing general practitioners, the Nurses Union, and all the specialist colleges representing psychiatrists, paediatricians, surgeons and others, as well as peak organisations representing mental health nurses and community child health groups. In all, nearly 30 organisations involved in health care. Together they are calling for an end to the detention of children.

Building on Zachary Steel and Derrick Silove's research, as well as international studies, the submission by the Medical Alliance lists symptoms among young detainees recorded by doctors, psychologists, psychiatrists and other health carers who have worked in the camps.

The list includes muteness, listlessness, suicide ideation, bed-wetting, sleep walking, night terrors, panic attacks, stuttering, disruptive behaviour and impaired learning development.

Dr Simon Lockwood, the long-time GP at Woomera, is so concerned about the epidemic of mental illness that he arranges to brief immigration officials in Canberra.

For more than two hours in a room full of senior bureaucrats, Simon Lockwood presents statistics and case studies about Woomera's catastrophic impact on families, on children.

'I saw so many proud fantastic people just break down to a level that you would find hard to believe, grovelling on the floor in my clinic and saying, "Please, help get me out of here." I found that really difficult to cope with,' he says.

'Then towards the end of the meeting one of the bureaucrats said to me, in front of everyone there, "That sounds all well and good to us Simon, but we don't want to make it so nice for them in detention that they don't want to leave." I knew I'd spoken for two hours probably for nothing.' He returns to Woomera embittered by government inaction. 'They knew [what was going on] and they did nothing,' he says.

Louise Newman's first visit to a detention centre provides a dramatic first-hand example of the system's disastrous shortcomings. She meets an Iranian woman in Villawood who is trying to breastfeed her young baby, but who has developed a chronic infection. Villawood management blames the woman for refusing to take her medication. Louise Newman is aghast to find the woman has been left drooping with fever in a wheelchair. To top it off management hasn't realised she's also become mentally impaired by post-natal depression.

Louise Newman harangues officials for immediate action. 'It was unbelievable really. They seemed to have the view that she was deliberately behaving like this just to annoy them!' So she leaks the story to the ABC's *Lateline* program. Within 24 hours, the woman is transferred to hospital.

Over the next six months, Louise battles immigration officials who want to return the Iranian mother and her baby to detention, despite the woman's mental collapse. She and other doctors at Sydney's Bankstown Hospital unite to ward off repeated attempts to re-detain the woman. Louise Newman arranges for a bedside hearing with the New South Wales Public Guardian. They eventually win a drawn out fight with the immigration department to keep the mother and baby out of detention.

It is an exhausting and frustrating process to ensure adequate emergency care for just one detainee. It will be repeated many times and often without an appropriate medical resolution.

'Most clinicians have this sense, probably overblown I might say,' says Louise Newman, 'that our word on clinical issues should be respected, that things we want to happen for patients should happen. Well, we learnt quickly that wasn't the case with the immigration department. It was usually the opposite. You could have five psychiatrists warning about what will happen to a child and urgently recommending the child be released and they just say "Sorry, other things take priority."'

'The problem I had with [the department] was that they're not doctors,' says Dr Simon Lockwood, 'they're not nurses, they're not psychologists and yet they would do the opposite of what was recommended by an expert in child psychiatry, for example. But on what basis? Because no-one died [in Woomera from suicide] bureaucrats believed that no-one made genuine attempts, but I can tell you being the doctor looking after those people and saving their lives, that that wasn't the case. There were lots of times I thought someone was going to die.'

Blocked from doing their jobs properly, many doctors and nurses become frontline dissenters and backdoor researchers.

'You know the department wasn't even collecting its own data on crucial issues like how many people have been diagnosed with depression, or were being prescribed anti-psychotic or anti-depressant drugs,' says Louise Newman. 'They didn't want to know. They didn't keep data on rates of self-harm, anything like that.'

The government and its department has a range of stock responses to deny there is a calamity behind the razor wire. There is 'wilful ignorance'. Followed closely by 'blame the victims'. If there is no formal data proving there is a calamity, then there is no calamity. And that means any problems are not the department's fault, but someone else's. Mainly the asylum seekers.

Immigration minister, Philip Ruddock: 'We're not going to unwind the detention arrangements merely because ... of the potential harm that they may suffer. This is a situation in which they have placed themselves.'

The nation's medical experts are, well, wrong.

'They would say there was no evidence that detention causes damage,' says Louise Newman. 'Every step of the way there was absolute denial. Not just minimisation, it was denial that there was any connection between length of time spent in detention and mental disorder.'

'When we said we were seeing people with clinical disorders, they would say they must have already had them before coming to Australia,' she says. 'And when we say that children are having developmental problems, they say it is because they are being neglected by their parents.'

Philip Ruddock wades in even further, declaring that 'most Australians' do not believe that 'depression is a mental illness'. He regularly describes self-harm and suicidal behaviour as 'manipulative', 'inappropriate' or even 'offensive'. This counters the government's own extensive programs to de-stigmatise mental illness.

'You know it really was a major assault on caring for the mentally ill,' says Zachary Steel. 'If you can treat the mentally ill with this kind of disregard, it's restigmatising everything, unwinding all our public education campaigns.'

The government digs deep into its political bag of tricks for yet another tactic: discredit the experts.

Louise Newman believes she is the first to be warned during a meeting with the then immigration minister, Senator Amanda Vanstone and some of her staff in June 2004. Dr Newman points out during the meeting that 'there's plenty of evidence that detention causes harm to people'.

A senior staffer snaps, 'Oh you mean Zachary Steel.'

'Yes, and others. There's plenty of research around,' says Louise Newman.

'Oh well – just watch this space. We're getting organised and we're going after that so-called research,' the staffer sneers.

Soon after, Professor Derrick Silove and Zachary Steel become the targets of complaints of unethical research by a Sydney psychiatrist. Despite having no background in either research or detention centres, Dr Doron Samuell produces a report which concludes the research by Steel and others is flawed by political bias.

'I see the research that they undertook as being an effort at advocacy rather than science,' says Dr Samuell.

The complaints against the researchers are all dismissed by the University of New South Wales.

During the exhausting four years of campaigning for improved health care in detention, Louise Newman, a scientist and an atheist, says there was one surprising group she came to envy for their robust endurance: nuns.

'I am not a religious person at all but they seemingly had this capacity to just stand it [the pressure]. Maybe because they had a clearer sense that what they were doing was right and then, you know, they could just pray about it. They obviously drew strength from that. And sometimes I thought "That would be nice."

'Some of those old nuns were very calming to talk to. And no nonsense. You know they'd just say "Well you're doing the right thing dear. Yes it's difficult, but just keep going."'

The years of denial by the government and the department seem even more bizarre with hindsight. Nowadays Dr Newman and other outspoken colleagues like Dr Michael Dudley, the chair of Suicide Prevention Australia, have been appointed by the immigration department as expert consultants on how to deal with mental illness in detention. The department has also asked them to help review a major research project on the issue, in part relying on Zachary Steel's reports.

The nation's medical experts have been, well, right all along.

'I'm talking about a 360 degree turnaround,' says Louise Newman, who now also trains departmental staff. 'They now say "Oh yeah you were all right. Of course it's obvious that long-term detention causes psychological damage." They even agree that people who are damaged can't be treated inside detention anymore.'

So what was it all about? Louise Newman wonders. Does Philip Ruddock, the prime architect of the system, really think it was all worth it? All those children hurt? All those broken people? All those compensation cases now lining up? All those hate-filled radio talkback shows she had to endure!

For years the activists, the advocates, the insiders like Paris Aristotle, the lawyers and now the doctors had all thrown themselves into the razor wire. Bloodied, exhausted, disillusioned, they vowed to fight on. But they all wanted to know, what was it going to take to break the government's resolve to maintain this harsh, hurtful system? How much longer could the government keep up its propaganda?

'Journalists, I have to say, were as big a problem as the immigration department,' Kate Durham says. 'They didn't believe us. No-one was prepared even to visit the visitors' centres in detention. [A newspaper editor] told me that he tore up my letters when they came. His offsider sneered at me at the National Gallery's opening "Where are your asylum seekers tonight, Kate?" Yes, we had a big row there. Finally after I got a tabloid to report the fact that detainees were charged for detention (by the day), a radio journalist told me that it was "rubbish", because the immigration department had denied it. I learnt how hard it is to have your tongue removed when you have so much to say.'

In 2002 Kate travelled to Nauru 'disguised as a housewife' to secretly film for the BBC inside the island's pitiless, filthy detention camps. 'Try to imagine a makeshift town compressed into what felt like a baking tray.' When she criticised the unsanitary conditions she was assaulted by a camp manager who grabbed her around the throat and pushed her into the ground. She was arrested. She was released when she flaunted her husband's QC credentials. But even though the documentary she helped film contained the first footage of the Pacific Solution, it was never shown in Australia. Instead she and her husband, Julian Burnside, virtually gave away nearly 1000 copies.

'The point is that our symptoms, our grief, began to mend when journalists did something with our stories. The only cure for it was public acknowledgment of the great wrongs the government was doing,' Kate says.

Which is why Ngareta Rossell is crestfallen to see the front page headline on 17 December 2002, in Sydney's largest selling newspaper, the *Daily Telegraph*. It reads 'Five star asylums', referring to the hotel-standard accommodation of most detention camps.

'Condemned by their critics as concentration camps, Australia's detention centres provide asylum seekers with everything from DVDs and pay-TV to classes in yoga, flower-arranging and driver education,' the article claims. It also lists an array of glossy services like mini-swimming pools for children, electric guitars and hair dressing. Advocacy groups are stunned. They have never seen any of these services inside detention.

The story comes straight from the immigration department's website. No reality checking by the journalist, David Penberthy (now editor of the *Daily Telegraph*) who said he wanted to write 'a long overdue counter-attack on the concentration camp line'.

Ngareta is determined to tackle him about his story. And she has a plan. But she waits four months, to let tempers cool. 'You probably got a lot of flack for that story', she says when she and David Penberthy finally talk on the phone. He has had his car tyres let down and a glass of wine thrown over him at a bar because of the story.

'But I can tell you've never been to a detention centre and I go all the time, so why don't you come with me for a visit?' Ngareta says. 'No strings attached, just come out, meet some of the detainees, see what it's like. I go out every week. I can pick you up from your office on Wednesday about 2 pm.'

Ngareta hears a short 'Uh' intake of breath and then David Penberthy says: 'Okay, yeah, yeah, that would be good.'

Over the next six months, Penberthy visits Villawood ten times with Ngareta.

As they leave Villawood one day, says Ngareta, another male visitor mentions to David Penberthy that there was a 'terrible article in a newspaper describing detention as an expensive hotel'.

David Penberthy at first stays mute and walks on to where their car is parked. But then he runs back, 'Geez mate, I have to tell you I wrote that story and I'm sorry I did.'

A year after his first article, David Penberthy goes on to write about his experiences in a series of articles in the prime minister's self-proclaimed favourite newspaper. Penberthy's articles, delivered into the homes of the Howard Battlers, describe in aching detail the plight of some of the rejected asylum seekers, left sitting in detention.

'Terms such as "queue-jumper" do not do this bloke any justice. They are also factually wrong.

'"People say we come through the back door, but where is the front door? Where is the queue? You can't jump it, because there isn't one.

In Iran, the moment you tell the authorities you want to leave you become an enemy of the state."

'... It is not the conditions, but the duration of detention that is manifestly cruel. Even if that doesn't bother you, think about it in selfish taxpayer terms.

'It's bloody expensive. The deliberate sloth in processing claims is part of a publicly-funded warning to those who would deal with people smugglers – come to Australia illegally and you'll languish in detention, possibly for years.

'Nice way to make the point.'

'And so we turned David Penberthy,' says John Highfield. 'And that was a signal to me that the movement was finally having an impact, finally breaking through the propaganda.'

By 2004 there are regular media reports about the dreadful effects of long-term detention on men, women and children. There are piercing signals that Australia's mandatory detention system has become dangerously inhumane.

The sheer number of riots and hunger strikes inside the detention centres is the first giveaway, according to prison experts, who say management is failing whenever there are successive riots in a closed institution.

'It is no coincidence that riots occur in a system that lacks accountability,' says Professor Richard Harding, Western Australian inspector of Custodial Services. 'We do not have riots in our detention centres because we have a riotous group of refugees; we have them because we run appalling systems.'

There has also been a blizzard of official reports criticising the operation of Australia's immigration detention regime. These come from Amnesty International, Human Rights Watch, the United Nations Working Group on Arbitrary Detention, the United Nations High Commissioner for Human Rights, the Commonwealth Ombudsman, various federal parliamentary committees, various state government child protection authorities, the Medical Alliance (covering just about all of the nation's health professionals) and the government's own advisory body, the Immigration Detention Advisory Group.

The government dismisses or skirts around them all.

'The report is a very disappointing effort. It contains fundamental factual errors ... Yet again a UN human rights body has produced a report misguidedly critical of Australia,' says a joint press release from ministers Philip Ruddock and Alexander Downer to the UN Working Group on Arbitrary Detention in December, 2002.

'You can take it that I am very disappointed at the quality of the work that the Ombudsman has done,' says Philip Ruddock of a 2001 Ombudsman report detailing how some detainees were not given the same basic rights as convicted criminals.

In May 2004, the most comprehensive and devastating investigation yet of mandatory detention is tabled in federal parliament. The Human Rights and Equal Opportunity Commission's 900-page report called *A last resort?* specifically deals with children in detention, and has taken almost three years to compile. Its researchers have conducted extensive first-hand interviews, trawled through boxes of internal ACM and immigration department documents, and received more than 300 submissions. The report details gross violations of children's rights and affirms the medical profession's claims about detention's catastrophic psychological effects. Its factual accuracy is never challenged by the government. It calls for all families to be released from detention.

The government nevertheless rejects the report's major findings and recommendations. To implement such a policy would be to 'send a very dangerous message' to people smugglers that 'if you bring children you'll be able to be out in the community very quickly', says Senator Amanda Vanstone.

The government also releases the report on the same day as the budget to ensure minimal publicity.

'I remember having a conversation,' says Trish Highfield, 'with a staffer in [then immigration minister] Vanstone's office about the HREOC report and he scoffed "Oh, you know what the government thinks of the HREOC report." And I said to him "How dare you treat a report like that with so much contempt? So many people in the Human Rights Commission, so many doctors and nurses, so many other decent Australians put so much work into this! How dare you be so disrespectful!'"

But in the lead up to the 2004 federal election later that year, the government is so sensitive about children in detention that it pretends there is only one child still locked up. Amanda Vanstone tells the *Sydney Morning Herald* that she is 'very pleased that we're now down to one child in detention centres'.

The 'one child' is in Baxter detention centre, and is the baby of asylum seekers who arrived by boat. In fact there are 75 children in detention at the time, including 59 around Australia and 16 on Nauru. Conveniently overlooked by the government are the boat arrival children imprisoned in Nauru, Christmas Island and the Port Augusta Residential Housing Project, and the children who arrived by plane and are imprisoned in the Villawood and Maribyrnong centres.

The refugee movement rallies for the election. Maybe this time. Surely with the medical profession now on side and with no more boats panicking voters, the electorate will pressure the government to relent.

But it is never a vote-changing issue for most Australians, who remain fearful of on-going Islamic terrorism. Terrorists had struck in 2002 in the Bali bombing which killed 202 people, including 88 Australians. On 9 September 2004, a month before the election, a car bomb planted by Muslim extremists ignites outside the Australian embassy in Jakarta, Indonesia, killing nine people.

On 9 October 2004, John Howard's government is returned for the fourth time with a record majority and control of both houses of parliament. 'Who do you trust?' has been the campaign theme. Boat people are not a key issue, but John Howard's mandate to continue the harsh detention regime as part of border protection is clear.

It is the lowest point for the refugee movement, which believes it now faces at least three more years of human carnage, especially among long-term detainees like Kashmiri asylum seeker Peter Qasim, who has been locked up for more than six years.

'There was utter despair,' says Jo Szwarc, who is working with Paris Aristotle at the Victorian Foundation for Survivors of Torture, and who has widespread contacts in the refugee advocacy movement. 'The feeling was we were stuck with the government's policies, that there could be no change.'

But then Jo Szwarc gets an offer he can't refuse. He will go to work with federal Victorian Liberal backbencher, Petro Georgiou. The course of mandatory detention is about to unexpectedly shift. And it is all crystallised over a big Greek Christmas lunch in Melbourne.

Petro Georgiou has gathered together the staff he needs, including Jo Szwarc and a political gun, Michael Kapel. Over lamb, seafood and white wine, Petro Georgiou tells them: 'I've had enough. We're going for it.'

CHAPTER 8

Petro's charge

'You know this will be ugly,' Petro Georgiou says.

His handpicked refugee policy hit team pour more wine. It is Christmas Day 2004 at Petro's house in Melbourne's eastern suburbs. They all know exactly what 'ugly' means.

'I knew it was going to be extraordinarily difficult; we probably had a five percent chance of succeeding,' says Michael Kapel, a long-time aide and friend.

Tough-minded and insightful, Michael Kapel, at 42 the youngest of the team, states the obvious: Petro will face a ferocious pre-selection challenge, not to mention dirty tricks, public renunciation by colleagues and media attacks.

The group quickly dismisses all the reasons not to go ahead. Kapel never hesitates. He had worked for Petro from 1996 before leaving to consult for corporate Australia in 2001. He would rejoin Petro in 2005 for this campaign as a volunteer.

'Petro said "Will you help?" and I said "You're paying for lunch for the rest of the year",' says Michael Kapel.

The other newly appointed staffer is also a longtime friend, although Jo Szwarc swings the other way: he votes Labor.

Szwarc and Petro Georgiou have been friends since their student days at Melbourne University. There they discovered a shared passion for human rights, even though 'we may have politically expressed it differently,' says Szwarc. Petro Georgiou headed into the Liberal

Party where he helped give birth to multicultural Australia. Jo Szwarc stood as a Labor candidate in local council elections before moving into government bureaucracy, the Victorian Law Reform Commission and human rights organisations such as Amnesty, the Victorian Foundation for Survivors of Torture and the Red Cross.

He doesn't hesitate when Petro approaches him soon after the 2004 election to help reform refugee policies.

'I was delighted,' says Jo Szwarc. 'I thought if anyone could [change the policies], he could. It certainly wasn't going to happen from the other [Labor] side of politics. I mean that had just been smashed [in the 2004 election], they were in disarray. I'd say to people Petro is now the only effective opposition on this issue.'

The Labor Party had called for children to be released from detention in 2002, finally breaking the lock-step bipartisanship on refugee policy. But it balked at calling for further reform, even though some of its members were passionately opposed to the detention regime. One of Labor's high profile shadow ministers, the former West Australian premier, Carmen Lawrence, had resigned from the frontbench over the issue. Along with left-wing MPs like Tanya Plibersek she had lobbied intensely for the party to reinstate permanent visas for refugees and to return to processing asylum seekers in the community. The reformers mobilised a ginger group called 'Labor for Refugees', and launched a major push at the Australian Labor Party national conference before the 2004 election. But party officials rallied enough votes to narrowly defeat their proposals.

'The conference did pass some significant changes,' says Tanya Plibersek, 'but the policy as a whole was still far from perfect. Removing children from detention and dumping the Pacific Solution were significant reforms, but I was disappointed we didn't go further.'

Unlike the Liberal Party, which has a tradition of conscience votes, all Labor MPs are bound by the collective vote of their parliamentary party in caucus. The last two federal Labor MPs to cross the floor, Senator George Georges in 1986 and Senator Graeme Campbell in 1988, were both suspended from the party.

But Petro Georgiou had received a Labor blessing of sorts. A few years earlier Petro had also protested the Howard government's attempts to more narrowly define what constitutes a refugee. One day he and Michael Kapel were at lunch in Parliament House when former Labor prime minister, Gough Whitlam, slowly made his way into the dining room. He surprised everyone by moving past his own table towards Petro, who jumped up to shake his hand.

'Gough, how are you?'

'Petro,' boomed Whitlam. 'You're a good man, Petro. You are doing good work on refugees. Keep it up.' And then just as Gough was about to turn away, he added: 'I know it was you in '75, Petro. But I forgive you.' And then Gough moved back to his own table.

That Christmas afternoon in 2004, Petro Georgiou lays out his plan. He is going to introduce a private member's bill aimed at abolishing indefinite mandatory detention unless he is offered substantial reform.

Petro faces an uphill charge, and there will be no turning back. Michael Kapel and Jo Szwarc pour more wine.

'No, no. I'm not going to sit around and be responsible for this happening whilst I'm part of the government,' Petro tells them. 'I've crossed my bridge on this. No, no. This is it. We're going there.'

Petro often talks in clipped, definitive phrases, as if he's moved way past the need for argument or explanation. It contributes to his cranky, taciturn image. Today no explanation is needed.

'We knew exactly what he meant. None of us at that lunch was in any doubt that Petro had decided to confront the prime minister and roll the policy,' says Michael Kapel.

Or to put it another way, laughs Michael: 'Two Jews and a Greek heading over the cliff together!'

They get down to details. This may be a morality mission, but Petro Georgiou maps it out with the cold-eyed expertise of his years as a brutal, machine politician.

First, timing. Now is the time. Leaving it much longer will mean it's too far away from the 2004 election and too close to the next election. Only three asylum seeker boats have made it into Australian waters since December 2001. Electoral hysteria has subsided, and some softening in community attitudes about asylum seekers has occurred. Refugee activists and the medical profession have successfully seeded concerns about the effects of detention on children and mental illness.

Second, Petro needs to gather around him a core group of like-minded Liberal parliamentarians, so he cannot be dismissed as a lone wolf. They are confident of finding at least two contenders for this punishing role. They also need to rally support among refugee advocacy groups and religious leaders.

Third, they assess small (but growing) levels of discontent across government ranks about mandatory detention policies. It is a potent point of leverage. Potential for breakouts exist on a number of fronts: in the lower house *and* upper house. Not just among the so-called moderates of the party like Petro Georgiou, but across factions. And not just among Liberals, but among some members of their Coalition partner, the National Party. The numbers are small and unpredictable, but it will keep John Howard guessing.

'The thing is you can't underestimate the effect on John Howard or any Liberal having lived through the [former Liberal prime minister Malcolm] Fraser and [former Liberal Opposition leader Andrew] Peacock periods, understanding the consequences [for a leader] of a major breakout with people crossing the floor,' says Michael Kapel, 'Petro and John Howard had both lived through that period. Petro had an acute insight into how the prime minister was likely to react to his first real internal crisis with MPs possibly crossing the floor.

'We knew we were unlikely to get the numbers, but John Howard couldn't be sure about how many we did have.'

To exploit this, Petro decides to break his private member's bill into two parts. The first part deals with the immediate crisis of children, mental illness, long-term detainees and the agonising temporary status of those who are found to be refugees, but have been left in limbo in the community. The second part deals with fundamental reform of the system to abolish long-term detention and provide for independent judicial review of detainees. It opens the way for nervous MPs to support bits of his bill, without having to wholly oppose John Howard.

If this was a western, it would be like creating the sound of many rifles in a canyon, when there were really only a few.

But why has Petro Georgiou waited so long? And why won't he consider smaller and perhaps more achievable reforms? How is it that Petro Georgiou now sounds more like Ian Rintoul, who also wants to smash the system of mandatory detention, and not like Gerard Henderson or other more traditionally-aligned voices, who are working for reform within the system? The Labor Opposition will not even contemplate abolishing mandatory detention at this time.

Because Petro has been battling quietly behind the scenes for three years. Because he and others have repeatedly sought, and been given assurances, that women and children would be put into alternative accommodation and that medical resources to treat spiralling mental illness in detention would be bolstered. Because those assurances have not been met. Because incremental reform has not worked.

'I had thought that doing deals to mitigate the worst excesses of some of the policies was enough,' says Petro Georgiou. He had led another backbench rebellion in 2000 over the introduction in the Northern Territory of mandatory sentencing for petty crimes (which would have inordinately applied to Aboriginal children). John Howard was forced to back down. Petro had also argued successfully against post-*Tampa* legislation which would have so narrowed Australia's definition of a refugee that had it been operating during World War II, it would have excluded Jews fleeing Nazi Germany. He also lobbied against expanding immigration department powers to enable body searches of children.

'So how will you feel, Petro,' one of his colleagues asked accusingly 'if a secreted weapon is used to stab one of our Australian immigration officers?'

'I will feel just as sad,' said Petro, 'as if a wayward youth stabs a police officer, but we still shouldn't conduct cavity searches of minors!'

But Liberal moderates like Petro Georgiou have been reduced to a largely ineffective rump, bargaining at the edges of government policy.

'When I stopped an extreme culture from becoming more extreme

I called it a victory,' says Petro Georgiou. 'If we could save something then I believed it was a good bargain. But at the end of the day, the bargains amounted to nothing.'

'Petro was enormously disillusioned,' says Michael Kapel. 'He had been through a tortuous process, trying to achieve reforms in detention policy and then believed there was an agreement for change. Ultimately he realised that it would never be implemented and he felt let down. And all the while things were getting worse in detention centres.'

Petro attended his first meeting with John Howard about refugee policies after the 2001 *Tampa* election. Multiple meetings followed over the next three years with a varying group of backbenchers and the prime minister, and separately with the then immigration minister, Philip Ruddock.

In August 2002, Petro took the argument to the party room: 'We are neither a country under siege, nor have we lost control of our borders,' he said. 'We have gone further than every other western country in the severity of our detention regime and now find ourselves punishing those who our own processes are finding to be legitimate refugees ... This is not good public policy ... We do not require mandatory detention but discretionary detention ... I believe that the policy has become unsustainable and whether it occurs now or later it is inevitable that it will be changed.'

In December 2002, Petro believed they had reached a deal when Philip Ruddock and John Howard agreed that the vast majority of women and children should be accommodated more humanely outside detention centres. The minister even went into parliament to table a series of 'Migration Series Instructions' declaring that 'every effort should be made' to place women and children in alternative detention housing outside the camps 'as soon as possible'.

'Do you feel triumphant?' Petro was asked at the time.

'No,' he said. 'I just feel better.'

Not for long. Only 83 out of more than 2000 children would be transferred by the end of 2003.

'Dear Prime Minister,' Petro Georgiou wrote in April 2003, it had become clear that 'the department had failed to make any attempt and did not intend to implement or pursue the use of residential housing projects ... achieving the agreed changes by administrative measures has not been successful.'

Petro suggested for the first time that he might introduce his own legislation. More meetings took place with John Howard and Philip Ruddock. All played out quietly behind the scenes, no dramatic show-downs, no party room threats, no media.

Petro wrote again in August 2003: 'Dear Prime Minister ... I have written to you and along with some of our colleagues I have also met with you and the minister raising the concern that the agreement we reached was not being implemented. A number of explicit assurances were given that the agreement would be met. It is deeply regrettable that the assurances ... have not been met ... I advise that I see no alternative to legislative measures.'

More meetings. But it became plain that it was going to take years before a comprehensive alternative housing scheme for families would be ready. Petro realised that the deal was a dud.

Three years of back room negotiations, by December 2004, have produced almost nothing. Petro has been out maneuvered. He is determined it will not happen again. Empty promises will not be met by empty threats.

And so it begins.

Petro Georgiou does not have to look hard to find his first parliamentary ally. He flies to Sydney to ask Bruce Baird to support the private member's bill. Bruce is a former New South Wales minister who had been instrumental in winning the Sydney 2000 Olympics. He was one of the first Liberals to protest the treatment of refugees after touring detention centres in 2000 for a federal parliamentary report. 'A gulag, dirt floors, people wandering around with spaced out looks, they were called by numbers not names,' he says of what he saw.

He was especially appalled by the attitude of the immigration officials who tried to censor what the MPs were seeing and hearing. At Port Hedland officials had put up photographs of the children being taken on an excursion to McDonalds.

'You would have thought it was a holiday camp the way they were talking and then we found the Juliet [isolation] block where they would lock up 30 people sometimes including children with one toilet. And they'd tried to keep that from us. We were saying to the officials "Why didn't you tell us about this beforehand? You've got a prison within a prison! If the guards don't like someone they can put them in here and there's no way for people to question that! Why have you got children in here?" And there was this one official who was like Dr Death and she never conceded a thing, just saying "Oh these people [detainees] would say that wouldn't they, oh we conform to the international standards." We were all pretty angry actually.'

Bruce Baird has also become one of the party's most active parliamentary advocates for individual asylum seekers over the years, helping at least 50 people to get out of detention.

Like Petro, he has been unsuccessfully pushing for reform. He had even toured Europe studying alternatives to the Howard/Ruddock refugee regime and written a private report for his colleagues proposing time limits for processing detainees.

The trip was an unnerving experience, he says, because Australian immigration officials suddenly popped up and followed him around various European cities. 'I had not asked them to accompany me,' he says. 'But they would sit in on all my meetings. And they would interrupt all the time, contradicting my concerns. I lost my temper with one of them in the end.'

Bruce Baird knows exactly what lies ahead for the rebels. He's been through it before.

In a June 2001 bipartisan report, called *A report on visits to immigration detention centres*, he and his parliamentary committee colleagues recommended a 14-week time limit on detention and separate accommodation for families. But they and their report were dismissed by immigration minister, Philip Ruddock, as 'naïve' and lacking 'life experience'.

PHILIP RUDDOCK: If you are emotionally influenced in relation to the way in which people are detained in Australia, and it appears that

that is the most significant event in your life, all I'm saying is such people have not had the benefits of life experience.

Philip Ruddock liked to point out he had years of experience visiting refugee camps around the world. 'I know what a refugee camp looks like,' he once told Petro Georgiou. 'But Philip,' said Petro, 'we are not a Third World country!'

Bruce and other Coalition members who'd written the report were savaged in the party room. 'The PM orchestrated [an attack on us] the next day in the party room so the right wing got up first and said how horrified they were about this report and how it would go down badly in their electorate because it didn't reflect what the voters wanted. I found it all a bit overwhelming, like being in the middle of a herd mentality. I just sat there. It made me feel quite sick actually,' says Bruce. 'I wish now I'd taken them on. But I gathered strength along the way.'

Bruce Baird had come to Canberra rightly expecting to be eventually offered a ministry in the Howard government. Moving against the prime minister would obliterate that hope. But not moving would mean the continued obliteration of young lives behind the razor wire. He agrees to support Petro's push.

When federal parliament resumes in February 2005, Western Australian MP, Judi Moylan, goes straight to see Petro Georgiou. Moylan had been dropped from the Howard ministry in 1998 and had been a member of the same human rights sub-committee as Bruce Baird, which had produced the detention centre report in 2001. She has become one of the party's most ardent behind-the-scenes advocates of reforming refugee policies. Now she has important news.

'Petro, I'm thinking about introducing a private member's bill,' she tells him.

He smiles. 'Mine's already being drafted.'

Judi signs on immediately and will be the most fiery member of the rebellion. And one of the toughest.

'I probably showed temper more than the others with the prime minister,' Judi Moylan says. 'I'm very direct. Usually the more I spoke [the more] he was in a very bad mood.

'But this was about first principles of human rights. In my view, the first principles have to be about how this is impacting on human dignity; about how we treat other people.'

She is haunted by the vacant stares of mothers and their children when she visited detention centres.

'No laughter, no laughter of children playing. Just nothing. The silence was actually deafening.'

She can't forget a rainbow-coloured beach ball she saw stuck in the barbed wire at Maribyrnong. It was stranded above one of the tiny outdoors areas available for children to play in. A larger recreational area was available for children only when guards had time to escort them, and only for ten-minute intervals.

'I found it extremely distressing to see people in Australia living in these kinds of circumstances, particularly children and their families.'

But it is a difficult message to communicate to her largely rural electorate in Western Australia. 'Can you put yourselves in the shoes of these people?' she says during a large town hall meeting of fearful constituents.

'I got letters accusing me of being a traitor. Someone sent me an application to join the Democrats. Another wrote to me saying "How will you feel when these people take your children's place at university and take your children's jobs?" It went on and on in that spiteful, hate-filled way. Very distressing, sometimes unsigned,' she says.

But after seeing detention centres, Judi returns home 'thinking I can't continue to close my eyes to what's going on'. Like Bruce, she also becomes involved in helping individual asylum seekers.

So they form a rebel band of three – Bruce, Judi and Petro – each of them political veterans and each without future prospects in a Howard ministry. They are resolved to no longer be mere supplicants pleading for reform. They are armed and ready.

To the prime minister, it must seem a predictable and perfunctory diary entry in early March 2005: meeting scheduled with Judi Moylan, Bruce Baird and Petro Georgiou regarding refugee policies. Next.

'This isn't working,' Petro tells the prime minister, reiterating his disappointment with the failed 2002 deal. 'I'm introducing a private member's bill, John.'

'Oh, really?' says John Howard, turning to Petro disdainfully. 'And who's going to second it?'

'I will!' 'I will!' chime in Judi and Bruce.

'They will,' says Petro.

The group now has the prime minister's full attention. John Howard asks them to hold off, to let him see what he can do, to give him two weeks. The rebels agree.

'Petro was very big on following process. He didn't want to be accused of ambushing the prime minister,' says Michael Kapel. 'Petro and John Howard had known each other well since the Fraser government. I think it gave Petro a good sense of the way in which the prime minister would respond at most of the key junctures. There was quite a lot of discussion in the office like: "Well, John's going to do this so we'll have to do that before he does it."'

And so it goes for nearly two months. The rebels threatening to introduce the bill, the prime minister pleading for one more week, two more weeks to coax reforms through Cabinet. The rebels wait. But Cabinet produces a lemon: the introduction of a new bridging visa which applies to only a small number of long-term detainees; after two months, only ten long-term detainees are released.

And then the poignant prediction made to Zachary Steel by his boss and former anti-apartheid campaigner, Professor Derrick Silove – that bad systems inevitably collapse under their own weight – starts to materialise. Political momentum breaks the rebels' way.

It begins with the shocking revelation that a former Qantas air hostess, Cornelia Rau, who suffers from schizophrenia, has been mistakenly locked up in immigration detention for ten months. Not only has she been denied adequate psychiatric care while in detention, but she has been kept in virtual isolation in a 'behaviour modification' compound in Baxter for more than three months, where guards can watch her changing.

How is it that a tall, blonde, blue-eyed Australian resident could disappear inside Australia's immigration detention system? How was her obvious mental illness not identified? Is mental illness so wide-spread that she seemed as 'normal' as most other detainees? Wouldn't that mean there really *is* widespread mental illness in detention and not deceitful, manipulative behaviour as Australians have been repeat-edly told?

'When you're in the system,' says David Manne, of the Refugee and Immigration Legal Centre, 'there's also the very real possibility of being locked up in solitary confinement for weeks or months with no access or ability to communicate with the outside world at all. We're looking at a system in which people are permanently, indefinitely imprisoned with no right of review at all.'

The government is forced to announce an independent inquiry headed by former federal police commissioner, Mick Palmer. It's not long before Mr Palmer and his team are asked to investigate a series of immigration department scandals, including more than 200 other cases of wrongful detention, which suddenly cascade into the media.

Like the case of Vivian Alvarez Solon, an Australian citizen, and mother of two, who also suffers mental illness. Solon is not only wrongly detained, but then is wrongly deported to the Philippines. Despite having head injuries from a recent car accident, and suffering convulsions at the airport motel on the eve of her unlawfully forced departure, Vivian Solon is dumped by Australian officials in a wheel-chair at Manila international airport. She is finally taken to a Catho-lic hospice for the destitute and dying where she languishes for four years, before being brought back to Australia.

But one scandal especially ignites Petro Georgiou: the story of a little girl named Naomi Leong, who had been born in detention and who was now marking her third birthday still in detention, listless and mute, banging her head against walls in Villawood.

Leading medical experts like Dr Michael Dudley, a child and adoles-cent psychiatrist at Sydney Children's Hospital, had been requesting that little Naomi be allowed to visit a nearby playgroup with children her own age at least once a week for two hours. Nothing happened.

'I mean [playing with other children her age] is crucial to social development and emotional development in children and also, a sense of identity development and so on,' said Dr Dudley. 'She's basically been brought up in a prison, in a highly abnormal environment with highly distressed people.'

'Petro hit the roof,' says Michael Kapel. 'He felt the Naomi Leong case was outrageous, because he'd done a deal in 2002 for children like her to be out of detention. In fact she had been identified as a tiny baby in 2002 and now in 2005 she's still in Villawood, banging her head against the wall and showing other signs of emotional distress and we're still nowhere with the promised reforms.'

Being jerked around by the immigration department didn't improve Petro's mood. After requesting permission to officially visit detainees in his capacity as a member of the government's Immigration Policy Committee, Petro ends up in the same infuriating mirror maze as the refugee advocates.

He writes directly to the then minister, Amanda Vanstone: 'Dear Amanda ... I was informed through your department that in order to speak to detainees I would have to nominate them in advance. I explained I did not have the names of detainees ... I asked for a list ...' but was told the department would not supply such a list.

'It was a Kafkaesque situation. It ended in yet another huge row with the minister,' says Michael Kapel. 'Government MPs were expected to sign off on legislation and regulations related to the *Migration Act*. But the department would provide little information about what was going on in the camps. It drove Petro and other committee members mad.'

Petro Georgiou eventually visits the Maribyrnong detention centre in Melbourne and along with Bruce Baird, the Baxter detention centre in Port Augusta in South Australia. Michael Kapel recalls Petro standing grim-faced outside Baxter after seeing so many tormented minds.

'My God,' Petro says to him. 'What have they done?'

For Bruce Baird, the visit is an especially devastating experience. Five years ago he had first visited detention centres and recommended time limits on processing asylum seekers. Now he is seeing people who have been locked up for three years or longer 'and we saw them one after the other that day, most of them severely depressed with appalling psychological trauma.' It is agonising. 'We were part of a system that had created this.'

Petro sends the prime minister a list of detainees he believes need urgent psychiatric help. He requests they be dealt with expeditiously by the department. Instead, he discovers the department is in the Federal Court trying to block two of the men on his list from obtaining independent psychiatric assessments. This is despite having already been told by three doctors that their treatment in detention has been inadequate.

'We knew that the people on our list needed urgent medical assistance. We had met many of them in Baxter and it was obvious they were in bad shape,' says Michael Kapel. 'Instead, the department made an application to the courts to prevent some of them from receiving that assistance. It sent Petro ballistic.'

The Federal Court delivers a damning judgment that the Commonwealth has breached its duty of care in relation to the treatment of the two men. Both are transferred to psychiatric hospitals.

Enough. Petro Georgiou heads to the party room on 24 May 2005, unveiling his private member's bill to his colleagues and the media. Bruce Baird declares his support. Judi Moylan argues for a conscience vote. John Howard objects. Petro counts five MPs, including rural Victorian backbencher Russell Broadbent, who might cross the floor. It will take 13 to cross before the bills can pass, assuming support from the Labor Party and independents.

'They all preferred to do a deal. Crossing the floor without the numbers would not defeat the policy,' says Michael Kapel. 'I think the prime minister took a long time to appreciate that it was really about achieving a policy outcome rather than destabilising the government.'

John Howard unleashes a rip-roaring party room debate lasting two and a half hours and involving 43 speakers. The prime minister declares that a strong majority favour maintaining mandatory detention, and he reminds MPs of the historic scars of previous splits.

Some backbenchers in marginal seats claim the rebels are undermining their re-election chances. 'I won my seat because of the *Tampa*, because of our tough stance against these [boat] people! You are attacking my seat!' was a common refrain.

But as the debate proceeds, it becomes obvious the rebels' support is growing. Seven MPs now say they might cross the floor. Another two express partial support for Petro's bills. Another ten speakers, while supporting the government, nevertheless have concerns about the way the policy is being administered.

'You know at first the usual suspects got up and attacked us, "terrible, terrible tutt, tutt,"' says Michael Kapel. 'But then people we hadn't expected started getting up to say "look this is really important, we may not support all of Petro's bills, but there are real problems with the detention policy". And we got an extra two votes and then another two maybes. And I suspect John Howard must have thought "Oh I don't like the look of this."'

The treatment of asylum seekers and immigration detainees is starting to bite. But not just in the party room. The rebels are receiving thousands of emails, phone calls and letters from the community. An unprecedented avalanche of public support rains down.

'The reaction was tremendous,' says Jo Szwarc of the 7000 emails and hundreds of calls received by Petro's office, virtually all supportive. 'The office manager who'd been there for years was saying, you know, as we're filling up new folders, she said she'd never seen anything like this ever. I was very struck by how many ordinary people took the time to do that. It was terrific.'

After Judi Moylan appears on ABC TV's 7.30 *Report*, her office receives 8000 messages of support in just a few days.

'Dear Judi … when you said the words "compassion" and "human dignity" it was like rain in the desert. Many of us on the other side of the continent are with you all the way … Dear Ms Moylan … you restore my faith in politicians as people of moral maturity and compassion … Dear Ms Moylan … I am writing to express my admiration and respect for you and Mr Georgiou … I send heartfelt thanks and wish you every success …'

Judi Moylan notes in her diary that her 'staff are deeply moved to tears by the overwhelming number of heartfelt letters and expressions of support'.

By now the National Council of Churches and religious leaders are also publicly supporting the aims of the bills. Bruce Baird, an active Christian, is in regular contact with various Anglican, Catholic and Uniting Church leaders who write letters to the prime minister and other MPs calling for more compassion for refugees. Their moral standing provides extra political ballast for the rebels.

Newly re-elected Victorian rural MP, Russell Broadbent, has already decided he will risk his volatile seat, the most marginal in Victoria, to back the rebels. 'This was a matter of national interest. It was about who we were as a nation. Blind obedience had never been a value of mine,' he says. But he has kept a low public profile on the issue. Up until now.

Russell Broadbent is not a headline grabber. But the former businessman's direct, instinctive style, often lands him in dramatic political chokeholds. Like when he tells the prime minister in the national media that nuclear plants would be built 'over my dead body' in his region. If he joins a fight, he sticks.

On the eve of the rebels' negotiations with the prime minister, Russell takes a call from Petro. The question is will he become part of their negotiations with the prime minister in Sydney?

Russell Broadbent is due to open a new Catholic school chapel in the Gippsland town of Leongatha on that day, Friday, 10 June 2005. It is to be attended by local dignitaries, local media and the Catholic Bishop Jeremiah Coffey. All especially important to a marginal seat politician. But he agrees to fly to Sydney instead, and sends his abject apologies to the Catholics. They work out where he is going and send a swift reply: 'Go with our blessing.'

'That meant a lot to me,' says Russell Broadbent, who is not Catholic. 'It was a powerful statement for me.'

And then there were four rebels. John Howard, is obviously annoyed to see Russell Broadbent risking his seat for this rebel cause. 'He looked at me when I walked in. He wasn't happy,' says Russell Broadbent. 'At one point in the meeting when I said something to try to break the tension, he said "Oh don't start on me with your Irish charm!" He was quite aggressive.'

'Russell was amazing,' says Judi Moylan. 'Of the four of us, he had struggled so hard to be [elected] and yet here he was with us. It took real courage, real courage.'

There are three major meetings with the prime minister. The first on a Friday in the prime minister's electorate office in Bennelong, Sydney, is testy but positive, with the rebels believing the prime minister agrees to consider serious reform. There are never any staff in the room. Just the PM and the rebels. '[Howard] had very good command of the detail of the whole system. And so did Petro,' says Russell Broadbent.

Petro is the ever-cautious technician. He's been down this road many times before. He wants to ensure that this time they negotiate from a position of strength; that they all maintain a hard line.

'I was always pleased when we got an extra little concession [from the prime minister],' says Bruce Baird, 'whereas Petro would not show any obvious signs of huge enthusiasm and just continued to push on. So his poker playing skills were absolutely essential.'

On Monday night the second meeting is held at the prime minister's Canberra residence, the Lodge. By now the media is onto the story and stake out the entrance. The rebels arrive hopeful of significant concessions. But the meeting is a debacle. John Howard is combative and offers little. He tries to break the rebellion. He and Judi Moylan clash.

'You don't have a mortgage on compassion,' Howard tells her.

'You are responsible for an unethical policy,' she says.

'It felt like we were back to square one,' says Russell Broadbent.

Petro steps in to break the impasse by moving them all closer to the cliff's edge. Since their negotiations are getting nowhere, he says, he will introduce his private member's bill into parliament in the morning. Howard warns Petro he will embarrass his party.

'I'll tell you what's embarrassing, John,' says Petro.

'Three years ago you agreed to let out a three month old baby who'd been born in detention. She's now three years old and she's smashing her head against a wall inside Villawood. That's an embarrassment to the party, John.

'We've got psychiatric patients I went to you about, who should have been released for treatment, but instead that was blocked by the department and now a court has found the government has breached its duty of care to these people. That's what I call an embarrassment to the party.

'And we've got 140 people locked up for three years or more with no convictions and no evidence that they pose a threat to anyone. Let me tell you, John, *that's* an embarrassment! I'm introducing the bill tomorrow.'

After dodging the media outside the Lodge, the rebels meet back at Judi Moylan's apartment where she cooks a stir fry dinner. The mood is bleak. Maybe they really will have to cross the floor after all.

'If anyone thinks it is easy going against your colleagues, your party, your government, they're wrong. It was a terrible feeling,' says Judi Moylan.

But the group knows that public support is gathering and that John Howard is increasingly on the back foot over the effects of the policy.

The government has released three-year-old Naomi Leong from detention after a public storm over her retarded development. The report by former Federal Police Commissioner, Mick Palmer, will be public in a few weeks and early leaks indicate it will be a devastating indictment of the immigration department. Each day seems to bring a fresh allegation against the department, which is forced to apologise publicly for failing to maintain appropriate standards. In a brilliant media stroke by advocates, photos of children in detention are put on the front pages of the *Sydney Morning Herald*, *The Age* and the *Sunday Telegraph*. It is a shocking sight.

Petro Georgiou believes it is time to press even harder.

But the prime minister's troops aren't done yet either. John Howard's supporters open fire in media interviews.

'There is an arrogance in the thinking by a few individuals who are at odds with the vast majority of the ... party room to hold the government to ransom,' says rural Victorian Liberal MP Sophie Panopoulos (now Mirabella). 'If you spit the dummy because the vast majority of people in your own party won't agree with you ... you in effect behave as a political terrorist.'

When given the opportunity to admonish such extreme language, the prime minister instead praises 'a very rich and diverse Coalition Party'. But there is scant tolerance for the diversity represented by the rebels who find themselves targeted around Parliament House.

'I'll tell you how it feels when you become an invisible person,' says Judi Moylan. 'I was shunned in the corridors. I passed a colleague and said "Hello" and this individual turned and refused to speak to me. People have been told not to associate with me. I'm the rebel, the dangerous woman who might influence you. Once I was at dinner with colleagues and another colleague approached one of my friends and took them to task for having dinner with me, saying how could they even consider it.

'It felt lonely. It felt uncomfortable. There's a lot of hurtful stuff that goes on. Like being called political terrorists; being told you're blackmailing the prime minister; being told you're a traitor; being snubbed and isolated.'

Russell Broadbent says he has no doubt such tactics would have been organised 'from the top', meaning the prime minister's office. 'I remember one of my colleagues chatting with me and they said "Oh I forgot I'm not meant to be talking to you today!"'

The message had gone forth, says Russell, that the rebels are to be attacked and crushed in the party room. It is toe-to-toe.

When a Liberal colleague derides the rebels for failing to understand the instability facing marginal seat MPs, Russell Broadbent strides across the party room to end up just a few centimetres from the colleague's face: 'I would like to speak with you,' Russell says. 'Can't you see I'm having another conversation?' his colleague replies, taken aback. 'No,' says Russell. 'Now you are having one with me! Because if anyone knows about being a marginal seat holder it is me!'

One of the prime minister's most loyal allies, New South Wales MP, Bill Heffernan, is seen loitering outside Petro's office apparently trying to collect intelligence on who is attending meetings. He almost falls into the opposite wall when a group of supporters and staff come out of Petro's office. 'Just like the class snitch,' says one.

Michael Kapel borrows a Kurdish lament to sum up their situation. 'I used to joke with Petro, "We have no friends but the mountains" because we could see the Great Dividing Range when we looked out of our parliamentary office. It was all the usual stuff. Some of them cut you dead, sly looks, don't talk to you, ignore you in the corridors, talk behind your back; all standard third-rate petty bullying. But that was pretty much normal for us anyway, so I'm not sure our office took much notice!'

Petro is particularly impervious to intimidation, partly because he is such a veteran machine politician and partly because he habitually ignores people and comments he regards as unhelpful or stupid. So when a Cabinet minister threatens him after a party meeting, Petro wanders off without even hearing the warning 'Wait until your pre-selection, Petro, we're going to get you.' Judi Moylan does hear it and later tells Petro. 'Let them come,' he says.

'I think they realised quickly that it was impossible for them to pressure Petro to back off,' says Michael Kapel. 'Their strategy was to bring pressure on the others and try to split the group. But the four of them stayed together.'

Bruce Baird also faces a backlash in his conservative electorate in southern Sydney, where racial tensions boil over at the end of the year during the Cronulla riots. Unlike the others, Bruce is still receiving reams of aggressive, hostile messages urging him to back off. 'Yeah I felt vulnerable,' he says, 'but I also felt totally convinced of my position'. Polling in his electorate put his net favourability rating at only 22 percent, after he first spoke out on refugees in 2001.

'This whole business is exacting a toll on us,' Judi Moylan writes in her diary in early June. 'But the guys are rock solid.'

Some Coalition members privately support the rebels, apologising for not offering more public encouragement.

'Look I respected that,' says Judi. 'One of my colleagues, who has very different views to me on many things, came to see me in my office bearing roses and chocolates and said "I just want you to know whatever your decision, I'm still your friend." I even had quite a few messages from people in the Labor Party as well. One of the [Labor MPs] delivered cakes to me one day. So there were some nice things.'

Bruce Baird receives a couple of calls from then Opposition foreign affairs spokesman, Kevin Rudd [now prime minister] and his wife Therese Rein. They urge him on and wish him all the best.

As the political pressures and media controversy escalate, a senior Cabinet minister intervenes, pulling aside Michael Kapel one evening in the parliamentary dining room.

'You know the prime minister is becoming quite angry about this,' Michael is told. 'Petro should accept the deal on offer. He's put up a good fight, he's had his flurry, but it is time to make this all go away. Howard will never be turned on this and Cabinet is locked into the existing policy. Petro won't win this, so it's time to shut this down.'

'Listen mate,' says Michael Kapel, 'Petro's not backing down unless there's a serious policy reversal.'

'What? He's going for broke on this?' says the Cabinet minister, incredulous.

'He's not backing down,' Michael says.

The minister is stunned, 'Oh my God.'

'They didn't get what Petro and the group were about,' says Michael Kapel. 'They didn't understand the level of their commitment to an outcome.'

'Howard had a view that Petro and Judi just wanted to make names for themselves,' says Russell Broadbent.

Negotiations with the prime minister have broken down. Petro is preparing to announce to the party room that his bill will be introduced into parliament and that he will cross the floor. But then Russell Broadbent does a nifty two-step. He pops his head into Petro's office before the party room meeting. 'Any change?' Petro shoots back a curt, colourful response indicating that nothing had changed. Russell continues on to the prime minister's office. John Howard is angry, animated. 'You were the ones who walked out on this! I was prepared to keep talking,' John Howard says. 'Well I think Petro wants to keep talking,' says Russell. 'Does he?' John Howard is surprised. 'Ok.' Russell goes to see Petro again. 'Howard is willing to keep talking,' he tells Petro. So the three meet with minutes to go before they are due in the party room. John Howard and Petro Georgiou agree: delay the bill again and hold more talks.

Dealing directly with the head of the prime minister's department, Peter Shergold, who 20 years earlier had worked with Petro at the Australian Institute of Multicultural Affairs, Petro prepares a draft document outlining proposed reforms.

It becomes the basis for negotiations that resume one last time between the prime minister and the rebels in Parliament House. Despite his recent choreography, Russell Broadbent still has to find his own chair.

The meeting turns into an excruciating three-day endurance test. Deals are made, but seemingly resiled from by the government once put on paper.

John Howard tells Petro to trust him; that he will deliver. 'No. No. We tried that already, John, and you couldn't deliver, remember?' says Petro. 'No, no. We're not going down that path again.'

A fresh agreement is typed up, amended and then rewritten again and again under Petro's eagle eye. No more empty bargains.

But Judi Moylan believes the constant bureaucratic watering down of their agreements signifies that the prime minister is not negotiating in good faith. She loses her temper.

'Prime Minister I don't think you are genuine about this and I think I have wasted six months talking to you about this!' she says, storming out.

Petro grinds on. Judi comes back. Negotiations continue.

'Petro was fantastic,' says Judi Moylan. 'He contributed most to the intellectual exercise of putting it together and I think Petro was a good foil for me, because when I was getting to the point of exasperation, he was a calming influence.'

It is a gruelling, brutal stare-down for all involved. Can the group stay the course?

'I'd go to my office and find a private moment and groan,' says Russell Broadbent. 'I felt the weight of a nation's heart on me. And then I got a call from my daughter who was outside a restaurant in West Australia and she said, "Dad I'm so proud of what you're doing. I feel like running down the main street and shouting out *That's my Dad in there!*"'

John Howard realises the rebels will not back down. After two days, significant concessions finally begin to flow from the prime minister.

Bruce Baird and Russell Broadbent wonder whether they should stop pushing for more. But Petro drills deeper: all children and their parents to be released, all long-term detainees to be reviewed by the Ombudsman with a view to releasing those who pose no public risk, time limits on processing asylum applications, and fast-tracking temporary protection visas into permanent ones.

On the third day, Russell Broadbent notices his chair is finally included in the meeting's configuration for the first time. In fact, it is placed directly opposite the prime minister. And as John Howard outlines the full range of major reforms he'll now agree to, he looks straight at Russell Broadbent. It is not quite a king's ransom, but the reforms will end the worst excesses of the regime for hundreds of families, either in detention or on temporary visas.

'That's it,' the prime minister says. He leans forward. 'Well? Well?'

'That's reasonable,' Russell says.

'Yes, that's reasonable,' agree Bruce Baird and Judi Moylan.

All eyes to Petro Georgiou.

'You got what you wanted,' says John Howard. 'This is it.'

'Yes,' says Petro, 'this is it.'

It is 17 June 2005. After four years, dozens of meetings and countless broken promises since, the deal is done. The framework of mandatory detention remains intact, but families, many long-term detainees, and temporary visa holders will be spared further anguish.

'We don't really need to put out the complete text of the agreement,' John Howard says.

'Oh yes we do,' says Petro Georgiou, who is wary of backsliding.

After everyone has left, Russell Broadbent finds Petro alone in the Cabinet room rereading the text of the agreement. Over the next few weeks, the gates open at detention centres. The longest serving detainee, Peter Qasim, is finally given a visa after nearly seven years. He remains in a psychiatric hospital after mentally collapsing two months prior. By 29 July, all of the remaining 43 children, including a five-year-old Iranian boy, are released.

'You know Petro was so strong and workmanlike throughout the whole process, he never got emotional,' says Russell Broadbent. 'But the day they let out the last children from detention, when he saw the photo of the five-year-old in the newspaper, then he lost it.'

Petro's staff present him with a framed copy of the photo. It sits on a bookshelf in his office.

A few days later, Bruce Baird addresses both sides of parliament: 'Let us never again see children in detention in this country. They should not be behind barbed wire or razor wire. It is an indictment that we have let it happen. Both sides of the House have been involved in that, but we are changing this process through the bill.'

Some activists and advocates criticise the deal as being too little, too late. Dr Louise Newman and Ian Rintoul are among them.

'Look at the time I said it had done nothing to change the system of mandatory detention which remained. That it didn't go far enough. But it did have an immediate effect. And that was good,' says Louise Newman.

'It was an imperfect result, but it had an immediate impact on people's lives,' Petro says. The rebels' breakthrough is complemented by the Palmer Report which recommends wide-ranging departmental reform.

Trish Highfield and Zachary Steel feel a wave of relief. No more families with shattered spirits and broken minds, at least for now.

'Heroes come from the least expected places,' says Zachary Steel.

'Thank God for Petro and Judi Moylan and the others,' says Trish Highfield. 'They got the children out. Yes, it took too long, but they did it. You know I remember talking to Petro years earlier and he listened for an hour while I told him about what was happening. Back then most people tried to get rid of me so I said to him "You probably need to go", but he said "No, I want to hear it all." I always remember that. He wanted to know everything.'

Over the next couple of years, two of the most high profile advocacy groups, Rural Australians for Refugees and ChilOut, wind down their activities.

The rebel Liberals pay tribute to the advocacy movement which Michael Kapel says was responsible 'for a turnaround in the media coverage of asylum seekers. A couple of years previously the government was briefing the media heavily about boat people as illegals and queue jumpers. But those activist groups really took up the cause, visiting individuals, making case studies known to the media.'

'There were a lot of women,' says Judi Moylan. 'I was amazed by the generosity of their spirit.'

'Many of them are not public figures,' Petro Georgiou wrote of the advocates. 'They do what they do ... simply in response to the plight of fellow human beings. These people are sometimes described as "ordinary". Their hard work, generosity and empathy show them to be extraordinary.'

And then there is payback.

Both Petro Georgiou and Judi Moylan face ugly pre-selection onslaughts, Petro against a former staffer for Alexander Downer who is praised by the prime minister and supported by three government ministers. Petro trounces the challenge by three to one. Judi also hangs on.

But the truce is short-lived. The group is shocked to find themselves fighting for their deal all over again. None of them anticipate John Howard's breathtaking backflip just one year later in 2006.

'I think the right-wing decided they were going to run over us this time,' says Bruce Baird. 'They were angry that we had gotten what we wanted.'

The prime minister introduces legislation to excise *all of Australia* from the migration zone. It means the Australian mainland ceases to exist, at least for boat people who try to step onto its shores. All future boat people will be exiled to the Nauru detention centre, including children.

The move is designed to appease an angry Indonesian government, which protests Australia's recognition of 42 refugees from the controversial Indonesian-run province of Irian Jaya, or West Papua. John Howard wants the controversial new legislation passed ahead of a visit to Canberra by the Indonesian president, Dr H Susilo Bambang Yudhoyono.

But it clearly breaches the agreement so painstakingly reached just 12 months earlier. The Petro Four gather once more. This time, the prime minister sends immigration minister Amanda Vanstone to negotiate with them. And he sends a clear message that he will not be turned. When approached by a Victorian frontbencher who says 'you cannot roll over to the minority', John Howard reportedly replies: 'We're not going to.'

This time there is no deal.

'It is the most profoundly disturbing piece of legislation I have encountered since becoming a member of parliament,' says Petro Georgiou. The rebels believe they have no choice. They tell a rowdy party room they cannot support the legislation. Judi Moylan, who is attacked by six different speakers, tries to respond by reading out a list of 26 Liberals who have crossed the floor in the past, including Philip Ruddock in 1988 to protest John Howard's call to cut Asian immigration. 'It is a tradition in our party to have the freedom to vote according to our conscience,' Judi Moylan says. 'If people can cross the floor on tax, why not on how we treat human beings?' But she is shouted down. John Howard is forced to intervene to allow her to finish her list.

Just a year ago they were all relieved to have avoided the trauma of splitting from their colleagues to sit on the opposite side of parliament with the Labor Party. But on 10 August 2006, Petro Georgiou, Judi Moylan and Russell Broadbent cross the floor to vote against the legislation. 'The path I take today, I did not choose,' says Russell Broadbent. 'It chose me.'

Bruce Baird abstains, following an appeal to the rebels from the prime minister. But he is attacked as a bleeding heart on refugees by Sydney radio talkback host Ray Hadley, who encourages people to complain directly to Bruce's electorate office. Scores of angry phone calls pour in. Bruce Baird is forced to close his office in Caringbah in southern Sydney after a few irate constituents storm the office yelling abuse at a staff member manning the phones. One man throws objects at the staffer.

'They were all aged over 60,' says Bruce who has never before or since faced such ugliness.

Just like the year before, John Howard cannot predict how all his MPs will act on this issue. In a move that takes his colleagues by surprise, National Party MP, John Forrest, also abstains from the vote and resigns as party whip, a position responsible for maintaining party discipline in parliament. He cites his experiences with refugees – many of whom now live and work in his rural electorate in northern Victoria – as the breaking point.

'Having formed some very strong friendships with the many [refugees] in my electorate,' he states in his resignation letter, 'it appears I have a different compassionate view to the majority here. In my humble opinion, this legislation offends many things I believe about my country.'

There is only one extreme reaction from a colleague: 'Why are you sticking your neck out for a bunch of rag heads?' Most support his right to dissent. A senior government member says: 'Jeeze mate, you've shamed us.'

'I barely ever said boo in the media. But I thought deeply about this,' Forrest says. 'It was horrific at the time, but I am satisfied I did the right thing. Just this year (2008) at our local Australia Day celebration, Middle Eastern refugees provided catering for free, and were pleased to share in the celebration. And at a citizenship ceremony in Mildura recently, more than ten refugee families became Australians. Surely this is the outcome all Australians should celebrate.'

The bill nevertheless passes through the House of Representatives where the government holds a sweeping majority. But in the Senate, where the government's majority is wafer thin, just one rebel government senator could defeat the bill. Four days later when the legislation is due to be debated in the Senate, a 66-year-old senator from Victoria, Judith Troeth, a former teacher and farmer and a grandmother, visits the prime minister's office.

She has harboured growing concerns about the effects of detention for years. A year earlier she had surprised colleagues by offering to support Petro Georgiou's private member's bill. This time around Judith Troeth has been part of discussions with the immigration minister to find an acceptable compromise.

In a strange twist Judith's son, Simon, is also present, because he is a senior advisor to Amanda Vanstone. Simon assures his mum that they are both 'mature enough' to cope with their different roles. 'It's quite funny when we go to meetings,' Judith Troeth says. 'I either kiss him hello or kiss him goodbye at which everybody falls apart.'

But in the end, the government concessions do not substantially change the effect of the bill. Judith Troeth tells the prime minister she can't support the legislation. She will cross the floor in the Senate thereby ensuring its defeat.

'We had a civil discussion about why I would not support the bill for about 45 minutes,' says Judith. John Howard says later that he can do the math.

He withdraws the bill.

'Yeah, when John Howard told the party room he was withdrawing the bill, that was one of the magic moments in politics,' says Bruce Baird, who retired from federal parliament at the 2007 federal election. 'We certainly celebrated that night. That and the 2005 deal for me is right up there with the Olympics. In many ways, it is better.

'You know still at least once a week someone will come up to me and say "I really appreciate what you did,"' Bruce says. 'It used to be constant. I was even finishing an ocean race one day and as I was getting out of the water someone came up! It really is very touching.' By the time Bruce retires, his approval rating in his electorate has doubled. He says it can only be attributed to a turnaround in attitudes towards his stance on refugees.

A Melbourne secondary school hangs banners thanking the MPs and quoting from Russell Broadbent's parliamentary speech: 'The Australia I know is a place where people find a sense of belonging and it is a place of hope for generations of new immigrants.'

This time, as the 2007 election approaches, most refugee advocacy groups maintain a strategically low profile. 'When we had tried to make it an issue previously, it had gone against us,' says Kate Gauthier from the national lobby group, A Just Australia. 'In 2007 we decided to keep it out of the headlines and not back Labor into a corner. We thought instead that we would get greater concessions out of them in a post-election, depoliticised environment than in a highly media-contested election environment.'

When the Howard government is swept from office in 2007 by Kevin Rudd and the Labor Party, Petro Georgiou and Russell Broadbent buck the anti-Liberal trend and record small swings towards them.

'You know the miraculous nature of my re-election can't be under-estimated,' says Russell Broadbent. 'I think even people who disagreed with me respected what I had done.'

Judi Moylan wins her seat with a negative swing far smaller than most of her colleagues. The national swing to Labor is twice the aver-age of the past ten federal elections, and the largest shift in national votes since 1975, when the Whitlam government was annihilated.

John Howard, Australia's second-longest serving prime minister, loses his own seat. He becomes only the second sitting prime minis-ter, and the third party leader since Federation, to be defeated in his own electorate.

Petro Georgiou is not one to dwell on what they achieved, simply observing, 'It was the right thing to do.'

More than 12 000 asylum seekers had come across the seas to Australia under the Howard government, including more than 2000 children. Nearly all were fleeing horrific regimes in countries like Iraq and Afghanistan against which Australia would go to war. Despite being labelled liars and cheats, the vast majority were declared genu-ine refugees. Yet nearly all were left to languish in hostile, remote Australian detention camps where they were given numbers behind the razor wire. The camps were condemned as inhumane by count-less local and international medical, legal and human rights groups. How many detainees have been permanently scarred by psychologi-cal damage? How many were wrongfully deported? Why was it done when it played no role in deterring others? Why was it done at all?

'I felt that we were pandering to that group in the community who were fairly vocal at the time who were supportive of Pauline Hanson's One Nation,' says Judi Moylan. 'The very worst aspect of this was putting those [refugee] children and their families behind barbed wire. It was unnecessary and we've seen of course that no harm has come from overturning that policy. The sky hasn't fallen in. So why did we do it? I wish I understood. But I don't.'

'Why didn't they [the government] get it?' says Bruce Baird, about why human rights were dismissed in the name of mandatory detention. 'They didn't want to get it. John Howard made it plain around the time of the 2001 election, he said to us in the party room, 'It is my aim to win back the One Nation supporters.' Politically they believed [such harsh policies] as well as September 11 [terror attacks] were why they won the elections in 2001 and 2004.'

Russell Broadbent agrees it 'grew out of the Hanson phenomenon. Everyone became so fearful. It was all about protecting the blue collar vote (the so-called "Howard Battlers"). Voices of reason and compassion were pushed by the way.' But he never felt disillusioned because 'what we did shows how the process in the end worked really, really well'.

Petro says division and fear were stirred by the government and 'Australia lost its head for a while and was stampeded. But in the end Australians recovered their moral compass as they always do. We are not a fundamentally racist country. We just have hot flushes every now and then.'

But many advocates like Trish Highfield remain shaken that such a policy was allowed to stand for so long. She now has a long, dark memory. 'It has changed me forever. It makes me realise you have to be on alert the whole time. You can never trust governments. You can't take our democracy for granted. We caged children and we live in a civilised country! I still feel angry about all the politicians and even all those press gallery journalists who never visited a detention centre when they were reporting government policy. And I will always remember the names of those departmental officials who were part of this. We all know who they are. I will never forget. I will never forgive.'

It's not over, they say. What happened must be put right.

◎

Not long ago, John Highfield bumped into an Afghan refugee visiting Australia from New Zealand, where he is a citizen. The man had been one of those rescued by the *Tampa* and sent to Nauru by the Australian government. After being recognised as a refugee, as most were who had been on the *Tampa*, he was told he was to be resettled in New Zealand. Here is what he said:

'When we arrived in New Zealand, we were taken for processing. I thought, *oh no, here we go again, more processing, more being locked away*. We were taken to an office and were wondering what is going to happen? When we went in we suddenly saw a large banner saying "WELCOME". And the New Zealand prime minister was standing up and she made a speech welcoming us. She told us we were safe now; that this was our new home and that the people of New Zealand were glad to be able to help us. It was the most wonderful thing. Our hearts just soared.'

CHAPTER 9

Why, Mr Ruddock?

What follows is an edited transcript of a series of interviews I conducted with former immigration minister, Philip Ruddock. He agreed to participate despite knowing this book was devoted to telling the stories of some of his most ferocious critics.

Philip Ruddock is a gracious, courteous man, who enjoys describing the many accomplishments of his family. His wife, Heather, and their two daughters, are all lawyers. One of his daughters, Kirsty, famously left Australia, partly because she passionately disagreed with her father's refugee policies. She once said she found it 'hard to reconcile some of the things my father is doing at the moment with some of the things he taught me to believe in'. She is now back. The family remains close-knit and has since celebrated the arrival of grandchildren.

Philip Ruddock, 65, is now a humble backbencher, and deputy chair of the parliamentary human rights sub-committee that once included Bruce Baird and Judi Moylan. This same sub-committee issued the 2001 report damning detention centres. He is also now the longest sitting federal MP.

There is no doubt that he has thought more deeply than most politicians about how Australia should respond to those fleeing murderous tyranny.

He is Australia's longest serving immigration minister, 1996–2003, and oversaw the largest migrant intake (742 000) since Harold Holt's

900 000 in 1949–56. In a portfolio notorious as a political graveyard, Philip Ruddock bloomed. It transformed him from 'Philip who?' into an unyielding frontline warrior who claimed to be protecting Australia from the gathering hordes. The quietly spoken lawyer and stamp collector received rousing applause when he attended New South Wales Liberal Party State Council meetings. His 30-year parliamentary anniversary in 2003 was celebrated by 1500 people at Sydney's ritzy Convention Centre in Darling Harbour. There was a protest outside. But he became the target of protests wherever he went. Sometimes he still is. He was made attorney general where he also became contentious curbing civil liberties in the fight against terrorism. He was a Liberal Party hero.

He has few regrets from those heady days. Philip Ruddock says he had to act to rescue what he saw as a crisis in the integrity of the Australian immigration system. 'Support for migration was at its lowest level in decades,' he says, and this was fuelling the popularity of Pauline Hanson's 'One Nation' party. He feared that people smugglers were readying 10 000 asylum seekers for Australia. And he had a powerful self-belief that because of his experience visiting overseas refugee camps, he knew who were the most deserving refugees. 'I've spent more time in refugee camps than most,' he says.

Philip Ruddock remains an unshakable ideologue when it comes to the policy of locking up or turning back boat people via mandatory detention and the Pacific Solution. 'Our determination brought it [people smugglers and boat people] to an end,' he says.

He fought hard for his policies; he was one of the most determined, knowledgeable and involved leaders the immigration department had ever seen. And he fought on all fronts; attacking the judiciary and lawyers who tested or modified the system he was constantly amending, negating Australia's medical experts, renouncing refugee advocates including his former Liberal Party prime minister, Malcolm Fraser, and repudiating criticisms from various government-funded watchdogs like the Commonwealth Ombudsman and the Human Rights and Equal Opportunity Commission (HREOC).

Ironically, Philip Ruddock probably fought least with the parliamentary Labor Party over the issue, even though refugee policy became a defining election issue in 2001.

Some colleagues and friends say he has been dramatically changed by the experience, that he is no longer the same Philip Ruddock who in 1988 crossed the floor of parliament to vote with Labor against calls by John Howard to slow down Asian immigration. He was also an active member of Amnesty International, which presented him with an honorary lapel pin for his extensive human rights advocacy. But in 1999 Amnesty International requested Philip Ruddock stop wearing the pin while he was carrying out ministerial duties, because of the organisation's strong objections to his policies. He refused. Throughout our interviews, he still wears the Amnesty pin.

'I think he lost his way keeping his Cabinet position under John Howard. He still can't see anything wrong with what happened and has convinced himself that he took appropriate action,' says Bruce Baird.

'I asked him what did he think he was doing,' says migration agent and friend, Marion Le. 'He said "Nation building." I said "What kind of nation did you think you were building, Philip?" I don't understand what happened to him. He used to say how much he hated razor wire in refugee camps.' Marion Le says Philip Ruddock also helped when she was campaigning to free children locked up in Port Hedland under the Labor government in the early 1990s.

Philip Ruddock says he always believed in an orderly program. 'We can't take everybody,' he says. 'We must have the right to choose who comes here.' He said much the same as Opposition spokesperson in 1992 when Labor introduced mandatory detention.

His focus was on the poorest and most desperate refugees, he says. These were the people who waited their turn patiently in camps, especially in Africa. These were 'real refugees' in Philip Ruddock's mind, according to advocates who worked with him.

It is while recounting a visit to an African camp in Kakuma northwest Kenya, that Philip Ruddock shows the most emotion during more than four hours of discussion. Only on a few other occasions, when pressed about the extent of psychological damage in detention camps, does he break his lawyerly flow with combative sarcasm: 'They're *all* refugees, they must *all* be taken! Don't ask any questions please!' or with angry accusations against detainees: 'Would I sit behaving like that in front of my children knowing it was going to damage them? What's happened to personal responsibility?'

People smugglers and refugees with money threatened the good order Australia desired in its refugee program. As you will read, Philip Ruddock believes that even Jews fleeing the Nazis during World War II should have joined an orderly departure program if they wanted to come to Australia.

Margaret Piper, former head of the Refugee Council of Australia, describes Philip Ruddock's approach to refugee policy as akin to a hospital offering elective surgery, but no emergency department.

Adhering so strictly to a predetermined refugee schedule made for some cold-hearted decisions. Marion Le was shocked when Philip Ruddock initially refused visas in 1999 for some women who had been raped.

'And I said to him, "You know Philip, they've all been raped and most of them don't want to tell their husbands. They're a mess psychologically. They don't want to go back because they have to face their rapist again,"' says Marion Le. 'I said "I listen to them, I'm asking you listen to me please." And then he said, "Marion you expect rape in war." And I said "Alright Philip you can expect it, but I don't accept it." His big fear was creating a precedent and opening the so-called floodgates. That was always his big concern.'

Philip Ruddock still believes the refugee system, even in his time, was too generous. Australia probably lets through many people who are not legitimate refugees, he says. And while he reiterates that immigration detention was an administrative edict, and not deliberately punitive like gaol, he slips frequently into comparisons between asylum seekers and gaoled criminals. Ironically, many reports found those sentenced to gaol had more certainty and rights than immigration detainees.

A wily and skilled dog-fighter in interviews, Philip Ruddock provides great lashings of bureaucratic jargon, theory, history and repetition to sometimes avoid the pointy end of a question. But he is pleased to joust, saying he has always been prepared 'to defend the policies I believed in. I think I had a duty to do that'.

It remains to be seen whether Philip Ruddock continues to claim prime responsibility for the policies as the years pass, the cheers recede and the questions about how people were treated continue to follow him.

REFUGEES SHOULD APOLOGISE

MARGOT O'NEILL: Did you ever feel the need to apologise for saying that people threw children overboard when they hadn't?

PHILIP RUDDOCK: Well my view at the relevant time was that it was not proven and if you're saying at a later point in time 'You should apologise for having said that', I would say 'Were people apologising for having tried to enter Australia without lawful authority?' I didn't get too many apologies for that.

MARGOT: But does that make it fair to say something as heinous as that about people?

PHILIP: If somebody came to me and said 'I'm sorry that I was seeking to enter Australia unlawfully' and I might well say 'Well look I'm sorry that in relation to the way in which you behaved at that particular time or it was alleged you'd behaved was wrong.' I would probably apologise for it, but I don't recall too many people apologising for having sought to breach our law by arriving without lawful authority.

MARGOT: Would you expect Jews to apologise when they jumped in boats and tried to escape from Nazi Germany?

PHILIP: What I do say in relation to the Jewish community is that I cannot recall any who sought to access Australia unlawfully.

MARGOT: But you know that they jumped in boats and went around the world and were often turned away. Did they have the right to try and do that at the time?

PHILIP: I think that to equate those circumstances with what we had here is flawed. Of course Jews were entitled to flee from Germany and to seek a sanctuary.

MARGOT: Would you have been annoyed if they'd come here by boat?

PHILIP: Yes.

MARGOT: Even if that was their only option.

PHILIP: Yes. Well I don't know that it's their only option. My view is that we took a lot of German Jews as part of an orderly program.

MARGOT: An orderly program?

PHILIP: And so you know I would take the same position in relation to German Jews.

CHILDREN IN DETENTION

MARGOT: Do you believe that detention damaged children?

PHILIP: Well let me ask you this question, do I believe that children might be damaged if they're facing persecution? I suspect they are. Do I think children are damaged if they're in gaols here in Australia? I suspect they are. Do I think children are damaged if they're in the care of welfare agencies? Do I think children are being damaged now because they can't be adopted and they're only going to be put under continuous foster care arrangements?

I think children are damaged in a variety of circumstances, and I'd like to think that people were focussed on dealing with the whole variety of those circumstances. But does it mean that because children are damaged you have no gaols? Does it mean that if children are damaged when they're fostered, that no children should ever be fostered? You see the difficulty in relation to detention was that people brought their children with them and in my view it would have encouraged more people to try and bring children with them if it was thought that those who arrived without lawful authority and were single were detained, but those who came with a spouse and children were automatically released. So I don't think that it was appropriate to be seen to be unwinding the mandatory detention policies, other than to look at alternative detention models.

MARGOT: Do you believe children were damaged in mandatory detention?

PHILIP: Well I don't know. I know it's asserted.

MARGOT: Commonsense dictates, doesn't it, that children would be damaged in detention; all the madness of lip-sewing, riots, children running around seeing people self harming, slashing themselves.

PHILIP: Yes and that was happening in Italy, in Europe, people were throwing themselves overboard because they thought if they put enough pressure on we would get outcomes, they will have to relent. But this was designed to appeal, in our view, to our sensitivity as a developed Western country; we don't like this sort of thing happening, so it's just easier to let them go ... But you know (the system progressed over time) and if you moved to a place like Baxter, you were dealing with people living in individual rooms, what could you do if something nasty was happening, you could take your kid to your room, you could lock them up with you, you didn't have to be around all this sort of thing, seeing all this sort of thing if it was going on.

Look I'm not defending it, don't get me wrong. I'm saying in relation to these reports, did I have a reaction? Yes I did. And if I was able to take decisions that were consistent with mandatory detention I would.

MARGOT: Do you honestly say you don't know whether or not children would be psychologically damaged from being in that environment?

PHILIP: Look I'm surmising as I say in relation to a whole lot of situations that children can be in, which we think are necessary, that they can be damaged, I'm not saying they can't be damaged. I didn't assert that. And if you put it in the book that I've asserted it, it would be wrong. I'm not saying that they couldn't be damaged ...

MARGOT: No I just asked you before and you said 'I don't know that they are damaged.'

PHILIP: No I don't, anymore than I know that children in foster care are damaged, I surmised that many are. I mean if you get an inadequate parent where they haven't done an adequate assessment the child could well be damaged. And do I know that they've been damaged? No I don't, I've not see any evidence of it. But do I surmise that it could happen, yes I do.

THE MINISTER VERSUS NEARLY EVERYONE

MARGOT: [Given the number of reports from HREOC, the Ombudsman, medical specialists and so on] I would say you had enough information in front of you to realise there was a crisis with children inside detention, and yet you left them all there.

PHILIP: I mean look, this was a campaign and it was orchestrated and it was orchestrated to get every possible group it could to ...

MARGOT: But what does it matter if it is a campaign if what they are saying is true? Does the Ombudsman write a report that he thinks isn't true? Would the Ombudsman have been part of a campaign?

PHILIP: It's about abandoning a policy that even this [Rudd] government today believes should be maintained. And that is that if people come without lawful authority they should be available for processing and if necessary available for removal. Now that's what it is about and there are some people who are saying that if you put children into the mix, the results should be different. You should not be available for processing, you should be in the community. They'd say 'Oh look we'll get a promise from them they will be available ...' I am saying that this was a very determined campaign by a group of people ...

MARGOT: Involving HREOC?

PHILIP: No, involving this woman from the Psychiatric Association [Dr Louise Newman]. You know these are people who had a view that the policy was wrong, they weren't about telling me how we could maintain the policy and deal with these issues consistently with ensuring that people were available for processing and if necessary for removal.

CHILDREN PAID THE PRICE

MARGOT: If you turned that around the other way, another way of saying it is this, that you were willing for the children to pay that price ...

PHILIP: No.

MARGOT: ... to maintain your policy.

PHILIP: No.

MARGOT: But that's the completely clear interpretation of it as well.

PHILIP: No, not at all.

MARGOT: But you didn't help the children, you didn't get them out.

PHILIP: No I'm ... well I did ...

MARGOT: You left them there.

PHILIP: No I sought to develop alternative detention models, I ...

MARGOT: But Petro [Georgiou] and Bruce Baird and Judi [Moylan] say they came to you for years about that and it never happened and that just a trickle of people went out there ...

PHILIP: Well we ...

MARGOT: ... that there was no substantial change.

PHILIP: Well let me just say that I was dealing with this issue and developing these arrangements before they even took them up. But I would be the first to admit that when you were dealing with a bureaucracy when you have to acquire sites, when you've got to put in place arrangements, that they take time.

MARGOT: But you got Nauru up and running really quickly, and Manus Island.

PHILIP: And some people would say that improvisation in relation to those matters, which it was, was not a good thing, they were very critical of it … I just simply say that I think [Petro and others'] expectations of the speed that you can get proposals like that through, funded, properly approved was optimistic and yes I understand their disappointment … And yes I was frustrated too.

MARGOT: Okay here's the point though. When you're getting medical report after medical report suggesting that various children should be released and you don't …

PHILIP: No I'm getting medical reports which say that 'This child is in need of care' and I'm saying they should receive that care. If I get reports that say 'We think this child requires care and the only way in which it can be dealt with is to release them,' I say 'Find another way …'

MARGOT: They're saying detention makes them sick.

PHILIP: … and I'm saying 'find another way'. I want to make this point very clearly. I don't think that there is any system in which people break laws where we essentially say 'Those who have broken the law should be freed into the community and absolved of any accountability …'

MARGOT: They haven't been convicted of anything though have they?

PHILIP: No they've been detained for processing administratively. It's not a question of conviction, it's administrative detention. And I'm saying that those who think that the system is in some way harming them should help improve the system, but in the same way that I would say you don't absolve a person of their criminal behaviour by releasing them from gaol before a sentence has been properly served because a psychiatrist comes in and says they're going to suffer in some way.

MARGOT: It's just too bad is basically what you're saying.

PHILIP: No I'm not saying it's too bad, I am saying you address the issue within the framework.

MARGOT: And what about if detention itself was contributing to the damage for a six-year-old child?

PHILIP: You address the framework.

MARGOT: Release the child from detention?

PHILIP: No, I mean there may be circumstances in which that should happen, but people then say you don't release the child from detention, you release the parties who are with them as well. That's what they argue.

MARGOT: Do you ever worry about any of the children who were damaged in detention and feel a little responsible for what happened to them?

PHILIP: No look I don't sit there and say to myself 'I am in some way personally responsible in relation to ensuring that the laws of Australia were upheld.' ... I mean I would say in relation to any of these children if they have been in any way injured through the experience, the totality of the experience, you ask yourself 'Who put them in that situation?' I'd say parents who put children on boats where they could lose their lives like that. You know others would say 'But think of how much they were suffering' and I'm saying 'Do you put your kids through that?' I mean I don't go and put my kids into a situation where I believe it is life threatening.

MARGOT: But they left a situation they thought was life threatening. I don't think they did it because they thought it was fun.

PHILIP: Well I think that's an assumption that you're making.

THE CASE OF SHAYAN BADRAIE

Shayan Badraie was the catatonic six-year-old boy secretly filmed for *Four Corners* on ABC TV. He was held in detention for 17 months and his story was recounted in Chapter 3.

MARGOT: [That long-term detention does damage children] has been conceded by the government in a court case against Shayan Badraie.

PHILIP: Come on, the Badraie case is a case that has been run in relation to a set of circumstances, which I still think have not been fully scrutinised.

I mean it was a situation in which this child was removed from his mother, his natural mother and was with his father and I think there were some legitimate questions raised by psychiatrists as to whether the bedwetting and the other conditions which it was said that he was suffering were related to detention or related to the wider range of circumstances. Now how government settles this matter now, a long time afterwards and so on given the extent to which some people have wanted to make it a totemic case, is another matter.

MARGOT: It just sounds like you cherry pick medical reports because there were such a lot of psychiatrists and other medical people advising you regularly that this child was sick and that he was getting worse in detention and what needed to happen was for him to be out of detention.

PHILIP: And that happened.

MARGOT: But it seemed to have taken too long. In fact one of the issues is there's a report in which you've written next to one of these medical reports advising that Shayan needs to be released, you've written the word 'Bucklies' [that is, Buckley's], you know, like that's never going to happen. And I'm wondering why you would write that against such a report, especially when it was not the first of its kind, it was at the end of a long line of medical reports urging the boy be released, including one by Paris Aristotle and Harry Minas [from IDAG].

PHILIP: Well I don't have those documents ... and I asked the department whether I could get access to those documents now and I haven't been able to refresh my memory in relation to that.

MARGOT: So you can't remember writing that?

PHILIP: I can't, but I mean I'm not saying it didn't happen. But I suppose somebody's got a handwriting expert there. But the point I would make is that when I was satisfied that on evidence that had been presented to me and I may not have been satisfied on the initial approaches that there were appropriate alternative arrangements that could be made, I was prepared to put them in place. It's just that some people thought there was only one appropriate arrangement to be made and that was for Badraie, his step-mother and father to be released. I mean that was all they would accept.

MARGOT: Well what's wrong with that when you've got a sick child? What is wrong with getting that child out when he was so sick, why not release his family?

PHILIP: The view I took and I would have still taken was that for those who were advocating this was a precedent and the precedent is if you do it for one you must do it for all. It was about unwinding mandatory detention. And the reason I looked for alternative detention models and the reason in Badraie's case that he was taken to hospital, his condition was treated and he was then returned, which is what happened. And then to see what the reaction was to that and then to arrange for the fostering was in my view the appropriate direction to take.

MY ONE REGRET

MARGOT: Is there anything you regret that you said or did?

PHILIP: The only thing that I'm very angry with myself for allowing to happen was to have agreed to an interview when I was at a Crocfest [which is] an indigenous program where indigenous people have school, learn to sing and dance and then present on a stage in front of other school kids and that sort of thing as part of a festival and I went to it at Mount Tom Price [in Western Australia]. Kerry O'Brien wanted to interview me on the Badraie matter and I was being interviewed with him asking the questions on the telephone with an earpiece and a local person there holding the camera and this was being beamed back to the 7:30 *Report* here in Sydney and I referred to Shayan Badraie as 'it'. And I could have kicked myself.

THE BAKHTIYARIS

The Bakhtiyari family were accused of being Pakistanis, and were deported after four years in and out of detention. The family included six children whom psychiatrists say were damaged. Their story is told in Chapter 5.

MARGOT: You have five children, ultimately six, who are here for four years. And I'm just looking at it from the children's point of view, it's a nightmare, it's a disaster for these children. The South Australian child protective services goes in and assesses them in Woomera, and says these children are in deep trouble and they need to be released from detention.

PHILIP: Why didn't they say that we've got a way of handling them, we've got these special arrangements that we can put in place that will ensure they are available? I mean look what I found in relation to all of these things, and I think you'll find in the groups now that are there, who believe that if you are able to argue these matters strongly enough you would unwind mandatory detention.

MARGOT: Why wouldn't you have just intervened to get those five children out of detention?

PHILIP: And what just leave them alone in the community?

MARGOT: No with their mother.

PHILIP: Or their father I think wasn't it?

MARGOT: Yeah the father was actually out. Why not intervene to just get them out of Woomera, get them away from all the shampoo-swallowing madness that was going on in there.

PHILIP: The intervention always was to try and get the process speeded up. I mean that's where it lay.

MARGOT: Why not on compassionate grounds?

PHILIP: No. I mean what you're assuming is that you can develop compassionate grounds and consider cases where a lot of the essential decisions as to character and so on haven't even been dealt with, and you just release some on the basis on what is in fact a fairly inexact science.

MARGOT: We're talking about children who are being damaged here.

PHILIP: No we're talking about my view which is that the focus had to be on more protection officers, faster decision making, getting extra members to the Refugee Review Tribunal. I mean what was not generally understood particularly by the advocates was the need to be able to develop facilities that would be able to detain people properly and humanely, the need to be able to train staff.

MARGOT: Do you think we got it wrong about the Bakhtiyaris? That they were Afghans not Pakistanis after all?

PHILIP: I mean what you're asking me to do is to form a view on the basis of material, where I can't and now no longer have access to, what may or may not have been countervailing material.

MENTAL ILLNESS IN DETENTION

MARGOT: What about people being damaged in detention and all the medical research that was put forward starting with Zachary Steel and Aamer Sultan and then moving on to the Medical Alliance? What do you feel about that?

PHILIP: So some of these people have been released and are psychiatrically sick and you tell me it's from detention? Maybe they came with it?

MARGOT: And maybe it got worse when they were here.

PHILIP: Maybe it did get worse and maybe it didn't. And maybe they've been treated. You know I mean I'm deadly serious. I mean I am not a researcher in relation to these matters. Do I accept that people who were institutionalised might suffer harm? Yes I do. And do I take the view that we change our institutional arrangements totally because some people may be adversely affected? That means we would never have a gaol ... look I tell you if there was some way of dealing with people who were criminals effectively without having a gaol, I would think it would be a great thing to do.

MARGOT: These people weren't criminals, they were asylum seekers.

PHILIP: No these were people who came without lawful authority who needed to be held for processing and removal. It was administrative detention, they were not being gaoled.

MARGOT: What about your response to people who were lip sewing or were slashing themselves, that this is manipulative behaviour, your response can be seen as stigmatising the behaviour of mentally ill people.

PHILIP: I don't think so.

MARGOT: So they weren't mentally ill?

PHILIP: Look I'm not saying that some may not have had pre-existing conditions and others that may have been generated by their experience en-route and here.

MARGOT: What about their experience in detention?

PHILIP: What I'm saying, I'm saying that you have a variety of circumstances and I'm not saying there can't be people like that there. That's the point I'm making. But nevertheless it's not only been our experience, it's been the experience of others that some people think that if they put you under a degree of duress it will influence the way in which you respond and that by demonstrating, protesting and the more exaggerated that can be for a people like us is designed, in my view, deliberately to put you under pressure.

MARGOT: How did you know it wasn't mental illness?

PHILIP: I make the point again that there are lots of people who are held in detention in Australia, in our gaols and I think gaols and detention facilities for young people and so on often leave quite a lot to be desired, but you don't see this sort of behaviour. And I don't think you would ever have found Australians who were incarcerated sewing their lips up.

MARGOT: You find people self-harming in gaols and in juvenile detention, slashing up, cutting themselves and it's accepted by the federal government, by virtually all the mental health community, that it's often symptomatic of depression and I just have to ask you again, what made you so sure that they were just being manipulative?

PHILIP: Well no. Look, the point I would make is that I would expect that if people were in need of medical or psychiatric assistance they would receive it and my expectation was that those people who needed that care would be put in an appropriate environment or institution ... I mean we had doctors in these places, we had psychiatrists in these places we were quite prepared for people who needed to be treated for psychiatric illnesses to be treated in centres.

MARGOT: That's patently not true though ... The Palmer Report found there were inadequate psychiatric services and there were court cases to get people independent psychiatric help. There were numerous reports from the Ombudsman, to HREOC, to the UN Committee, to the Medical Alliance all of which said that it was inadequate.

PHILIP: Well I mean I'm not going to argue that when you're faced with very large numbers of people and you're having to find the resources that there may not have been circumstances in which, if you'd had appropriate notice and were in a position of what you're having to deal with, you wouldn't have done it a lot better. I'm not saying that, but I think that's a different issue ... But what you're saying is that everybody has a [mental health] condition. I don't accept that.

MARGOT: But I'm not saying that, I'm saying that you didn't know and yet you were making statements about their behaviour.

PHILIP: I may not have known. I'm saying that in relation to those people who had conditions and were in need of care were receiving it and there were others who were endeavouring to put us under duress.

MARGOT: How is it possible you end up with a system, which you were there for seven and a half years developing and leading, where they detain an obviously mentally ill woman [Cornelia Rau] and can't tell that she's mentally ill?

PHILIP: I think some people who are mentally ill can be very plausible.

MARGOT: Just on your judgment about mental illness, you once said that you didn't think most Australians believed depression was a mental illness. But do you believe depression is a mental illness?

PHILIP: Did I ever say that?

MARGOT: On the *Insight* program, I checked the transcript.

PHILIP: Did I? Can't remember saying that. Do I think depression is a condition for which people should be properly treated? Yes I do.

MARGOT: But you won't say it's a mental illness. Do you have a problem saying that?

PHILIP: Look I think there are questions of degree in relation to that. I think for some it can be and for others it's a condition that can be fairly readily treated. Yeah I would have some difficulty in saying that all depression means that you're dealing with somebody who is mentally ill. I would have some difficulty saying that because I think people can have depression for relatively short periods of time related to particular circumstances which properly treated and addressed and the underlying cause being addressed is essentially cured.

MARGOT: So there'd be obviously medical colleges that would have a problem with you saying that ...

PHILIP: Would they? I don't know, I'm just simply saying that I think there are people who have depression, but if you went out and said they're mentally ill would be quite offended.

MARGOT: Do you accept that in most detention centres there were extremely high levels of mental illness, especially among people who'd been there for longer than six months?

PHILIP: Look when you say mental illness I accept there would be some. Do I accept that there are high levels? I probably don't.

WHY WERE YOU SO DEROGATORY ABOUT BOAT PEOPLE?

MARGOT: Looking back at your quotes about boat people there was never anything positive about them. In fact at times it sounded quite derogatory.

PHILIP: Did it, how?

MARGOT: You said they were liars, manipulative, illegals, rich demanding people who asked for shampoo, some of them even had mobile phones, well most Australians don't have mobile phones how dare they have mobile phones.

PHILIP: Do you think I should have stood up there and said 'These are the most deserving people in the world and we think that they should get on boats and just turn up regardless.' You see I mean for me I think people who have a need for assistance should get it.

MARGOT: But most of these people were refugees.

PHILIP: The point I make is if they were refugees in need of resettlement they should have been prepared to go through the proper process to determine that. That's the only point I make. And you say I was derogatory. I don't think my comments would have been other than to outline information that came to us. I mean I did hear, and I think the claims would have been about individuals rather than the class if I can use that term, that there were people who were very demanding and that made the process of management very difficult.

There were some people who came with large amounts of money. I mean the Derby Bank was somewhat surprised at the amount of money that had to be deposited for safe keeping in the bank that belonged to people who'd come on boats. That doesn't mean they all had money, it meant that some did ... There were some people demanding of shampoos. Yes I mean there were demands that were made.

MARGOT: Didn't you have a special responsibility as a national leader to choose your language carefully?

PHILIP: I think you're looking at it with a degree of hindsight ... It's a chicken and egg situation. In my view, this was not a matter in which whatever I said would influence the view of the Australian public about there being a right and a wrong way to come and I think with hindsight people pick up comments. I mean I was there for seven and a half years. I did a lot of interviews, I would be pressed for information and for commentary. These statements that you put together as if they represent the words you are uttering every day don't reflect the reality. What you're doing is putting together a mosaic over a long period of time and suggesting that constituted the full story and ...

MARGOT: I don't think that it's misrepresenting you to say that you talked about them often as being manipulative, as being illegals, as being rich ...

PHILIP: You say often ...

MARGOT: Yeah.

PHILIP: ... and I say there would have been occasions in which I was asked to respond, to give information and if you want to put it all together you would see it differently to the way in which you'd see the comments in isolation and in context.

MARGOT: You're not concerned that some of your rhetoric may have left people with a derogatory view of these so-called illegals?

PHILIP: I think that if you have a framework of law you bring it into disrepute if you don't uphold it.

THREE-STAR HOTELS

MARGOT: You say they [the asylum seekers] had the right to be held humanely.

PHILIP: Absolutely.

MARGOT: And Paris [Aristotle and other medical and human rights experts] say they weren't.

PHILIP: And I'm saying all the advice that I could get and implement to ensure that we detained people more humanely was seen and acted upon, that's what I'm saying.

MARGOT: Except for all the advice you rejected.

PHILIP: No, well I think you would need to go through and look at advice that was rejected, rejected, rejected. I'm not sure about that. I think it came down to a question of, you know, if it wasn't implemented tomorrow it was rejected.

MARGOT: Are you saying it wasn't always humane?

PHILIP: Well no [it wasn't]. You have to improvise initially ... I've made the point that there was a degree of improvisation because of the pressure that we were put under, but as we were able to apply the resources and do so it became progressively a better system.

Did I think Woomera, Curtin and, in the end, Port Hedland were as good as you could get? No ...

And you know I didn't build Curtin, Curtin was built by Labor. What was it? These were demountables. You know they were put on a base and a fence put up around it.

MARGOT: You could have made the decision not to use those places.

PHILIP: No, you could have made the decision not to detain.

MARGOT: Or you could have used somewhere else?

PHILIP: Well where else?

MARGOT: Not in the desert.

PHILIP: Where else?

MARGOT: I don't know. I presumed that departments have been nutting through these issues over the years.

PHILIP: They haven't been nutting over these issues for years ... You know Woomera was a facility, you say in the desert, it was accommodation that was surplus to requirements ... The military had moved out, but it was accommodation that Australian military personnel had to use, I mean I had to defend it and I made the point you know people were saying 'They're not air-conditioned', well they weren't air-conditioned, but this is how Australian servicemen lived when they [were] training there.

And originally you know Port Hedland was seen to be not unreasonable accommodation, you know these things develop a mystique of their own. These days to be humane you've got to give people essentially three-star motel-type accommodation, a bedroom and perhaps a bit of a sitting room and a bathroom each, which was what they were getting at Baxter ...

But I'll tell you that what we built [at Christmas Island] is something like accommodation for 400 people and I'm sure it'll have ensuites, I'm sure it will have playing grounds, exercise grounds, it'll have medical centres, it'll have educational facilities, everything that opens and shuts will be there, and people will say 'It's not humane because it's got a fence', that's what they'll say in the end.

I mean I was arguing for new detention facilities in Sydney, I wanted to get Villawood replaced ... And I couldn't get it done. I wanted to do it up in Brisbane and I couldn't get it done. And in the end there were elements of compromise, you had to get what you could get the money for and get it actually done.

You know when all is said and done, with hindsight what would I have done? Yes with hindsight I'd have gone to my colleagues and said 'I know that this is going to take X and it's going to require these additional resources' and perhaps pushed harder, but you don't have that hindsight, you're not in that position.

HOW DETENTION WAS RUN

MARGOT: Was it appropriate to contract out the running of the detention centres to a security company like ACM [Australasian Correctional Management] which was used to running gaols and not dealing with non-English speaking and traumatised asylum seekers?

PHILIP: It was a government decision to outsource. And so it then became a question of writing criteria by which people would then tender to provide a service. Now I don't recall St Vincent de Paul or the

Brotherhood of St Lawrence responding to any of our tenders to provide guarding arrangements. Who do you think does that sort of work?

I mean ACM provided guarding services for people who were in state corrective institutions and our expectation was that they would not deal with people as prisoners, but that they would ensure that people were detained ... we provided the housing, but you know they had to provide the medical services and this was all part of their contract. Now there was an expectation that it would be different to what you do in a gaol, the population is going to be different. But you know feeding, educating and they did include education, they were to provide teachers, they had to recruit a wide range of people.

MARGOT: There were penalties if people escaped, but not similar penalties if there was an assessment that they weren't adequately providing welfare services?

PHILIP: Look I don't have the contracts with me at the moment and I think you know these were not contracts that the government had necessarily drawn up before. This was a new activity for government.

So yes I would agree that you know it was a learning experience ... and there were aspects of the contract that we initially negotiated that with hindsight you might have done differently.

MARGOT: Like?

PHILIP: I mean the issue of ensuring that you deal with people in a civilised way. I mean they weren't gaols, it was administrative detention and so our view, or my view, was that in the way in which the organisation was responding you had to do a lot more in terms of training people to deal with people from culturally different backgrounds and ensuring that the staff were appropriately prepared for that. I mean again these things weren't as obvious initially because we hadn't had to deal with these sorts of populations in these sorts of numbers ... And you know I mean we were very conscious that this was not [the immigration department's] core business.

MARGOT: Why would you have allowed a system where people are given numbers not names?

PHILIP: Well look I mean I didn't micromanage to that extent and when I became aware that people were being given numbers not names I demanded that the system change. If you were running a humane detention regime you don't demean people by giving them numbers and not using names.

MARGOT: It went on for quite some time though.

PHILIP: Well look when you ask for explanations what do you get? You get you know 'We need to call the particular people over in [the pa] systems' ... and 'You've got people with similar names and you try to identify who you want', they were the sorts of arguments that were given.

DID THE SYSTEM GET OUT OF CONTROL?

MARGOT: The Palmer inquiry found a culture [in the immigration department] of denial and self-justification that left a whole lot of serious issues and questions even by senior management and certainly of serious inadequacy in psychiatric services. You were the minister for seven and half years, the longest serving in Australia. Don't you feel responsible for that culture?

PHILIP: I think this idea there was some sort of culture, failed to recognise adequately the difficulties under which people were work-ing, that's what I think ... Now does that mean that mistakes can't be made? No it doesn't, I mean mistakes can be made. And does that mean you can have individuals who may have a particular approach that you could think would have been identified and dealt with? Look in the [Vivian Solon] matter I mean I was very disappointed that there was an element of cover-up in relation to something where I think the officer concerned should have said 'Look it's become apparent there's a mistake here' and it should have been dealt with. Is that a culture in the whole department? I would say no, I would say it was a serious error of misjudgment on the part of the individual.

MARGOT: But the Ombudsman had to investigate more than 200 wrongful detentions.

PHILIP: And if you look at wrongful detention you find that it invariably emerges where the decision as to whether or not somebody was wrongfully detained was highly arguable at the time or where there were issues in relation to obtaining accurate evidence.

MARGOT: Arguable? On what basis do we detain when something is arguable, shouldn't the first recourse be not to detain? Depriving someone of their liberty is something that police do with huge amounts of legal restraints. We had immigration officers going into schools. Didn't it get out of control?

PHILIP: No. I think it's unfortunate that people focussed on the public service in the way in which you did because I think they've done an outstanding job in very difficult circumstances.

MARGOT: There was concern about the attitude that developed in the department, that every concession even to sick children was seen by the department, the government, and maybe by you, as potentially unwinding the whole system.

PHILIP: Well I think that's just wrong because I mean, in fact there were often concessions, but concessions would not be dealt with, as far as I was concerned, in a way in which you would parade them, because they then become a basis upon which other people think that you can then manipulate part of the system.

MARGOT: Indirectly it's a criticism of you, the Palmer Report, because you were there for seven and a half years.

PHILIP: Is it?

MARGOT: Well isn't it? The most important thing to a culture developing in organisations, and this is generally accepted in management theory, is that the most important influence is leadership.

PHILIP: And the leadership I gave was that people should make lawful decisions ...

AUSTRALIA WAS TOO GENEROUS

PHILIP: Australia's [refugee processes have] always been described as being the Rolls Royce model. All you had to do was have the standard Commodore, but everybody was given the Rolls ...

MARGOT: Did you try and give us the Commodore?

PHILIP: I would have given you the Commodore.

You go to a place like Syria, 90 percent of Iraqis would be found not to be refugees. When they get here, 90 percent are found to be refugees.

I mean look, the fact is there were people who were getting claims up here and I can't say, you know it's very hard to say they're not refugees if they've been found to be refugees, but when you've got a system in which the assessment is merely on the basis of what they've told you and the likely rejection arises because you haven't been able to find any inconsistencies when they tell the story over and over again, which is usually the only basis upon which you can catch somebody out, claims tend to get up. But I tell you when you've got somebody who is in the country next door assessing these matters and they're the UNHCR [United Nations High Commission for Refugees], and there's no judicial review, you might be able to get an appeal but it'll only be one, a second look by a more senior UNHCR officer, yeah a lot of people decided if I've got the money and I can engage a smuggler in the end I'm going to have a better chance if I'm dealt with in the Australian system than if I'm dealt with in Jordan.

I think it gets down to the fact that you've got a system [in Australia] that has built into it all of our principles of natural justice and fairness and so on and you know better that ten non-refugees be admitted than one refugee be returned. You know that sort of thinking permeates along the decision-making, and you've got a judge who you know is dealing with one case, he's not seeing thousands of people. You know someone who's in the UNHCR, they say 'I've heard all this before.'

MARGOT: So did you have to degrade those principles or change them so that you were getting more rejections?

PHILIP: Well we couldn't do it could we, because in the end the courts had said that you can't remove the process of judicial review. We tried that through the privative clause [prohibiting most appeals] and it failed. And essentially the off-shore processing [in Nauru] ensured that we were able to put in place a simpler system that more closely replicated what the UNHCR adopted and that was with the Pacific Solution so-called, and by excising islands and so on and ensuring that if people landed there they weren't able to lodge claims, and then processing them off-shore, it certainly meant that they weren't able to access our judicial system and that did have an impact.

MARGOT: It feels to me like you want to say we let too many boat people become refugees.

PHILIP: I want to help refugees. I don't want to help non-refugees.

MARGOT: So you thought a lot of people got through here who maybe shouldn't have?

PHILIP: Well I'd agree with that.

WHO ARE THE 'REAL' REFUGEES?

MARGOT: [An advocate who has been in meetings with you] said ... you would hold up a photograph of a boy from an African refugee camp and say 'This is a real refugee and this is the kind of refugee that I want to help' thereby implying that boat people weren't real refugees ... Is that true?

PHILIP: Let me say I don't know that I've ever had photographs ... I've no pictorial representation ... [but] do I have a personal image of this? Yes I have a personal image of a friend of my daughter's whom I met in Nairobi who died in a plane as a young man. I've got an image in my mind of a young man whom I'd known personally who's now dead for whom this was a cause. And he had been there when the trains were coming down into Southern Sudan, bringing the northern goods and services for mining and that sort of thing, because they were trying to expropriate assets from the south. And they came with their mercenary guards on horseback to ensure that these trains wouldn't be attacked and their role was to live off the local population by essentially ravaging, men, women and children. And yes I saw these people, and I did ask the question, 'Is it durable for them to stay here?' And do I consider these people are worthy of helping? One thing I know is that they never had any money to pay a people smuggler, to get on a boat and to be able to make a claim in a place of choice.

THE ADVOCACY MOVEMENT

MARGOT: What did you think of the advocacy movement?

PHILIP: I mean it's called the doctors' wives syndrome. Trish High-field exemplifies [it]. I mean I don't know that Trish Highfield had ever been going around refugee camps before she even went out to Villawood ... Highfield became very emotional. I mean we tried to talk these issues through with them because her husband was on the ABC and that sort of thing, but I suppose she was seen as one of the classic doctors' wives ... who wasn't a doctor's wife.

Look I mean I don't think it has impacted on the great majority of Australians, but there are certain populations who do get engaged and you know I've got them in my electorate. In fact probably more in my electorate [Berowra, on Sydney's upper North Shore] than most others.

And mainly it becomes people who then took it upon themselves to go out there and visit and the only people they ever see are those who are in detention and you know nobody ever tells them about the particular people they're seeing because there are privacy require-ments. You know immigration is not going to say 'Look this is the other side of the story', because it breaches people's privacy. So all you'd get is what you'd hear from the very person that you're seeing.

PETRO AND THE REBELS

MARGOT: How did you feel about the Petro push with Bruce [Baird] and Judi Moylan and Russell Broadbent?

PHILIP: Look, frustrated that in terms of realising their ambitions that we couldn't do it as they would have liked, but also frustrated that they didn't understand always the difficulties of putting in place those sorts of arrangements.

MARGOT: And were you angry with what they did in 2005?

PHILIP: No I don't think I was angry. I was frustrated. But I like to think we're good friends.

THE PAULINE HANSON FACTOR

PHILIP: I think the Pacific Solution and all of the measures that we put in place to restore public confidence in the immigration program was dealing with the Pauline Hanson phenomenon.

Now some people will tell you that Pauline Hanson was typical of a xenophobic population which ... you have to essentially thrash into submission, you've got to convince them that they should no longer be a racist. My view was that you looked at what the root cause was, and I can tell you what the root cause was. The root cause was an immigration program that no longer is predicated on skill. A family reunion program that was predicated upon manufacturing relationships for the purposes of obtaining entry; and a border that essentially was not being managed. And it didn't start with the Middle Easterners. It started in fact with the Chinese, and Labor had to manage it in relation to the Chinese ... So you know these were not new issues, they were there. We had boats arriving at Holloways Beach [QLD], boats arriving in Broken Bay [NSW] and people saying 'What does this mean?' Is it a xenophobic population or is it a population saying 'Yes we want to help refugees by an orderly process of identification of people whom we know have needs that ought to be best helped.'?...

I'm saying 'One of the factors that we had to deal with was ... Pauline Hanson.' And do you reckon it wasn't an issue that needed to be dealt with? It was an issue that needed to be dealt with and it needed to be dealt with by ensuring that the factors that she would identify which reflected badly on all of us were in fact dealt with.

And you know surprise, surprise, we weren't a xenophobic population at all, we were a population that was concerned to have good immigration policy, that would deliver a program of 80 000 when Labor left office, but 160 000 when we left office.

MARGOT: Do you think she was xenophobic, Hanson?

PHILIP: Look I think Hanson was a political opportunist of the first order, and she found it easy enough to go out and identify these issues and to express them in that way and people, not fully informed, related to those sorts of arguments ... I think she tapped into an anxiety about immigration which people couldn't clearly identify as being related to the skills change, or the family reunion rorting or the border protection issues and they get a simplistic explanation, they say 'Oh gee, we'll stop them all.'

THE BOATS STOPPED

PHILIP: You know what really worked? I mean the Pacific Solution is part of it, temporary entry was part of it, processing was part it, but the ante, you know the ante was being raised all the time, whatever you can do, we'll do more, that's what the smugglers were about. What ruined the smugglers was what I call consumer protection. They smuggled on vessels that were returned and the people suddenly went back to the smugglers and said you failed your duty to deliver us and we want our money back. So the smugglers then started going to ground, but those who wanted to remain in business then found that there wasn't a clientele because the people who were being in Indonesia and wanting to be smuggled were saying, 'We want a guarantee from you that you will deliver us. We will pay you COD.' But what you did have was a situation when you look at a very sophisticated organised crime and the reason it came to an end was when people no longer part with their money until they can be guaranteed of arriving in Australia. And arriving in Nauru or Manus was not the same as arriving in Australia. Being returned to Indonesia was not the same.

I WOULD DO IT ALL AGAIN

PHILIP: You know if you put me in the same situation, I mean my view of it would be if you were faced with the same situation you'd go and argue the case, because the case is absolutely compelling. I don't think that any government would survive a situation where they allowed entry to Australia to become a free-for-all.

The job is difficult, but I can tell you it's a hell of a lot easier for those now following who have to, you know just do the tidying up rather than having to manage that whole process.

I mean I was there for seven and a half years and during most of that time we were dealing with those sorts of issues, some people are kind enough to recognise that I probably had a rougher patch than most.

Most of the time it's not an issue, it's not an issue at the moment. But I would be reasonably certain that if it became an issue again tomorrow there'd be different players, but they would still have to respond in the same way.

I actually clipped these [recent newspaper articles] to show you.

MARGOT: Yeah.

PHILIP: I mean we are in a situation where we had no boat arrivals and Europe at the moment is in a situation where the European community is moving to put into place mandatory detention including mandatory detention of women and children.

DID YOU LOSE YOUR COMPASSION?

MARGOT: People like Marion Le say you changed from the person who hated razor wire.

PHILIP: Look razor wire has always been used as a descriptor to demonise the system. I in fact went out of my way to try and develop facilities that didn't need or require that medium.

MARGOT: But they all had it.

PHILIP: No they didn't. Nobody saw razor wire when they were at Baxter.

MARGOT: No okay, it has an electric fence though.

PHILIP: Well I'm just making a point that nobody *saw* razor wire at Baxter. The way in which it was designed was you lived in ... and what people said was 'You couldn't look out.' Well there's a degree of truth in that, the facilities were built so that you couldn't see any razor wire.

I would say that I was still of the view that where there were compassionate circumstances a minister ought to be able to intervene and later the accusation, and still the accusation that's being made, is that I was the most interventionist minister that Australia ever had in terms of a willingness to examine the circumstances that might be different, but nevertheless compelling. And I might say I wouldn't issue press releases every week saying 'I've granted this many visas this week', my view was that if that was the way in which it was seen it would encourage more people to simply say 'Oh well eventually they'll tire and let us go.' So you know my view ... yes I mean in relation to the system ...

MARGOT: Well if it needs that much ministerial intervention is there something wrong with the system?

PHILIP: My view is that if you essentially build a system which allows a degree of intervention by individual decision-makers, firstly you'll find in terms of transparency people will have different views and my view has always been that in the end the person who is responsible ought to be the minister. Most of my interventions were in fact around families and spouses, often with dependent children.

MARGOT: Okay, and the other half were interventions on detention cases or ...?

PHILIP: No but some were detention.

WOULD YOU HAVE WAITED IN A CAMP?

MARGOT: Do you reckon you would have waited in a camp?

PHILIP: Well there may be circumstances in which I'd have no choice. If I'd had no means or little knowledge of what you could do ...

MARGOT: The odds are against you getting chosen from a camp and resettled in a western country.

PHILIP: It is true ... when you are dealing with a total of about 200 000 places a year and America was taking 70 000 and after 9/11 they took no more from Iraq or Iran or Afghanistan, so it dropped down to about 20 000. So it might have been around, you know, our 12 000 was probably about ten percent of the world's total for resettlement. And what is being said is most of Europe can get away with taking none because they are unable to manage their borders, but we here in Australia should abdicate making choices in favour of the most vulnerable simply because we can manage our borders, but some people think it's immoral to do so.

For me you know the person who is in a refugee situation and has fled and has no means, has lost everything, and is just there at the behest of the UNHCR and you know often they have to wait four years, sometimes decades and people did in Afghanistan, they have in Kakuma.

And what surprises me sometimes is that some of these people who address these things in terms of resources, take the side of those who have the money to travel, and sometimes quite a lot of money to travel. Now I'm not saying that because you've got money you're not a refugee, I'm not saying that at all. But what I am saying is that if you've got bona fide claims, and aren't making a decision of choice, you wait where you first flee.

MARGOT: Isn't that unrealistic? Human nature means people will try to get to a better life if they can.

PHILIP: I'm sorry, human nature has been accommodated and there are no longer boats.

MARGOT: Did you understand why some families who had the means got out because they'd just had enough of all the decades of civil war and repression and violence and ...

PHILIP: I don't think that's enough.

MARGOT: Did you have empathy with them?

PHILIP: Look I can have empathy with people … If you were going to put together an endurance test as the test for entry we'll only take the survival of the fittest, that may be the game that you would play. But I mean it's not what you're doing, I mean they're playing with people's lives.

My perspective is not that I am lacking in compassion for people who are refugees, I feel very strongly about refugees, I always have … we can't take the whole world, we can't take the whole world's refugee population. In the end you have to make choices, and the difficulty about making choices is when you set criteria, if it is to be meaningful, in the end it means you have to be able to manage the process of selection. And if people say 'Well we don't give a damn about your rules, we're coming whether you like it or not', you have to be prepared to respond to that and it's not easy, but it is important public policy and I think the great majority understand it.

Epilogue

On Tuesday, 29 July 2008, the new Labor immigration minister, Chris Evans, announced that immigration detention centres would be used only as a last resort and never for children. The legal framework for indefinite mandatory detention, however, endures.

'Mandatory detention,' said Minister Evans, 'is an essential component of strong border protection.'

At the time of his announcement, there were 352 people in detention, mostly Chinese men in Villawood, and 16 children with their parents in residential or community housing.

All future unauthorised arrivals will still be detained, but only for identity, health and security checks. If there are no concerns, they will be released into the community for further processing.

Children, and unless there is a security concern, also their parents, will be detained for these initial checks in residential housing projects or community accommodation, both on the Australian mainland and on Christmas Island.

Only two groups face longer detention in camps: those who pose a risk to the community, and those who repeatedly refuse to comply with their visa conditions. Their cases will be subject to independent and regular oversight by the Ombudsman.

But while the Labor government has also shut down the centres on Nauru and Manus Island (PNG), it has not returned Australia's outer islands to its migration zone and will process any future waves of boat people on Christmas Island. They will be denied access to the full weight of Australia's legal system, but will, for the first time, have access to funded legal assistance. This off-shore system, which is located 2300 kilometres northwest of Perth, will also be scrutinised by the Ombudsman.

In keeping with an election promise, the minister also abolished temporary protection visas (TPVs), which had been introduced by the Howard government nine years earlier. After being marooned in the community as uncertain exiles, those found to be refugees will now be given permanent visas.

A surge of excited, stunned emails swirled among advocates as the news spread. Celebratory drinks were arranged. For some, the changes are not enough, and the fight goes on. But mostly there was weary relief. It had been seven long years. For some, even longer.

Their achievements – as individuals and as a collective political force – are significant. In 2001, those who argued for refugee human rights were often derided or vilified as 'unAustralian'. By 2005, when Petro Georgiou and the Liberal dissidents ended the most debilitating effects of the system, public opinion had shifted markedly.

What now? Lives have been transformed, careers reshaped and some patriotic hearts broken.

Some advocates stay in touch, some don't. Many have forged life-long bonds. Some have lost regular contact with the asylum seekers who once dominated their lives. That's okay, they say. Everyone needs to get on with life. Maybe they'll have dinner once every year or two. And remember.

They all share a memory of a time in Australia when there were razor wire cages in deserts brimming full of distraught, numbered children and their parents, just about all of whom were recognised as refugees fleeing blood-soaked regimes.

Without exception, those featured in this book say they would do it all again. They hope they won't have to. But they're not sure anymore. How will Australia react the next time refugee boats arrive?

In this epilogue refugee advocates have been given the last word. In their own words they'll let us know what they are doing now, what they think about the Labor reforms, and how the advocacy experience changed them. There are also attempted updates on some of the former detainees.

ADVOCATE UPDATES

Trish Highfield

I still work at my local pre-school with children of the same age as many of those gaoled for years behind razor wire. They were put there for no other reason than punishment against parents for daring to seek a safe and secure life. This was done by an uncaring government.

When I experience the daily joy of the young people now in my care, my anger only grows. I'm furious over the cruel incarceration and damage to hundreds of children by an immigration department that responded to political demands. A department that wilfully ignored the advice of experts on the terrible damage to those captured by Australia's mandatory detention system. With a few honourable exceptions, the politicians on both sides were complicit. My ongoing contact with a child of detention returned to her homeland convinces me that self-serving authorities do not want to understand the long-term damage done to these children in Australia's name. As the wonderful psychologist Zachary Steel once put it to me: 'it's the scattering of our sins, all over the Middle East'.

Children must never be imprisoned. The July 2008 changes announced by the Australian government go some way towards redressing a bad system. However, Australia still needs to adopt something like the Canadian model, which stipulates that each refugee claimant child, unaccompanied or with family, has an independent, official advocate to oversee welfare, education and health needs during the entire claim and settlement process.

John Highfield

Although the ocean environment of Sydney's northern beaches helps to soothe some of the bad memories from the hard battle to get the children free, in retirement I'm still taken by the hypocrisy of a system which wasted millions of taxpayer dollars on debased community fears.

That the pejorative language, heard so often during my ABC reporting years, is still used by official and educated circles to demonise those who seek Australian protection, is appalling. It's as if an Australian government never ratified international covenants and conventions agreeing to treat people who are in fear of persecution with dignity and compassion. The new deal announced by the Labor immigration minister, Chris Evans, is of concern because of the lack of legislative intention. Unless clear law proscribes behaviours, the lesson of the ten dark years teaches that systemic abuse and neglect is all too easy.

Zachary Steel

I have recently handed in a PhD that I have been trying to complete since 1999, based on a large survey of 1200 Vietnamese refugees living in Sydney. The findings showed that the Vietnamese community have been very successful in their resettlement, with one of the highest rates of citizenship of any community group. They have progressed economically and have one of the lowest rates of mental disorder in Australia. As the majority of Vietnamese arrived in Australia before immigration detention centres were built, this success story stands as a testament to what a compassionate refugee program can achieve.

The most significant change is that the burden of proof has been reversed, with detention now used only where there is a demonstrated risk. This is a very important outcome and finally aligns our detention policy with our international human rights obligations. Also, temporary protection visas have, for the most part, been abolished. Both of these changes are very important and after many years, breathe humanity and compassion into the system.

There are still, however, many areas that need attention.

I am still trying to undertake research with refugees and other marginalised groups. The experience over the last few years demonstrated to us the importance of clinical research in identifying areas of concern in helping the process of advocating for change. With future work in Australia and overseas, we are hoping to focus research more on the next step identifying treatments and interventions that help refugees and trauma effected populations recover from their experiences.

My reflections are both professional and personal. At a professional level it is extremely important to advocate on behalf of vulnerable populations. Asylum seekers always represented an easy target. The last 15 years have been like watching a school bully targeting the weakest child in the playground. This diminished us all. Both in language and policy we need to show respect and understanding for the circumstances that make people flee their homelands. This does not mean an open border policy. Australia's off-shore refugee program is a great achievement of which we as a nation can be proud. For years this has been obscured. In the future I hope we can be proud of both our off-shore and our on-shore programs.

It took many people to stand up and try to bring about change. At times it seemed impossible. Mandatory detention was supported by both Liberal and Labor and there was widespread community support, built on years of negative language and fear-mongering. Many things didn't seem to work at first, but it did bear fruit in the end. As the true stories began to emerge the lies could not hold any more. I have been deeply inspired by the people I have met in these years, the advocates and the refugees.

Aamer Sultan

I am pursuing my career in medicine, studying to be a general surgeon and living in western Sydney. My experience (three years in Villawood detention centre as an Iraqi asylum seeker) significantly changed my personality and disillusioned me from the myth of a fair and humanitarian West. I find that I'm still adjusting to my new life here, and that while I want to spend a lot of time alone, at times I also feel quite lonely. Something seems to stand between me and happiness at this point in my life. But I still regularly see my good friends like Zachary and all the old advocacy gang.

Paris Aristotle

I'm now in my twentieth year as the director of the Victorian Foundation for Survivors of Torture. I still sit on the Immigration Detention Advisory Group and the Refugee Resettlement Advisory Council for the new federal Labor government. The main focus of my work with regard to immigration detention is the development of the Community Care Pilot. The aim is to see it become a national program for caring for vulnerable asylum seekers living in the Australian community and a real alternative to detaining people in immigration detention centres. I also hold a position as a part-time commissioner of the Victorian Law Reform Commission.

I feel very optimistic about the direction Chris Evans is moving in this policy area. Naturally the 'devil is in the detail' and there are still concerns about issues such as excision and the use of Christmas Island for detaining people. However, the changes introduced by Chris Evans have moved Australia to a dramatically more principled, just and humane approach to dealing with seeking protection. [The government is] also more financially responsible and has begun the process of restoring Australia's international human rights reputation.

It wasn't that we mandatorily detained people who had arrived in an unauthorised manner that I thought was the problem. It was how and why we did it that troubled me. The way in which mandatory detention policies were implemented and operated will be remembered as a terrible period in Australian history. It was sad and left a trail of damaged and distressed people in its wake ... good people from all areas and many different walks of life.

The abuse of authority and power, the powerlessness of the people it targeted and the psychological trauma it created was pervasive. The separation of families, the damage to children and the way in which the system justified itself in the name of a supposedly greater good, in this instance border protection and anti-people smuggling, diminished the nation and therefore hurt us all. It had the characteristics of a system as fundamentally flawed as the one surrounding the stolen generations.

However, out of all that mess thousands of good people stood up, and in a myriad of ways, made the best contribution they could to help change what was happening. From that I think we can draw hope for the future in this area.

As for how it changed me ... I'm still not sure about that.

Julian Burnside

I am still working full time in commercial litigation, and still doing human rights cases.

If the reforms announced by the Labor government are faithfully implemented, they are a great relief. The acid test will be what happens if another boat of asylum seekers arrives on our shores.

I am still politically active, particularly in connection with the 'anti-terror' laws, and campaigning for a federal bill of rights.

I don't reflect on the past seven years much. When I do, my main reaction is one of grief. I had held it at bay until I heard Chris Evans announce the changes. I thought that, at last, I could afford to recognise how painful those years have been. I could not do that before; it would have disabled me.

The entire experience changed me; for the better, I hope. The idea of standing up for social justice is no longer an academic ideal for me: it is a lived experience.

Kate Durham

Right now I am recovering my wits (laughing at odd moments). I just felt dumb, dull and uncomprehending for a long time. Trying to find something worthwhile, artistically. Nothing drained me more than the SIEV X paintings. Crying into your paint isn't a necessity.

Regarding how I feel about the Labor reforms: very warmly, but what about Christmas Island? What about the detainees from Nauru who were told they would be sent by force unless they leave voluntarily? Some were killed on their return to Afghanistan, some still write to us.

More human rights work? I can't face it. But among our Melbourne and Shepparton art groups there's always activities happening. I did an embroidery project in Shepparton with the Country Women's Association. They all met Afghan women and sewed for a show for a year, it was called 'Sewing all the way to here', and it was a minor, but pretty moving exhibition of love of home and handiwork of both Australians and Afghans. Currently trying to get Afghani music recorded.

Becoming a refugee advocate has changed me permanently. I'm

much more critical of what I read and see. More likely to see sham and falsity.

I feel even more guilty about what I have.

Petro Georgiou

I am still the federal member for Kooyong.

In May 2008, I supported Minister Evans' announcement that the temporary protection visa regime was to be abolished.

I also welcome the recent changes to detention policy. I believe that these reforms are substantial and are a further step towards the establishment of a fairer, more humane and accountable approach to the treatment of asylum seekers and others subject to immigration detention.

I do not, however, believe the task of reform is complete. Under the new system, it appears that people may still be detained – even indefinitely – at the discretion of the department and the minister. The new system, which will require that the decision to detain a person be justified, requires only that a department official justify the decision to another departmental official. This means that the department retains the right to be judge and jury in its own cause, with no external oversight for a least the first six months of a person's detention. Further, it appears the reforms will be carried out by administrative fiat. I would like to see these reforms legislatively mandated.

Finally, I am concerned that the new Christmas Island facility will be maintained as a 'maximum security environment'. I believe that a gaol-like institution is completely unnecessary, inappropriate and a potentially harmful place for vulnerable asylum seekers.

I continue my refugee and human rights work through my position as member for Kooyong. I am a member of the Joint Standing Committee on Migration which is currently conducting an inquiry into immigration detention in Australia. I am also a member of the Standing Committee on Legal and Constitutional Affairs.

In early 2008, I introduced a private member's bill to establish the position of an Independent Reviewer of Australian terrorism laws. The

Independent Reviewer of Terrorism Laws Bill provides a mechanism to ensure that Australia preserves both our security and democratic principles. Labor did not grant leave to move the bill in the House of Representatives. The bill is currently before the Senate after being introduced by Senator Judith Troeth.

Bruce Baird

I'm now chairman of the Tourism and Transport Forum and also chairman of the Refugee Resettlement Advisory Council (RRAC).

I'm very positive about the changes introduced by Chris Evans in removing the Pacific Solution, temporary protection visas and releasing most asylum seekers from detention after they have cleared health and security checks. These were all on our agenda, but were not possible to achieve during the negotiations with the then prime minister, John Howard.

In my role at RRAC I'm obviously involved directly with refugees and was appointed by the current Labor government to that role.

I regard the period as one which was tough and challenging, sometimes very painful, but nevertheless deeply satisfying at the end of the day. The fact that we have relieved a lot of suffering for asylum seekers coming to Australia and shortened the processing time and removed families out of detention centres makes the whole process worthwhile.

Judi Moylan

I was re-elected to the federal parliament in 2007 for the seat of Pearce and continue to take an interest in policy in relation to refugees. I am deputy chair of the Families, Community, Housing and Youth Parliamentary Committee, on the Speakers Panel, a member of the back-bench Economics Committee and continue to chair the Parliamentary Diabetes Support Group and work the vast expanse of the electorate of Pearce.

I welcome any changes that wind back keeping refugees in detention centres any longer than is absolutely necessary, and am pleased to see TPVs abolished. Speeding up the decision-making process in relation to long-term detainees, some of whom are stateless people, is an important step forward.

I continue to assist whenever possible, but immigration is not the central focus of my work in parliament. I continue to take an interest in some of the refugees I assisted, and meet them from time to time.

The release of families and children from detention centres was a very emotional time for me personally. It reminded me of how important it is to take a close interest in the detail of legislation, particularly when it goes to the treatment of others who are particularly vulnerable. I have developed close friendships with the most marvellous people who shared a strong view that fair and compassionate treatment of refugees and other vulnerable people must be an integral part of the Australian ethos.

Russell Broadbent

I continue to work as the federal member of McMillan.

I am very pleased to have been re-elected especially when, at the time, the federal seat of McMillan was the most marginal seat in the state of Victoria.

Basically I share the same views as Petro on the changes introduced by Evans.

Of course, human rights and immigration issues continue to be a part of my day-to-day work.

I was part of one of the most dramatic and significant events of the Howard years that has also changed the lives of thousands of families *for generations*.

Ian Rintoul

I remain active with the Refugee Action Coalition, dealing with the unfinished business of undoing the legacy of the Howard years: justice for those detained and wrongly returned, including compensation. I hope the day will come when those responsible for the brutality of the Howard years and those who administered the detention hell holes are brought to account.

Over the last year, I have been campaigning for the re-instatement of the *Racial Discrimination Act 1975* (Cth) and against the racism of the intervention into Aboriginal communities in the Northern Territory, now extended by the Rudd Labor government. I am also concerned with union rights and the campaign to end all of the Howard government's WorkChoice legislation and re-establish the basic right of workers to strike.

I am a leading member of a now unified socialist organisation called Solidarity. In 2008, five years after an acrimonious split, Solidarity and the International Socialist Organisation rejoined.

The recent change to the administration of detention by the Labor government was a welcome shift. That it goes beyond Labor policy and now includes aspects of the Labor for Refugees policy (rejected in 2004) speaks volumes to the timidity of Labor in Opposition, and its unwillingness to stand up to the Howard government. But the changes announced by the minister do not go anywhere near far enough.

I wouldn't say [the refugee campaign] changed me – but it did reaffirm some deep beliefs – that governments will spend millions of dollars, willingly tell lies and abuse human rights to gain political advantage or retain power. The road that led to the barbarity of the detention centres is not very different to the road that led to Guantanamo Bay.

Most of all it re-affirmed my belief in the fundamental decency of ordinary people, who in their tens of thousands saw through the racism and scape-goating. And that fundamental change comes from the grass-roots up.

The resilience and determination of the asylum seekers themselves to fight from inside the razor wire remains an inspiration, showing that human beings will struggle for justice and dignity in the face of the most inhuman adversity.

Marion Le

I'm still working as an advocate; a voice for the voiceless and a migration agent.

Regarding Labor reforms, this is a great step, but I still believe that the excision of Christmas Island, Ashmore Reef and other spots is a legal fiction, which should be revoked. It seems to me to treat Australians as dopes who will go along with the fiction that people who land on those places haven't really reached Australia and it also undermines our international reputation as a country which upholds democratic domestic law and human rights. I also query why Christmas Island detention centre is really there and I hope my dark thoughts never become reality about that place. I remember that under the Howard government some extraordinary laws were enacted and note they are still in place: our freedom has been more narrowly defined.

I am still actively involved: focussing at the moment on Iraqis and the fate of Albanian children [in Australia] who are locked away in their homes because of blood feuds from as early as the age of six, potentially for all their lives.

[The refugee controversy] didn't really change me, but it made me even more determined to continue to speak out against immoral and abusive treatment and to reflect on how thin the veneer of civilisation sits on us all. I spoke out from 1989 against holding people indefinitely in detention and cried out for the release of children: that no child should ever be held in detention for even one day. I have also said that if you treat people like animals, they behave like animals. For many years I felt very lonely and then there was the surge of others like ChilOut and Rural Australians for Refugees and Pamela Curr and now Chris Evans; I feel justified, at peace internally, but still ever vigilant!

Louise Newman

I am in an academic role: professor of Perinatal and Infant Psychiatry at the University of Newcastle. I do research into prevention of child abuse. I am also working with traumatised child refugees.

The changes are welcome and signify an important change in approach. However, I would like to see broader changes to immigration law.

I see refugee children and am involved in some of the compensation cases. I still see ex-detainees, many of whom need ongoing psychiatric care.

I am still coming to terms with the terrible disregard for human rights we witnessed and the lack of process for redress. Systemic reform is helpful, but the legacy of damage to human beings persists. I have become a more committed individual, but also more realistic and cynical about the political process.

Ngareta Rossell

I am collaborating with a colleague to make a feature film.

Congratulations to Chris Evans. It's one giant step for asylum seekers. One small step for the 49 000 people on bridging visas. And no step at all for the hardline bureaucrats who remain in their permanent positions within the department of immigration.

I consult with various refugee groups as well as with the media. I am a member of the Council for Civil Liberties.

I am constantly appalled that such an abuse of human rights not only manifested in Australia, but was endorsed by the majority (although not all) members of two major political parties. Conversely I feel privileged to have been in a position to work for change and awed by the courage, endurance and eventual triumph of the human spirit I witnessed on both sides of the wire. Did it change me? Yes. I can't do small talk anymore.

'Toby'

I am still a research scientist and still studying.

Regarding Labor reforms: a big improvement, but not all the way there yet. Basic rights need to be enshrined in law or better yet a bill of rights or the constitution.

I am not [working with refugees] at the moment. I was employed with a refugee welfare non-government organisation for a while, which mainly dealt with TPV holders. Still do the occasional bit of information gathering or connecting people with people.

I feel a little proud of what we did because we were on to the issue pretty early and worked very hard at significant personal cost. I certainly met so many amazing people, refugees and activists and formed some lasting and important relationships. So personally it was a valuable experience for me in that way. It rather sabotaged my career though, but I am getting that back on track now. I would not say that it changed me fundamentally, but it was a developmental experience. I certainly acquired or developed new skills, public speaking, media, political, clandestine etc. I also increased my awareness and understanding of the experience of human suffering and the political and social conditions in various parts of the world which cause these things. And I also came to understand the dynamics and nature of racism in this country much better.

Allan Clifton

These days, due to ill health [Allan has a terminal illness] I cannot engage in any employment. I spend what remaining time I have with my family and also tinker with my vintage Holden. I live just outside Adelaide, South Australia.

I see the changes so far introduced by Chris Evans as positive and humane, but I also worry and ask myself whether he will be strong enough to continue and expand Labor's current policy.

Since a very early age I have always tried where able, to assist others, no matter what their colour, language or nationality. To me that was a 'duty of care'. Woomera reinforced that duty to me. It also opened my eyes to the ugliness that lies below the surface in all humans. Unfortunately, this trait when coupled with the perceived, unchecked power of some politicians, gives rise to what occurred in that barren place. Did it change me? Of course it did. Not a day goes by that I do not see or hear the sounds and smell of the despair and fear that reigned within those compounds.

Eric Vadarlis

I'm back at working to save all the corporate souls! Got to pay those school fees. Engaged in full-time plus commercial litigation practice.

I think [the government's changes] were well overdue and they are wholly appropriate. It's a humane solution to a difficult problem. It's what we argued from day one when *Tampa* started. But in many ways they don't go far enough. The refugees are allowed into the country and then they are dumped, with no ongoing assistance at all. They can't speak the language, they have no job, so their integration into the community needs to be seriously addressed and very soon.

No refugee work anymore, they are mostly all out of detention. Many, many others (and not only lawyers) have rolled up their sleeves and have taken up the challenge and are running with it. But still involved in pro bono work for the general public.

Do I reflect on it? Yes, often. I think it brought on the discussion that Australia needed to have about its attitude to refugees. And boy, did we Aussies show our colours! It was frightening.

Did it change me? Yes, it reaffirmed in me Lord Acton's famous (1877) dictum – 'Power tends to corrupt, and absolute power corrupts absolutely' – and has made me even more cynical about all those in power. And I never imagined before *Tampa* that people could be so vicious and cruel. And that as humans, most of us would fail the humanity test. Sad really.

PS: Am glad that Howard got thrown out! He got his just deserts.

Shame that Ruddock got re-elected. What does that say about those in his electorate?

Pamela Curr

I'm working as campaign coordinator at the Asylum Seeker Resource Centre Melbourne. Will continue to (campaign for human rights) until I die or lose my marbles.

I am glad that temporary protection visas are being removed, relieved that the Pacific Solution is being dismantled, but bitter that the Indian Ocean solution (Christmas Island detention centre) remains in place and disappointed at the measly changes to mandatory detention.

I am saddened at the hoopla over the mandatory detention announcement. Australians used to know what being 'sold a pup' meant. This announcement does not signal an end to mandatory indefinite detention. What the changes amount to are, that the minister is stating publicly that he expects the department to 'be nice' – to think before they incarcerate – but still with only the merest infringement on their powers. An un-named 'senior' insider may examine their decisions and the Ombudsman retains his recommendatory power, that is, power only to comment. The legislative architecture to deprive a person of liberty indefinitely is still enshrined in law.

We must not be sucked in by spin – Labor or Liberal – it is still spin.

I used to have a belief and trust in the intrinsic goodness of the community. I used to believe that most people in Australia – not all – shared a desire for kindness towards those in trouble. I do not believe this anymore. The last decade has shown how callous we can be.

Last time we locked up those who fled Pol Pot's killing fields, Saddam Hussein's torture chambers, the Taliban's brutality and other victims of repression and persecution; locked them up until they went mad. What will we do next time? Shoot them?

What reassures me is that there are still Australians, not the majority unfortunately, but still a vocal and substantial number who resist the messages of hate. These people who continue to believe in and fight for human rights, often against their own interests, give me hope that we can install a human rights architecture which will not blow over at the sight of another boat.

Anne Henderson

I am deputy director of the Sydney Institute and have just completed a biography of Dame Enid Lyons. I no longer visit Villawood, but keep in touch with many of the asylum seekers I assisted. With friends I have since formed the Sanctuary Movement Lower North Shore, which raises money to assist refugees to come to and settle in Australia. I regard Labor's recent changes to immigration detention policy as a positive step forward.

Gerard Henderson

I am executive director of the Sydney Institute and a weekly columnist for the *Sydney Morning Herald* and the *West Australian*. I regard Chris Evans' changes to detention as a further development of the reform process that commenced in 2005.

Jacquie Everitt

I have finished my book on the Badraie family (*The Bitter Shore*) and their quest for refugee status. The book was so complex and took so long that the job I had been offered of running a small humanitarian aid organisation in Cambodia could wait no longer for me. Working with refugees was seductive, it inspired a powerful sense of possibility, which I cannot resist pursuing. My heart is set on hunting down a job in the humanitarian aid sector.

The announcement of the [Labor] changes came so quickly and unexpectedly, that they became a power in themselves. They are a big first step, initiated by a new minister who took the time to see detention and the Pacific Solution for what they were. The changes have shown us that each vote against the Howard government was important, that a good government can react because a policy is intrinsically wrong, and that human rights of the most disenfranchised among us are again important and to be protected. The second step must be to abandon the concept of Christmas Island as a refugee warehouse.

I vote. I beat the drum. I maintain the closest friendship with a handful of refugees whose lives and mine entwined during the dark days. We will remain together for life. I am part of a number of human rights organisations.

My experience was like a mourning process. Shock that people were locked up and ill in fair-go, sunny, beach-loving Australia; denial and a belief that it was a mistake and I could change it by writing a story in the *Sydney Morning Herald* that would let Australians know so their outcry would ensure mandatory immigration detention would be brought to an end. I felt guilt that I belonged to a society which turned a blind eye, and because I could not find the right mechanisms to persuade a minister to change his stance.

This was followed by a burning, relentless anger that the 'bad refugees' (the boat people) were being punished in a strategic way for not being 'good refugees' and sitting in a refugee camp somewhere they had never heard of. Resignation and acceptance are the final stages of mourning, instead I remained in a state of anger mixed with sadness that our country was governed by elected representatives who had no compassion, who sneered at people who did as 'bleeding hearts'. Worst of all was hatred for the people in power who did not care that a child became a sacrifice on the altar of government policy. After Minister Evans' announcement, I maintain the memory of the anger that it happened and an unhealthy cynicism that it could happen again.

Damien Lawson

For the last four years I was an advisor to Greens Senator Kerry Nettle, whose portfolio included immigration. I am now the national climate justice coordinator with Friends of the Earth Australia. A large part of my work is highlighting the displacement of people by climate change and advocating for Australia to assist climate refugees, particularly in the Pacific.

I live at Maroubra Beach with two boys, aged three years and six months, and my partner Kylie, who is a contemporary artist and also participated in the Woomera protest and refugee movement.

Regarding Labor reforms: they are a step in the right direction, but need to be enshrined in legislation. The Christmas Island detention centre is being retained and boat people incarcerated there will still not have access to the courts. Labor is retaining the legal and physical infrastructure that could allow a future government to easily return to the practice of the Howard years.

Regarding my period of refugee activism: I learnt many, many things. It taught me a lot about working with a diverse range of people. Despite my criticism that we should have been prepared for escapes, I believe our direct actions were the right thing to do. In hindsight, we should have done more and had a more organised underground, which may have contributed to a greater problem for the government. That time more than any other, taught me that movements are messy and diverse beasts that defy any attempt to put them in a straitjacket. In fact, it is this diversity that makes social change possible. This is an important lesson for the climate movement. Some of what I learnt at Woomera, I have applied in new actions like the recent climate camp at Newcastle, where we stopped coal trains for a day and had 57 arrests.

Michaela Byers

I am practising as a solicitor in Campsie and lecturing in immigration and refugee law at the University of Western Sydney.

I would like to see criteria on 'threat to the community'. I'm disappointed that decision making is still in the hands of immigration department officials. We need independent involvement, such as federal magistrates, to ensure no stuff-ups or cover-ups occur.

I am still doing refugee and human rights work. Some pre-2005 cases (that is, those mentioned in this book and prior to the Petro-led reforms) are still unresolved, but none of the children are in detention.

Pre-2005 was an extremely traumatic time. I took on too many complicated pro bono cases, but it seemed at the time that no one was legally assisting penniless families in detention. The experience has increased my distrust of the department and the company now running detention centres [Global Solutions Limited], and I am more determined than ever to change the system. Although dealing with cases one by one is still very exhausting.

Margaret Piper

I am a consultant with over 20 years' experience working in the refugee sector. Currently my work primarily centres on research, training and capacity building in the area of refugee settlement. In addition, I maintain a keen interest in policy development and program planning through the various fora in which I participate.

I am a member of the Refugee Resettlement Advisory Council, which advises the minister for immigration and his parliamentary secretary for multicultural affairs. I am also a life member of the Refugee Advice and Casework Service and I sit on a variety of local and international boards and committees involved in refugee affairs.

Clearly I am delighted with the detention changes which, incidentally, closely resemble a model I worked on with other refugee practitioners (including Sydney lawyers Nick Poynder and Kerry Murphy) in the mid-1990s.

Being around in the early 1990s, which were in many ways much harder than more recent times, helped me to survive the 1999–2005 period. I learnt at this time that maintaining dialogue was the critical factor, as was focussing on achievable outcomes (even if these were not those most desired) and ensuring that there were win-win outcomes. I also learnt that pushing the government up against a wall was counterproductive.

Jo Szwarc

I am now working part time at Foundation House and also part time for Petro Georgiou; so yes, I am still involved with refugees and other human rights related work.

I think the changes introduced by Chris Evans are very good and consistent with the reforms Petro Georgiou continues to advocate. But further reforms are desirable (for example, judicial supervision of detention), which will need legislative action.

I feel proud and honoured to have had the opportunity to contribute to the reforms of 2005. They made a positive difference to the lives of vulnerable people who we did not treat well and properly and diminished the risk that others like them would be treated badly in the future. Along the way I was inspired by encountering so many so-called 'ordinary' Australians (which they are not!) who were actively involved on behalf of asylum seekers and refugees in diverse ways. These feelings remain strong.

Michael Kapel

I am currently chief of staff to the Liberal leader of the Opposition in Victoria, Ted Baillieu.

FORMER DETAINEE UPDATES

Al Abadey family (Iraq)

The Al Abadey family all have permanent residency in New Zealand. The boys are doing well working in a family hairdressing and tailoring business and in a separate tyre business. The little girl, Afnan, is now topping her class at school. Sadly, their youngest son was killed in 2008 in a tragic accident.

Heman Baban (Iraq)

Heman Baban and his son escaped from Australia in March 2001 to Canada via the Australian underground. Have never been heard from again.

Shayan Badraie (Iran)

Shayan Badraie is attending a secondary school in Sydney, which has particular expertise with refugee children whose past education has been non-existent or interrupted. He speaks of becoming a doctor. He will be 14 in January 2009 and 'is a gorgeous boy with old-fashioned manners and a gentle demeanour'. The Badraies have now been in Australia since March 2000, and are still waiting to be allocated a date for citizenship.

Bakhtiyari family (Afghanistan)

The Bakhtiyari family are back in Afghanistan as far as anyone knows. In 2006 Alamdar and Muntazer gave interviews apologising for upsetting the Australian government and blaming some advocates and lawyers. They wondered whether they could come back to Australia to complete their education.

Hwang family (South Korea)

The mother and children of the Hwang family have permanent residency. They are also trying to bring the children's father back from South Korea. They're negotiating with the federal government for compensation for wrongful detention.

Naomi Leong (Malaysia)

Naomi and her mother, Virginia, have permanent residency visas. Virginia is working with the elderly as a nurse's aid. Naomi is settled at primary school and loves it. They recently appeared on the second-last episode of Channel 9's *Sunday* program where it was revealed Naomi's speech is developmentally delayed. Also that Naomi has difficulties with memory.

Peter Qasim (Kashmir)

Peter Qasim is still on a bridging visa and living in Melbourne. But he is finding it difficult to obtain employment because of his temporary status. He is on a removal pending bridging visa, meaning he suffers from the uncertainty that he could be deported or re-detained at any time.

Cornelia Rau (Australia)

Cornelia received a $2.4 million compensation package from the federal government. She still has not recovered. She is now an Australian citizen.

Vivian Solon (Australia)

Vivian Solon is living in Sydney, and fully cared for by the government. She is continuing with her physiotherapy and occupational therapy and is making progress. The federal government reportedly paid out $4.5 million in compensation. Vivian's children are still in Queensland.

The two escapees

'Mohsen', the Iranian, is an Australian citizen who now lives in western Sydney. He has bought a house, works as a tradesman and is planning to travel to visit relatives overseas soon. He keeps in touch with many of the people who assisted with his escape, his life underground and his successful bid for legality.

'Hassan', the Afghan, is now on a permanent visa and has had a child with his partner. Toby states that he 'had only one brief "hello" by phone over the years. He was in Melbourne.'

Timeline

1991

18 October   Port Hedland detention centre opens in Western Australia (104 Indo-Chinese asylum seekers are transferred from temporary sites in Darwin).

Perth detention centre opens.

1992

5 June   Parliament passes the *Migration Amendment Act 1992* (Cth), legalising mandatory detention. Labor government of Paul Keating introduces the law.

8 December   The High Court rules that the government's mandatory detention policy is a valid use of government power, provided it is to facilitate processing and removal and is not punitive.

1998   One Nation member of parliament Pauline Hanson proposes temporary protection visas (TPVs) for all asylum seekers. Immigration minister Philip Ruddock tells parliament this would cause too much uncertainty in people's lives and that parliament will not contemplate it.

Zachary Steel and Derrick Silove publish 'The mental health and well-being of on-shore asylum seekers in Australia'.

12 May   The Human Rights and Equal Opportunity Commission (HREOC) report, *Those who've come across the seas: Detention of unauthorised arrivals*, is tabled in parliament. It recommends that those whose detention cannot be justified should be released, subject to reporting requirements, until their status is determined. It proposes a range of community release options.

9 September   Peter Qasim arrives from Kashmir, is detained in Perth. (He's later transferred to Curtin, Port Hedland, Woomera then Baxter.)

1999

May   Aamer Sultan arrives from Iraq at Sydney airport, is taken to Villawood detention centre in Sydney.

12 June   Heman Baban, and his 19-month-old son Bawan, arrive from Iraq at Ashmore (and Cartier) Islands, and are taken to Villawood.

September   Curtin detention centre is re-opened in Derby in Western Australia.

20 October   John Howard's government introduces TPVs for all refugees who arrive without a valid visa.

22 October   Ali Bakhtiyari arrives from Afghanistan at Ashmore Islands, is immediately detained.

1 December   Woomera detention centre opens in South Australia's Simpson Desert.

20 December   The Al Abadey family (parents and their four youngest children, aged four, nine, 13, and 15) arrive

from Iraq at Christmas Island, taken to Curtin.

2000

26 March   The Badraie family (parents and five-year-old
Shayan) arrive from Iran on Ashmore Islands, taken
to Woomera.

May   The Al Abadey family is transferred to Port Hedland
detention centre.

June   Two days of detainee protests at Woomera. Nearly
500 detainees walk into town.

Mid-2000   Refugee Action Collective (later Coalition) is
formed.

August   Three days of riots and fires at Woomera. Tear gas
and water cannons used for the first time.

3 August   Ali Bakhtiyari recognised as refugee, granted a three-
year TPV and released from detention.

September   Zachary Steel and Aamer Sultan meet at Villawood.

4 September   *Not the Hilton: Immigration detention centres: Inspection report*
tabled in parliament by Joint Standing Committee
on Migration. Committee recommends further
monitoring of detention centres and future meetings
with detainees.

2001

15 January   The Bakhtiyari family (mother and five children
aged three, seven, nine, ten and 12) arrive from
Afghanistan at Ashmore Islands, taken to Woomera.
Unbeknown to them, their father had arrived in
Australia in 1999 and been accepted as a refugee.

February	Immigration Detention Advisory Group (IDAG) is established.
February	*Report of inquiry into immigration detention procedures* (Flood Report) tabled in parliament. It condemns the detention centre at Woomera, and its management, for treating children like criminals.
3 March	Badraie family transferred from Woomera to Villawood.
26 March	Baban family escapes from Villawood along with 21 others.
2 April	Vivian Solon found wandering streets of Lismore, hospitalised.
5 May	Zachary Steel, Aamer Sultan, Derrick Silove and RF Mollica publish 'Detention of asylum seekers: Assault on health, human rights, and social development' in *The Lancet*.
May	Riots at Port Hedland, tear gas used. Al Abadey parents charged with rioting, sent to prison, older boys sent to juvenile detention centre. Youngest children (aged five and ten) fostered to Port Hedland detainees.
June	Riots at Woomera. Water cannon used again.
18 June	Joint Standing Committee on Foreign Affairs, Defence and Trade's Human Rights Sub-Committee tables *A report on visits to immigration detention centres* in parliament. Highlights a number of human rights concerns. Recommends that the immigration department and ACM make substantial changes, which 'satisfy community concerns', and 'ensure that Australia's international reputation is not damaged by reports of its treatment of asylum seekers'.

20 July	Australian mother of two, Vivian Solon, wrongfully deported to the Philippines.
July	Al Abadey children transferred to Villawood; parents remain in WA prisons.
July	Trish Highfield meets Jacquie Everitt and Ngareta Rossell in the Villawood visitors' area.
7 August	Woomera housing project first accepts women and children detainees.
13 August	*Four Corners* program about Shayan Badraie is aired.
14 August	New refugee advocacy group ChilOut formed, focussing on getting children and their parents out of detention.
23 August	Shayan Badraie is released from Villawood alone to foster care.
26 August –3 September	MV *Tampa* crisis.
3 September	Operation Relex begins. It involves the Australian navy turning back refugee boats.
September	Al Abadey mother transferred to Villawood, reunited with children.
7 September	First Suspected Illegal Entry Vessel (SIEV) turned back.
11 September	Terror attacks on USA, war on terror begins.
26 September	First excision of islands: Ashmore and Cartier Islands in the Timor Sea, Christmas and Cocos (Keeling) Islands in the Indian Ocean.
September	Pacific Solution begins with Nauru detention facility opening in the South Pacific.

October	Manus Island detention centre opens in the Bismarck Sea, Papua New Guinea.
October	A new advocacy group called Rural Australians for Refugees (RAR) is formed.
October	TPV legislation tightened: those spending more than seven days in another country en route to Australia never able to become permanent residents.
7 October	Navy fires warning shots directly into the water ahead of 'children overboard' boat. Navy then rescues the 223 asylum seekers.
19 October	Sinking of SIEV X, an Indonesian vessel bound for Christmas Island: 353 people drown and 44 survive.
November	Christmas Island detention centre opens in Indian Ocean.
10 November	The Howard Coalition government is re-elected.
December	In co-operation with Dr Kevin O'Sullivan, Aamer Sultan publishes a study of the psychological effects of long-term detention.
December	Zachary Steel and Derrick Silove publish 'The mental health implications of detaining asylum seekers' in the *Medical Journal of Australia*.

2002

16 January	Shayan Badraie is reunited with mother and sister. All three are granted bridging visas to live in the community. His father remains in Villawood.
22 January	IDAG delegation visits Woomera amid a 16-day mass hunger strike.

26 January	Bakhtiyari children's uncle, Mahzar Ali, jumps shirtless into Woomera's razor wire. A TV camera films the jump.
February	A Just Australia, a new refugee advocacy group, is launched.
24 March	Cocos Island detention centre closes.
March	Woomera Easter protests, 50 detainees escape.
April	Al Abadey father transferred to Villawood, reunited with family.
5 May	Naomi Leong born to a pregnant detainee. Immediately transferred from post-natal ward to Villawood.
May	Alliance of Doctors and Health Professionals formed, uniting medical profession around the issue of effects of long-term detention especially on children.
24 May –2 June	Justice PN Bhagwati, representative of the United Nations High Commissioner for Human Rights, visits Australian detention centres.
28 June	Woomera hunger strike and 37 detainees escape, including the two oldest Bakhtiyari children.
2 July	Aamer Sultan granted a TPV and released from Villawood after 37 and a half months in detention.
18 July	Bakhtiyari boys make asylum bid at British consulate-general in Melbourne. Re-detained.
31 July	PN Bhagwati releases his report, *Human rights and immigration detention in Australia*. He finds multiple breaches of human rights. The report criticises lack of independent monitoring mechanisms, restricted

access to healthcare workers and lawyers, lack of protection of the family unit, the harmful policy of detaining unaccompanied minors, and the prison-like conditions.

July   Baxter detention centre opens in Port Augusta, South Australia.

9 August   Badraie family recognised as refugees.

23 September Curtin detention centre closes. Detainees moved to Baxter.

4 December   Ali Bakhtiyari's visa is cancelled and he is put back in detention, at Villawood.

5 December   Carmen Lawrence resigns from Labor's front bench partially in protest against the asylum seeker policy launched by the Federal Parliamentary Labor Party (also disagreed with Iraq war).

10 December Human Rights Watch releases *By invitation only: Australian asylum policy* report. The New York-based NGO, after eight months of investigation, condemns Operation Relex. It accuses members of the Australian Defence Force of mistreating asylum seekers. It catalogues use of inhumane treatment; people being held below decks in very crowded conditions for days, denied food, water, medical treatment, and being beaten with electric batons.

December   United Nations' Working Group on Arbitrary Detention releases its report on its visit to Australia in May–June. It condemns the government's policy of detaining asylum seekers, describing it as contrary to accepted international standards and of an arbitrary nature.

2003

January	Bakhtiyari mother and children moved from Woomera to Baxter detention centres.
10 February	Al Abadey family deported to Syria.
April	Woomera detention centre closes. Remaining detainees moved to Baxter.
June	Family Court orders the release into foster care of the Bakhtiyari children.
26 August	Bakhtiyari children's first day of what will be 16 months of freedom.
19 September	Port Hedland residential housing project opens.
7 October	Amanda Vanstone replaces Philip Ruddock as minister for immigration.
November	Port Augusta residential housing project opens.

2004

30 January	Labor Party national conference, Labor for Refugees loses fight to reform asylum seeker policy.
April	High Court again declares mandatory detention constitutionally valid.
29 April	High Court overturns Family Court decision to release Bakhtiyari children, orders they be re-detained. Government allows them to remain in Adelaide house with mother.
13 May	*A last resort?*, HREOC's report on its inquiry into children in immigration detention, is tabled in parliament. It recommends all children be released from detention centres and residential housing

projects immediately. It gives the government a four-week deadline to do so.

June
Port Hedland detention centre closes. Detainees moved to Baxter.

6 October
Cornelia Rau is transferred to Baxter detention centre from Brisbane women's correctional centre, where she has been held as an immigration detainee for six months.

9 October
The Howard Coalition government is re-elected, wins control of both houses of parliament.

18 December
Bakhtiyari mother and six children forcibly taken to Port Augusta from Adelaide and re-detained.

25 December
Petro Georgiou hatches his plan over Christmas lunch.

30 December
Bakhtiyari family deported to Pakistan.

––––––

2005

3 February
Cornelia Rau released from Baxter to hospital.

5 February
Cornelia Rau detention scandal hits the media.

8 February
Immigration Minister Amanda Vanstone announces Palmer Inquiry.

8 March
Ian and Janey Hwang seized from Stanmore Primary School and taken to Villawood, where they are left alone for two hours before their mother arrives.

5 May
Naomi Leong's third birthday. She has spent her whole life in detention.

11 May
Vivian Solon scandal hits the media.

23 May	Petro Georgiou goes public with his private member's bill.
24 May	Naomi Leong and her mother released from detention.
9 June	Sydney residential housing project opens.
17 June	John Howard announces changes to detention regime including the release of all children within six weeks.
14 July	Palmer Report published. It recommends wide ranging reforms of immigration department.
17 July	Peter Qasim released after almost seven years in detention.
20 July	Ian and Janey Hwang released from Villawood with their mother.
29 July	Last children released from detention centres.
July	Second excision of islands to the north of Australia.
11 December	Race riots at Cronulla Beach, southern Sydney.

2006

18 January	43 West Papuan asylum seekers arrive at Cape York, are flown to Christmas Island and detained.
March	Immigration department finalises an out-of-court settlement with Badraie family.
22 March	42 West Papuans granted TPVs. Indonesian government lodges official protest with Australian government, asks that they be sent back to Indonesia.

13 May　　　*Designated Unauthorised Arrivals Bill* (the DUA Bill) is introduced into federal parliament by John Howard.

10 August　　Petro Georgiou, Judi Moylan and Russell Broadbent cross the floor to vote against the DUA Bill.

14 August　　Senator Judith Troeth tells John Howard she will cross the floor. Government withdraws the DUA Bill.

2007

Perth residential housing project opens.

30 January　　Kevin Andrews replaces Amanda Vanstone as immigration minister.

24 November Federal election, the Howard government is defeated. The Kevin Rudd Labor government is elected. Chris Evans becomes minister for immigration and citizenship.

2008

8 February　 Last detainees leave Nauru, Labor government scraps Pacific Solution.

29 July　　　Labor immigration minister, Chris Evans, announces that immigration detention will be used only as a last resort and will never be used for children. The onus of proof is on the department to show need for detention after initial checks.

9 August　　Rudd Labor government abolishes temporary protection visas.

Notes

PROLOGUE

Page 6: 'Almost 12 000 asylum seekers ... 1999 and 2002': Department of Immigration and Citizenship (DIAC), search <http://www.immi.gov.au>; Barry York, Social Policy Group, *Australia and Refugees, 1901–2002: An annotated chronology based on official sources*, available at <http://www.aph.gov.au/library/pubs/online/Refugees_s3.htm>.
Page 6: 'At the time there were ... and Iraq (530 000)': United Nations High Commission for Refugees (UNHCR), *Statistical Yearbook, 2001*, available at <http://www. unhcr.org/statistics.html>. All world refugee statistics have been taken from UN-HCR (unless otherwise stated).
Page 6: 'Whole [Middle Eastern] ... minister, Philip Ruddock': 'Minister warns of boatpeople flood', *The Australian*, 16 November 1999; 'Refugee crisis warning', *The Age*, 18 November 1999.
Page 6: 'After the September 11 ... defence minister, Peter Reith': AFP, 'Australian government says asylum seekers a security risk', 13 September 2001; Reuters, 'Australia warns of boat people "terrorist pipeline",' 13 September 2001.
Page 6: 'Most terror experts laughed ... August 2002': Joint Standing Committee on Foreign Affairs, Defence and Trade (JSCFADT), Human Rights Sub-committee, *Aspects of HREOC's annual report 2000–01 concerning immigration detention centres*, Commonwealth of Australia, House of Representatives, Parliamentary Debates, Hansard, 22 August 2002.
Page 7: 'Then the government introduced ... obligations towards them': *Migration Amendment (Excision from Migration Zone) Act 2001* (Cth): *Migration Amendment (Excision from Migration Zone) (Consequential Provisions) Act 2001* (Cth).
Page 7: 'Once we had brought ... Ruddock, explained': 'NZ, Nauru to take boat people stranded off Australia', *Kyodo News*, 1 September 2001; 'Fortress Australia – the implications', *Sydney Morning Herald*, 3 September 2001.
Page 7: 'Australia is a signatory ... authorisation': *Convention relating to the Status of Refugees*, adopted on 28 July 1951, available at <http://www.unhchr.ch/html/menu3/b/o_c_ref.htm>.

Page 7: 'Each year worldwide … a year': UNHCR, available at <http://www.unhcr.org/statistics.html>; DIAC, search <http://www.immi.gov.au>.

Page 8: 'For most countries … 2000': UNHCR, available at <http://www.unhcr.org/statistics.html>.

Page 8: 'We are a humanitarian country … in Melbourne': 3AW Neil Mitchell, August 2001 quoted in David Marr and Marian Wilkinson, *Dark Victory*, Sydney, Allen and Unwin, 2003, p 47.

Page 8: 'It involved, in words quoted … seeker boats': Parliament of Australia, Senate, *A certain maritime incident*, 23 October 2002, available at <http://www.aph.gov.au/SENATE/committee/maritime_incident_ctte/report/index.htm>; Chris Sidoti, 'Truth overboard: One year after *Tampa*', Speech, Deakin University, 5 December 2002, available at <http://www.hrca.org.au/one%20year%20after%20tampa.htm>. The ship's log was tabled before the Certain Maritime Incident Senate Committee on 21 February 2002, nearly five months after the event.

Page 8: 'In one case the Australian warship … were also rescued': Parliament of Australia, Senate, *A certain maritime incident*; 'Boat children – what really happened – Children Overboard Inquiry', *The Australian*, 27 March 2002.

Page 9: 'In a staggering tragedy … the naval blockade': SIEV X <http://www.sievx.com/> details primary and secondary source material relating to the SIEV X disaster.

Page 9: 'We shall decide who … famously declared': AFP, 'Australian government says asylum seekers a security risk', 13 September 2001.

Page 10: 'The first half of 2005 … wrongfully deported': Commonwealth Ombudsman, 'Commonwealth Ombudsman takes on immigration detention investigations', Media release, 14 July 2005; Mick Palmer, *Inquiry into the circumstances of the immigration detention of Cornelia Rau: Report*, Commonwealth of Australia, Canberra, July 2005; Australian Broadcasting Corporation (ABC) TV, 'Govt searching for wrongly deported woman', *Lateline*, 4 May 2005, available at <http://www.abc.net.au/lateline/content/2005/s1360111.htm>; Commonwealth Ombudsman <http://www.comb.gov.au>.

CHAPTER 1

Page 17: 'A founding member … dispute and globalisation': This organisation has now merged with the Socialist Action Group to form a new group called Solidarity, see <http://www.solidarity.net.au>.

Page 19: 'But those refugees … punitive response': Australia's response to 'boat people' is discussed by Meredith Wilkie, Norman Aisbett, Chris Doepel, Vanessa Moss and Christabel Chamarette in 'Boat people symposium', Centre for Research in Culture & Communication, Murdoch University, 15 October 1996, available at <http://wwwmcc.murdoch.edu.au/ReadingRoom/boat/panel2.html>.

Page 19: 'There had been a … Vietnam War': JSCFADT, *A report on visits to immigration detention centres*, 18 June 2001, available at <http://www.aph.gov.au/house/committee/jfadt/idcvisits/IDCchap2.htm>.

Page 19: 'One newspaper … human flotsam': 'Keeping posted', *Cairns Post*, 19 November 2001.

Page 20: 'The then federal ... increase its population': *The Australian*, 29 November 1977.

Page 20: 'But because ... Fraser has said': Malcolm Fraser, Speech, Conferment of the Degree of Doctor of Laws, University of Technology, Sydney, 29 April 2002, available at <http://www.unimelb.edu.au/malcolmfraser/speeches/nonparliamentary/utsdoctoroflaws.html>.

Page 20: 'In April 1979 ... queue jumpers': *The Australian*, 24 April 1979, available at <http://www.ausref.net/cms/home/history-mission>.

Page 20: 'Despite the scale ... others in 1989': Department of Immigration, Multicultural and Indigenous Affairs (DIMIA) and DIAC fact sheets.

Page 20: 'But the welcome mat ... Michael Harper': 'Giant strides', *The Australian*, 3 May 1997. The boat arrived at Montague Sound, Western Australia, 31 December 1991. All but one were eventually allowed to stay on refugee or humanitarian grounds.

Page 21: 'Mandatory detention ... Gerry Hand': ABC TV, News, February 1992, excerpted in ABC TV, 'Immigration causing nightmares for Labor', *7:30 Report*, 1 February 2002, available at <http://www.abc.net.au/7.30/content/2002/s471733.htm>.

Page 21: 'Prime Minister Bob Hawke ... on,' he said': 'Prime Minister's ambivalent attitude to refugees causes concern to both colleagues and Opposition', *The Economist*, 16 June 1990, p 85.

Page 21: 'The whole system ... exceeded nine months': *Tang Jia Xin v Nick Bolkus, Minister of Immigration and Ethnic Affairs and Joanne Mcrae* [1993] FCA 372; (1993) 116 ALR 329 (6 August 1993).

Page 22: 'Dedicated immigration ... in South Australia': DIAC, *Fact sheet 81*.

Page 23: 'PHILIP RUDDOCK: We've even had ... high expectations': ABC TV, 'Rare bipartisanship in parliament', *7.30 Report*, 22 November 1999, available at <http://www.abc.net.au/7.30/stories/s67804.htm>.

Page 23: 'PHILIP: It's amazing ... a mobile phone': ABC TV, 'The queue jumpers', *Four Corners*, 16 October 2000, available at <http://www.abc.net.au/4corners/stories/s200031.htm>.

Page 23: 'Security at immigration ... conglomerate Wackenhut': DIMIA, 'Company takes up responsibility for immigration detention centre', Media release, 14 November 1997, available at <http://www.immi.gov.au/media/media-releases/1997/d97019.htm>; Letter to the editor of *The Australian* by acting director, DIMIA Public Affairs, 29 August 2003, available at <http://www.immi.gov.au/media/letters/letters03/australian_2908.htm>.

Page 23: 'At the time, Wackenhut was ... abuse and neglect': ABC Radio, 'Private detention centres reap mammoth profits', *PM*, 23 November 2000, available at <http://www.abc.net.au/pm/stories/s215963.htm>.

Page 23: 'George Wackenhut, the company's ... all along': 'The more punishment the better to fill George Wackenhut's coffers', *Sydney Morning Herald*, 12 December 2000.

Page 24: 'Former ACM operations ... has said': Human Rights and Equal Opportunity Commission (HREOC), *A last resort? National inquiry into children in immigration detention*, Transcript of hearing, Allan John Clifton, Adelaide, 2 July 2002, available at <http://www.humanrights.gov.au/human_rights/children_detention/transcript/clifton.html>; 'Woomera: victims of the war zone', *The Age*, 25 February 2007.

Page 24: 'At Woomera some ... Saddam Hussein': Transcript of speech by Nurse

Moira-Jane, Children Out of Detention (ChilOut) information night, 3 June 2002.
Page 24: 'Pressures inside ... by June 2000': Department of Immigration and Multi-cultural Affairs (DIMA), 'Immigration detention', *Fact sheet 82*.
Page 25: 'And at Woomera, ACM ... off skin': A registered nurse Mark Huxstep who worked at Woomera described what he was told could be the injuries arising from the use of a water cannon: HREOC, *A last resort?*, Chapter 8, Transcript of hearing, Brisbane, 5 August 2002, available at <http://www.humanrights.gov.au/human_rights/children_detention/transcript/brisbane_5august.html>.
Page 29: 'Traditional advocates ... Council of Australia': Refugee Council of Australia <http://www.refugeecouncil.org.au>.
Page 30: 'The Refugee Council ... Woomera in 2000': ABC TV, '... About Woomera', *Four Corners*, 19 May 2003, available at <http://www.abc.net.au/4corners/content/2003/transcripts/s858341.htm>.
Page 30: 'Philip Ruddock responds ... continue to address it': Commonwealth of Australia, Parliamentary Debates, House of Representatives, Hansard, 29 August 2000, p 19509.
Page 31: 'Then in 2001 ... the nearby township': HREOC, *A last resort?*, Chapter 8, available at <http://www.humanrights.gov.au/human_rights/children_detention_report/report/chap08.htm 8_3>.
Page 31: 'The Australian public ... nurse at the time': 'Woomera officer tells of boy raped and sold for cigarettes', *The Australian*, 15 November 2000; ABC TV, 'Detention danger', *Lateline*, 24 November 2000, available at <http://www.abc.net.au/lateline/stories/s216614.htm>.
Page 33: 'The following Friday ... Mr Heman Baban': Baban took his case to the United Nations' Human Rights Committee which found that the mandatory detention upon arrival and inability for courts or administrative authorities to order their release meant their rights were violated under the *International Covenant on Civil and Political Rights*, which Australia ratified in 1980. The committee also said Australia had an obligation to pay them compensation: *Omar Sharif Baban v Australia*, Communication No 1014/2001, UN Doc CCPR/C/78/D/1014/2001, 8 August 2003, available at <http://www1.umn.edu/humanrts/undocs/1014-2001.html>.

CHAPTER 2

Page 41: 'For instance, between ... to be refugees': HREOC, *A last resort?*, Chapter 3 <http://www.hreoc.gov.au/Human_Rights/children_detention_report/report/chap03.htm>.
Page 43: 'Paris Aristotle, the memorably ... for Survivors of Torture': Victorian Foundation for Survivors of Torture, Foundation House, see <http://www.survivorsvic.org.au/home.php>.
Page 44: 'But by scrounging ... asylum seekers': Derrick Silove and Zachary Steel, 'The mental health and well-being of on-shore asylum seekers in Australia', Psychiatry Research and Teaching Unit, University of New South Wales, 1998.
Page 51: 'Their research about ... truthful a manner as possible': Derrick M Silove, Zachary Steel, RF Mollica and Aamer Sultan, 'Detention of asylum seekers: Assault on health, human rights, and social development', *The Lancet*, vol 357, 5 May 2001, pp 1436–37; Zachary Steel and Derrick M Silove, 'The mental health implications

of detaining asylum seekers', *Medical Journal of Australia*, vol 175, 2001, pp 596–99, available at <https://www.mja.com.au/public/issues/175_12_171201/steel/steel. html>. Kevin O'Sullivan spent a year as the Villawood detention centre psychologist and he later worked with Aamer to better define 'Immigration Detention Stress Syndrome': Aamer Sultan and Kevin O'Sullivan, 'Psychological disturbances in asylum seekers held in long-term detention: a participant-observer account', *Medical Journal of Australia*, vol 175, 2001, pp 593–96, available at <http://www.mja.com. au/public/issues/175_12_171201/sultan/sultan.html>; ABC Radio, 'Ruddock attacks *Medical Journal of Australia*', *The World Today*, 10 December 2001, available at <http:// www.abc.net.au/worldtoday/stories/s436609.htm>; ABC Radio, 'Asylum seekers in detention', *Radio National*, 13 August 2001, available at <http://www.abc.net.au/rn/ talks/8.30/helthrpt/stories/s345280.htm>.

Page 51: 'The *Good Weekend* publishes … July 2001': 'The two of us', *Good Weekend*, 7 July 2001.

Page 52: 'Aamer is commended … Equal Opportunity Commission': HREOC, search <http://www.humanrights.gov.au>.

Page 53: 'He's accepted an … monitor detention centres': see DIAC, Immigration Detention Advisory Group (IDAG) <http://www.immi.gov.au/managing-australias-borders/detention/regulations/idag.htm>.

Page 56: 'Even when Paris … themselves on boats': see HREOC case study on their experiences, 9 July to 28 September 2001 in Woomera. See *A last resort?* Chapter 14, available at <http://www.humanrights.gov.au/human_rights/children_detention_re-port/report/chap14.htm 14_9>.

Page 57: 'Zachary Steel continues to … been in detention': Zachary Steel, Derrick Silove, Robert Brooks, Shakeh Momartin, Bushra Alzuhairi and Ina Susljik, 'Impact of immigration detention and temporary protection on the mental health of refugees', *British Journal of Psychiatry*, 188, 2006, pp 58–64.

Page 58: 'A man … Aamer says': 'The two of us', *Good Weekend*.

CHAPTER 3

Page 59: 'They arrive quietly … the footpath': see for instance 'Immigration home raids highlight sweeping powers', *Sydney Morning Herald*, 29 March 2001.

Page 61: 'JOHN HIGHFIELD: Well the Minister … not to be a refugee': ABC Online, 'Ruddock discusses refugee detention centre procedures', *The World Today*, 28 March 2001, available at <http://www.abc.net.au/worldtoday/stories/s267513. htm>. Transcript extract from *The World Today* (details above) first published by ABC Online, is reproduced by permission of the Australian Broadcasting Corporation and ABC Online, © 2001 ABC. All rights reserved.

Page 63: 'Nine adults and … escape from Villawood': 'Asylum seekers on run after Villawood escape', *Sydney Morning Herald*, 29 March 2001.

Page 64: 'Ali is part of the ethnic Hazara … human mine sweepers': Human Rights Watch, 'Backgrounder on Afghanistan: History of the war', available at <http://www. hrw.org/backgrounder/asia/afghan-bck1023.htm>; Human Rights Watch, 'Afghanistan: Massacres of Hazaras in Afghanistan', February 2001, available at <http://www. hrw.org/reports/2001/afghanistan/>; AFP, 'UN confirms Taliban massacre of ethnic minority', 11 September 1998, available at <http://www.rawa.org/mazar6.htm>; US

Embassy, Jakarta, 'Fact sheet: The Taliban's betrayal of the Afghan People', Press release, 18 October 2001, available at <http://jakarta.usembassy.gov/press_rel/The-Talibans.html>; Human Rights Watch, 'Afghanistan: Ethnically-motivated abuses against civilians', Press backgrounder, available at <http://www.hrw.org/back-grounder/asia/afghan-bck1006.htm>.

Page 65: 'After three years in various ... dead are placed': 'Behind the wiring of an easy lifestyle', *Sydney Morning Herald*, 21 April 2004.

Page 67: 'I want to offer ... malicious intent': Commonwealth of Australia, Parliamentary Debates, House of Representatives, Hansard, 7 December 2000, p 23658.

Page 70: 'After returning to Sydney ... Casework Service': Refugee Advice and Casework Service <http://www.racs.org.au>.

Page 70: 'She was immediately ... attention on them': Jacquie Everitt details this story in her book *The Bitter Shore*, Sydney, Pan Macmillan Australia, 2008.

Page 71: 'They find the ... Shayan Badraie': Shayan's story is detailed in HREOC, 'Case study: Shayan Badraie', *A last resort?*, Chapter 8, available at <http://www.humanrights.gov.au/human_rights/children_detention_report/report/chap08.htm 8_7>. Ngareta Rossell tells the story of her first meeting with Shayan in *Acting from the Heart: Australian advocates for asylum seekers tell their stories*, Sarah Mares and Louise Newman (eds), Sydney, Finch Publishing, 2007, pp 2–9.

Page 72: 'Every expert medical ... expert is ignored': Doctors' reports from West-mead Hospital on Shayan's condition can be found in 'Report of an inquiry into a complaint by Mr Mohammed Badraie on behalf of his son Shayan regarding acts or practices of the Commonwealth of Australia (the Department of Immigration, Multicultural and Indigenous Affairs)', HREOC Report no 25, Appendix B, available at <http://www.hreoc.gov.au/legal/HREOCA_reports/hrc_25.html>.

Page 74: 'Just over a week later ... widespread public protest': ABC TV, 'The inside story', *Four Corners*, 13 August 2001, available at <http://www.abc.net.au/4corners/stories/s344246.htm>.

Page 75: 'The group campaigns ... 800 children in detention': DIMIA statistics are cited in HREOC, *A last resort?*, Chapter 3, available at <http://www.humanrights.gov.au/human_rights/children_detention_report/report/chap03.htm 3_2>; ChilOut <http://www.chilout.org>. Junie Ong tells the story of her involvement in *Acting from the Heart*, pp 160–63 and the story of ChilOut is continued by Dianne Hiles on pp 163–67.

Page 75: 'Royal Australian and New Zealand College of Psychiatrists': <http://www.ranzcp.org>.

Page 76: 'PHILIP RUDDOCK: A lot of the psychiatric ... step-child': ABC TV, 'Ruddock replies to community concerns', 7:30 *Report*, 14 August 2001, available at <http://www.abc.net.au/7.30/content/2001/s346319.htm>.

Page 76: 'We love our children ... child from eating?': ABC TV, 'Four Corners program gives insight into plight of detainees', 7.30 *Report*, 14 August 2001, available at <http://www.abc.net.au/7.30/content/2001/s346329.htm>.

Page 76: 'The ABC produced ... take him home': Piers Akerman, 'Hidden truth of asylum seekers', *Sunday Telegraph*, 19 August 2001; Peter McEvoy on Akerman 'Getting the inside story' is reproduced in Margo Kingston's article 'Boat people media games', *Sydney Morning Herald*, 29 October 2001, available at <http://www.smh.com.au/articles/2003/11/26/1069522663624.html>; ABC TV, 'The inside story'.

Page 77: 'The immigration ... detention centres or detainees': 'Boat people media games', *Sydney Morning Herald*.

Page 77: 'Among those reports ... be released': Jacquie Everitt, *The Bitter Shore*.

Page 78: 'Now a 'gentle and quiet' teenager ... says Jacquie Everitt': Jacquie Everitt, *The Bitter Shore*.

Page 78: 'And then out to ... of the passengers': Marr and Wilkinson, *Dark Victory*, p 1.

Page 78: 'The *Tampa* rescues ... nation of Nauru': *A certain maritime incident*, 23 October 2002.

Page 79: 'There is no war; just ... support John Howard': ABC TV, 'Tampa issue improves Coalition election prospects', *7.30 Report*, 4 September 2001.

Page 79: 'Along with mainland detention ... for an actual war': A Just Australia and Oxfam, *A price too high: The cost of Australia's approach to asylum seekers*, August 2007, available at <http://www.oxfam.org.au/media/files/APriceTooHigh.pdf>.

Page 80: 'The *Tampa* also ... Rooms for Refugees': Spare Rooms for Refugees <http://www.spareroomsforrefugees.com/main.htm>.

Page 80: 'Kate also begins ... to Nauru': 'Detainees to cast off from Nauru', *The Age*, 14 October 2005.

Page 80: 'These are subsequently ... Australia's Pacific Solution': BBC, 'Australia's Pacific Solution', 29 September 2002, available at <http://news.bbc.co.uk/hi/english/static/audio_video/programmes/correspondent/transcripts/2279330.txt>.

Page 80: 'In the conservative ... for Refugees (RAR)': Rural Australians for Refugees <http://www.ruralaustraliansforrefugees.org.au>.

CHAPTER 4

Pages 83ff: 'Toby', 'Mohsen' and 'Hassan' are pseudonyms.

Page 84: 'Most of the ... escape, however briefly': ABC TV, 'Police say Woomera protesters planned to free detainees', *7.30 Report*, 1 April 2002, available at <http://www.abc.net.au/7.30/content/2002/s518373.htm>.

Page 88: 'He doesn't want to ... Western governments': Human Rights Watch, *Iran*, search <http://hrw.org>.

Page 89: 'It had been described ... was even worse': ABC Regional News, 'Woomera under scrutiny ahead of advisory group's arrival', 29 January 2002.

Page 89: 'Australia has traditionally ... reported the BBC': BBC News, 'Analysis: Australia's tough asylum policy', 24 January 2002, available at <http://news.bbc.co.uk/2/hi/asia-pacific/1780365.stm>.

Page 90: 'This was 'alien' ... go home': 'Go home, Ruddock tells Afghan protesters', *Sydney Morning Herald*, 21 January 2002; AFP, 'Self-mutilation won't sway us, Australia tells asylum seekers', 20 January 2002.

Page 90: 'Prime Minister John ... detention policy]': 'Time for a fair go at Woomera', *Sun Herald*, 27 January 2002; AFP, 'Australia warned of looming tragedy at Woomera detention centre', 29 January 2002.

Page 90: 'Many Australian commentators ... *Daily Telegraph*': 'Brutality not only barbaric, it's futile', *Daily Telegraph*, 22 January 2002.

Page 90: 'Yet as Paris ... under blankets': HREOC, *A last resort?*, Sharon Torbet, Submission 62a, Annexure 1, p 10, available at <http://www.hreoc.gov.au/human_

rights/children_detention_report/report/chap08.htm>.

Page 91: 'GUARD: Do you need ... DETAINEE: No': ABC TV, '... About Woomera', *Four Corners*.

Page 91: 'Unlike the Iranian escapee ... 9/11 attacks in 2001': ABC Radio, 'Advisory group head discusses situation', 'Processing of refugee claims to resume at Woomera', 'Woomera cross', *PM*, 24 January 2002, available at <http://www.abc.net.au/pm/indexes/2002/pm_archive_2002_Thursday24January2002.htm>.

Page 92: '[People all over ... he says': 'Go home, Ruddock tells Afghan protesters', *Sydney Morning Herald*.

Page 93: 'Paris and the ... safe for them': 'The day Ruddock came to the table on Woomera – Inside story', *The Australian*, 2 February 2002.

Page 94: 'But as the hunger strike ... his own hands': ABC Regional News, 'Woomera under scrutiny ahead of advisory group's arrival', 29 January 2002; HREOC, *A last resort?*, Chapter 14 Case study 3: Woomera, January 2002, group self-harm resulting in removal of unaccompanied children, available at <http://www.humanrights.gov.au/human_rights/children_detention_report/report/chap14.htm 14_9>.

Page 95: 'Under a banner ... inside Woomera': 29 January 2002.

Page 95: 'Further restrictions ... move back': ABC Radio National, 'Media freedom and Woomera', *The Media Report*, 31 January 2002, available at <http://www.abc.net.au/rn/mediareport/stories/2002/475505.htm>.

Page 103: 'There were 373 ... remain unresolved': DIAC.

CHAPTER 5

Page 104: 'The boys were ... marked for deportation': DIMIA, 'Brothers reunited with their mother', Media centre, MPS 66/2002, 19 July 2002.

Page 105: 'Hazaras, with their distinctive ... thousands of refugees': US Committee for Refugees and Immigrants <http://www.refugees.org>, see the World Refugee Survey.

Page 105: 'The children were ... concentrate on anything': 'Back to the ruins', *Sun Herald*, 24 March 2002.

Page 106: 'Please this is ... burning here': 'This isn't a camp, it's an oven and we are burning', *Sun Herald*, 17 February 2002.

Pages 108ff: 'Anna' and 'Nicholas' are pseudonyms.

Page 111: 'Federal police would raid ... eventually dropped': 'Homes raided in forgery probe', *The Age*, 2 December 2004.

Page 117: 'We have been sent ... by phone': 'Our life on the run', *Herald Sun*, 20 July 2002.

Page 117: 'This prompts ... of the Bakhtiyaris': ABC News Online, 'Ruddock tells SA govt to keep out of Bakhtiyari case', 16 August 2002.

Page 117: 'These children have ... Mr Rann says': AAP, 'Fed – Baktiari [sic] boys unlikely to be released – Williams', 17 August 2002.

Page 118: 'We believe his visa ... says Ruddock': ABC News, 'Boys' family lied about nationality – Ruddock', 18 July 2002.

Page 118: 'It emerges later ... of Quetta': DIMIA, 'Brothers reunited with their mother'.

Page 118: 'And it is not a ... Mr Ruddock warns': ABC Radio, 'Government looks at

refugee visa claims', *The World Today*, 23 August 2002.
Page 123: 'There was a brave ... Just Australia': A Just Australia <http://www.ajus-taustralia.com>.
Page 124: 'Meanwhile the ... to the wrong countries!': 'How tapes sent to Sweden alter thousands of lives', *The Age*, 27 July 2002, available at <http://www.theage.com.au/articles/2002/07/26/1027497412021.html>.
Page 125: 'The Refugee Review ... is dishonest': Refugee Review Tribunal, available at <http://www.mrt-rrt.gov.au/conduct.asp> and scroll down to Guidelines.
Page 126: 'Lawyers from three ... Mostly they lost': 'Flight ends long fight for Bakhtiyaris', *The Australian*, 31 December 2004.

CHAPTER 6

Page 134: 'Those whose rights ... have a voice': Julian Burnside, *Watching Brief: Reflections on human rights, law, and justice*, Melbourne, Scribe, 2007, p 45.
Page 134: 'When she is finally ... created in Canberra': You can see the memorial at <http://www.sievxmemorial.com>. The group creating the memorial initiated in the Uniting Church with Bellingen RAR and was led and funded by psychologist Steve Biddulph. They worked for over five years against government hostility, to create a national memorial to those who lost their lives.
Page 137: 'One night he ... I love you': 'Welcoming refugees into the family', *The Australian*, 10 February 2003.
Page 140: 'Julian Burnside was at Melbourne ... radio interview': ABC Radio, 'Australian lawyers barred from Nauru asylum case', *The World Today*, 26 April 2004.
Page 145: 'Inadequate resources ... scarred them all': see ABC TV, 'A place called Woomera', *Four Corners*, 19 May 2003.
Page 147: 'He has since ... by the immigration department': Z Steel, D Silove, R Brooks, S Momartin, B Alzuhairi and I Susljik, 'Impact of immigration detention and temporary protection on the mental health of refugees', *British Journal of Psychiatry*, 188, 2006, pp 58–64; S Momartin, Z Steel, M Coello, J Aroche, D Silove and R Brooks, 'A comparison of the mental health of refugees with temporary versus permanent protection visas', *Medical Journal of Australia*, 185(7), October 2006, p 35761; Z Steel, S Momartin, C Bateman, A Hafshejani, DM Silove, N Everson, et al, 'Psychiatric status of asylum seeker families held for a protracted period in a remote detention centre in Australia', *Australian and New Zealand Journal of Public Health*, 28(6), December 2004, pp 527–36; LK Newman and Z Steel, 'The child asylum seeker: Psychological and developmental impact of immigration detention', *Child and Adolescent Psychiatric Clinics of North America*, 17(3), 2008, pp 665–83; D Silove, P Austin and Z Steel, 'No refuge from terror: The impact of detention on the mental health of trauma-affected refugees seeking asylum in Australia', *Transcultural Psychiatry*, 44(3), 2007, pp 359–93; Z Steel and D Silove, 'Science and the common good: Indefinite, non-reviewable mandatory detention of asylum seekers and the research imperative', *Monash Bioethics Review*, 23(4), October 2004, pp 93–103; Z Steel, N Frommer and D Silove, 'Part I – The mental health impacts of migration: The law and its effects failing to understand: Refugee determination and the traumatized applicant', *International Journal of Law and Psychiatry*, 27(6), November–December 2004, pp 511–28.

CHAPTER 7

Page 149: 'Stanmore Primary ... are really upset': ABC Radio, 'Parents, teachers slam schoolyard raids', *PM*, 16 March 2005, available at <http://www.abc.net.au/pm/content/2005/s1325087.htm>; ABC TV, 'Immigration raid angers community', *7.30 Report*, 23 March 2005, available at <http://www.abc.net.au/7.30/content/2005/s1330414.htm>.

Page 150: 'Frightened and bewildered ... of a car': ABC TV, 'Vanstone backtracks on Hwang case errors', *7.30 Report*, 21 July 2005, available at <http://www.abc.net.au/7.30/content/2005/s1419657.htm>.

Page 151: 'Instead they ... traumatised': Paula Farrugia, *Psychological assessment: Ian Hwang*.

Page 151: 'Instead they were ... Jane Hwang': ABC TV, 'Vanstone backtracks on Hwang case errors'.

Page 152: 'The mother and children ... inside the immigration department': 'Flawed system', *The Australian*, 30 May 2008.

Page 152: 'Advocates have been ... as well': ABC News Online, 'Korean children granted permanent visas', 10 May 2008, available at <http://www.abc.net.au/news/stories/2008/05/10/2240900.htm>.

Page 152: 'He is now suing for compensation': Harry Freedman, solicitor.

Page 155: 'When Kylie arrives ... nervous collapse': ABC Radio, 'Another case of severe mental illness in Baxter emerges', *PM*, 10 May 2005, available at <http://www.abc.net.au/pm/content/2005/s1364442.htm>.

Page 156: 'For the first time ... in health care': Its official name is the Alliance of Doctors and Health Professionals. See ABC TV, 'Health professionals demand release of detained children now', *Lateline*, 8 May 2002, available at <http://www.abc.net.au/lateline/stories/s551410.htm>.

Page 156: 'The list includes ... impaired learning development': ABC TV, 'Australian doctors concerned over detention of children', *Lateline*, 19 March 2002, available at <http://www.abc.net.au/lateline/stories/s508624.htm>.

Page 156: 'Dr Simon Lockwood, the ... nothing,' he says': ABC TV, 'Woomera detention centre doctor speaks out', *Lateline*, 27 October 2004, available at <http://www.abc.net.au/lateline/content/2004/s1229335.htm>.

Page 157: 'So she leaks the ... transferred to hospital': ABC TV, 'Tribunal challenges detainee treatment', *Lateline*, 30 May 2002, available at <http://www.abc.net.au/lateline/stories/s569401.htm>.

Page 158: 'Immigration minister ... placed themselves': ABC TV, 'Ruddock defends detention of children', *Lateline*, 19 March 2002, available at <http://www.abc.net.au/lateline/stories/s508634.htm>.

Page 159: 'Philip Ruddock wades ... a mental illness': SBS, *Insight*, 8 May 2003.

Page 159: 'Louise Newman believes ... staffer sneers': ABC TV, 'Our work has been undermined, researchers say', *Lateline*, 9 February 2005, available at <http://www.abc.net.au/lateline/content/2005/s1299518.htm>.

Page 159: 'Soon after ... says Dr Samuell': ABC TV, 'Our work has been undermined, researchers say'; ABC TV, 'Vanstone rejects smear campaign claim', *Lateline*, 10 February 2005, available at <http://www.abc.net.au/lateline/content/2005/s1300408.htm>; ABC Radio, 'Health inquiry possible: Vanstone', *PM*, 10 February 2005, available at <http://www.abc.net.au/pm/content/2005/s1300340.htm>; ABC

Radio, 'Govt accused of cash for critique over detention centre research', *The World Today*, 10 February 2005, available at <http://www.abc.net.au/worldtoday/content/2005/s1300032.htm>; 'Lib's call to end detention gets expert backing', *The Age*, 11 February 2005.

Page 161: 'Which is why Ngareta ... most detention camps': David Penberthy, 'Five star asylums', *Daily Telegraph*, 17 December 2002; ABC TV, '5 star beat up', *Media Watch*, 17 February 2003, available at <http://www.abc.net.au/mediawatch/transcripts/s785747.htm>.

Page 162: 'Terms such as "queue-jumper" ... Nice way to make the point': 'Learning to play the waiting game', *Daily Telegraph*, 22 November 2003.

Page 163: 'It is no coincidence ... run appalling systems': Speech, Third meeting of the International Corrections and Prisons Association by Western Australia's inspector of Custodial Services, Professor Richard Harding, 30 October 2001.

Page 164: 'The report is a very ... December, 2002': Alexander Downer and Philip Ruddock, Joint media release, FA184, 13 December 2002.

Page 164: 'You can take it ... convicted criminals': 'Ruddock disappointed with "unbalanced" Ombudsman's report', *Lateline*, 2 March 2001, available at <http://www.abc.net.au/lateline/stories/s254233.htm>.

Page 164: 'The Human Rights ... *A last resort?*': 'No child shall be deprived of his or her liberty unlawfully or arbitrarily. The arrest, detention or imprisonment of a child shall be in conformity with the law and shall be used only as a measure of last resort and for the shortest appropriate period of time.' *Convention on the Rights of the Child*, article 37(b).

Page 164: 'In May 2004... and its catastrophic psychological effects': HREOC, *A last resort?*, available at <http://www.hreoc.gov.au/Human_Rights/children_detention_report/report/index.htm>.

Page 164: 'The government ... senator Amanda Vanstone': Amanda Vanstone and Philip Ruddock, Joint media release, 13 May 2004, available at <http://www.chilout.org/information/hreoc.html>. 'Detention policy damned as cruel to children', *Sydney Morning Herald*, 14 May 2004, available at <http://www.smh.com.au/articles/2004/05/13/1084289822162.html>.

Page 165: 'But in the lead up to the 2004 ... one child in detention centres': 'Detained children freed in policy flip', *Sydney Morning Herald*, 6 July 2004.

Page 165: 'The 'one child' is ... and Maribyrnong centres': ChilOut, Press release 16/2004, 6 October 2004, see also PR14/2004, available at <http://www.chilout.org/news/press_releases.html> quoting DIMIA.

Page 165: 'Terrorists had struck ... including 88 Australians': Russell Lain, Chris Griffiths and John M N Hilton, 'Forensic dental and medical response to the Bali bombing', *Medical Journal of Australia*, 179(7), 2003, pp 362–65, available at <http://www.mja.com.au/public/issues/179_07_061003/lai10499_fm.html>.

Page 165: 'On 9 September 2004 ... killing nine people': '9 dead, 161 hurt in Jakarta bombing', *Sydney Morning Herald*, 10 September 2004.

CHAPTER 8

Page 168: 'The reformers mobilised ... didn't go further': 'Left loses vote on refugees', *West Australian*, 31 January 2004; ABC News, 'Latham victorious as Labor adopts immigration policy', 30 January 2004, available at <http://www.abc.net. au/news/australia/nsw/200401/s1035165.htm>; ABC Radio, 'Latham refugee policy set to win conference vote', *The World Today*, 30 January 2004.

Page 172: 'Do you feel … feel better': 'Freedom fighters behind the scenes', *The Sunday Mail*, 8 December 2002.

Page 172: 'Only 83 out of more than 2000 … end of 2003': HREOC, *A last resort?*, Chapter 3, para 3.3, available at <http://www.humanrights.gov.au/human_rights/ children_detention_report/report/chap03.htm 3_3>; Chapter 6, para 6.4(a), p 145, available at <http://www.humanrights.gov.au/human_rights/children_detention_re- port/report/chap06.htm 6_4> (81 at Woomera, two at Port Hedland).

Page 173: 'He was one of the … of what he saw': Joint Standing Committee on Migration, *Not the Hilton: Immigration detention centres: Inspection report*, Tabled 4 Septem- ber 2000.

Page 174: 'In a June … for families': JSCFADT, *A report on visits to immigration detention centres*. Its recommendations are available at <http://www.aph.gov.au/house/commit- tee/jfadt/idcvisits/IDCrecs.htm>.

Page 174: 'PHILIP RUDDOCK: If you … benefits of life experience': ABC Radio, 'Ruddock rejects refugee report', *PM*, 18 June 2001 available at <http://www.abc.net. au/pm/stories/s314691.htm>; Government response, 9 December 2002, available at <http://www.aph.gov.au/house/committee/jfadt/IDCVisits/IDCresponse.pdf>; ABC TV, 'UNHCR goes up against Govt in plight of refugees', *7.30 Report*, 19 June 2001, available at <http://www.abc.net.au/7.30/content/2001/s315568.htm>.

Page 177: 'It begins with the shocking … her changing': For more on this you can refer to the Palmer Report and 'Chris Rau and her sister's "illness-mongers", Cor- nelia Rau's sister lines up the facts', 18 October 2005, available from <http://www. safecom.org.au/chris-rau-pilch.htm>; Christine Rau delivered the Public Inter- est Address 2005 for the Queensland Public Interest Law Clearing House, search <http://www.qpilch.org.au>. *Statement of Baxter detainees regarding Cornelia Rau in Red One Compound*, 10 February 2005, available at <http://www.safecom.org.au/cornelia- rau.htm>. P Prince, *The detention of Cornelia Rau: Legal issues Law and Bills Digest Section*, Parliamentary Library, 31 March 2005; HREOC, *Summary of observations following the inspection of mainland immigration detention facilities*, 2006, available at <http://www. humanrights.gov.au/human_rights/immigration/inspection_of_mainland_idf.html>.

Page 178: 'When you're in … of review at all': ABC TV, 'Govt searching for wrongly deported woman', *Lateline*, 4 May 2005, available at <http://www.abc.net. au/lateline/content/2005/s1360111.htm>.

Page 178: 'I mean [playing … highly distressed people': ABC Radio, 'Just another birthday behind the razor wire', *PM*, 5 May 2005, available at <http://www.abc.net. au/pm/content/2005/s1360970.htm>. ABC Radio, 'Naomi Leong's release highlights plight of children in detention', *AM*, 25 May 2005.

Page 180: 'The Federal Court delivers … psychiatric hospitals': *S v Secretary, Depart- ment of Immigration & Multicultural & Indigenous Affairs* [2005] FCA 549 (5 May 2005); ABC News Online, 'Detention ruling "no surprise" to advocates', 5 May 2005, avail- able at <http://www.abc.net.au/news/newsitems/200505/s1360926.htm>.

Page 181: 'After Judi Moylan … a few days': ABC TV, 'Liberal backbenchers want detention policies changed', *7.30 Report*, 24 May 2005, available at <http://www.abc. net.au/7.30/content/2005/s1376203.htm>.

Page 184: 'The government has … retarded development': ABC TV, 'Villawood

mother, child released from detention', 7.30 *Report*, 24 May 2005, available at
<http://www.abc.net.au/7.30/content/2005/s1376204.htm>.

Page 184: 'In a brilliant media stroke ... and the *Sunday Telegraph*': 'Meet the
barcode kids in detention', *Sydney Morning Herald* and 'The babes behind bars
revealed', *The Age*, 31 May 2005, available at <http://www.smh.com.au/news/Na-
tional/Meet-the-barcode-kids-in-detention/2005/05/30/1117305563811.html>
and <http://www.theage.com.au/news/Immigration/The-babes-behind-bars-re-
vealed/2005/05/30/1117305559364.html> respectively; 'We want to get out', *Sunday
Telegraph*, 5 June 2005; 'Our secret children – Villawood detainees may win freedom
at last', *Daily Telegraph*, 27 June 2005.

Page 184: 'There is an ... political terrorist': ABC TV, 'Petro Georgiou, quiet
achiever or political terrorist?', *Stateline*, 17 June 2005 available at <http://www.abc.
net.au/stateline/vic/content/2005/s1394865.htm>.

Page 185: 'When given the ... Parliament House': ABC Radio, 'Sophie Panopoulos
criticised over "political terrorist" tag', *PM*, 15 June 2005, available at <http://www.
abc.net.au/pm/content/2005/s1393119.htm>.

Page 189: 'We don't really ... wary of backsliding': Howard releases the statement
in the late afternoon of 17 June 2005: ABC News Online, 'Howard announces major
changes to migration laws', 17 June 2005 available at <http://www.abc.net.au/news/
newsitems/200506/s1394839.htm>; ABC TV, 'PM admits immigration changes long
overdue', 7.30 *Report*, 20 June 2005, available at <http://www.abc.net.au/7.30/con-
tent/2005/s1396449.htm>.

Page 190: 'The longest serving detainee... seven years': 'Free at last: The
longest held detainee', *Sydney Morning Herald*, 18 July 2005, available at
<http://www.smh.com.au/news/national/free-at-last-the-longestheld-detain-
ee/2005/07/17/1121538868829.html>.

Page 190: 'You know Petro ... then he lost it': 'Last of children in detention set
free', *The Age*, 30 July 2005.

Page 190: 'A few days later, Bruce ... through the bill': Commonwealth of Australia,
Parliamentary Debates, House of Representatives, Hansard, 21 June 2005, p 91.

Page 191: 'Many of them ... them to be extraordinary': Foreword by Petro Georgiou in *Freeing Ali* by Michael Gordon, Sydney, UNSW Press, 2005.

Page 191: 'Both Petro Georgiou ... hangs on': ABC News Online, 'Libs set to decide on Georgiou preselection', 23 April 2006.

Page 192: 'When approached by ... going to': Glenn Milne, 'Jakarta politics thwart
Georgiou', *The Australian*, 22 May 2006.

Page 192: 'But on 10 August 2006 ... It chose me': ABC TV, 'Liberals cross floor in
immigration bill vote', *Lateline*, 10 August 2006.

Page 193: 'Four days later ... minister's office': AAP, 'Troeth welcomes migration bill
climbdown', 14 August 2006.

Page 194: 'In a strange twist ... everybody falls apart': Michael Gordon, 'Why reso-
lute senator defeated asylum law', *The Age*, 15 August 2006.

CHAPTER 9

Page 198: 'She once said ... believe in': ABC TV, 'The gatekeeper', *Australian Story*, 16
September 2002, available at <http://www.abc.net.au/austory/transcripts/s672095.htm>.

Page 198: 'He is Australia's ... in 1949–56': *Prime Facts*, Chapter 17, the Australian Prime Ministers' Centre, Old Parliament House.

Page 199: 'His 30-year ... Darling Harbour': 'Multi culture at Ruddock bash', *Sydney Morning Herald*, 23 September 2003, available at <http://www.smh.com.au/articles/2003/09/22/1064082933432.html?from=storyrhs>.

Page 200: 'Some colleagues ... Asian immigration': 'In the name of the father', *The Age*, 22 November 2003.

Page 200: 'But in 1999 ... wears the Amnesty pin': ABC Radio, 'Ruddock stripped of Amnesty International badge', *AM*, 18 March 2000.

Page 205: 'PHILIP: It's about abandoning ... should be maintained': 'Rudd govt softens asylum seeker laws', *Sydney Morning Herald*, 29 July 2008, available at <http://news.smh.com.au/national/rudd-govt-softens-asylum-seeker-laws-20080729-3mgo.html>.

Page 209: 'In fact one of ... going to happen': Jacquie Everitt, *The Bitter Shore*.

Page 215: 'MARGOT: On the *Insight* program': SBS TV, *Insight*, 8 May 2003.

Page 223: 'You go to a place ... to be refugees': UNHCR grants all refugees from south and central Iraq refugee status. Syria does not recognise the word 'refugee'.

EPILOGUE

Page 239: 'I am a member of ... detention in Australia': See Joint Standing Committee on Migration, Committee Activities (inquiries and reports), available at <http://www.aph.gov.au/house/committee/mig/reports.htm>.

Page 246: 'Power tends ... corrupts absolutely': Historian, Lord Acton, 1834–1902, *Historical Essays and Studies*, Appendix, quoted in JM and MJ Cohen, *The New Penguin Dictionary of Quotations*, London, Penguin, 1992, p 1.

Page 251: 'Al Abadey family (Iraq)': Heather Tyler, advocate and author and John Highfield.

Page 252: 'Heman Baban (Iraq)': Trish Highfield and Ian Rintoul.

Page 252: 'Shayan Badraie (Iran)': Jacquie Everitt.

Page 252: 'Bakhtiyari family (Afghanistan)': Dale West, Centacare, and Marilyn Shepherd, advocate; Paul McGeough, 'Mrs Bakhtiari [sic] is one of ours, say Afghan', 28 September 2005, available at <http://www.smh.com.au/news/world/mrs-bakhtiari-is-one-of-ours-say-afghan/2005/09/27/1127804478530.html>.

Page 252: 'Hwang family (South Korea)': Michaela Byers.

Page 252: 'Naomi Leong (Malaysia)': Ngareta Rossell.

Page 253: 'Peter Qasim (Kashmir)': Andra Jackson, journalist, *The Age*.

Page 253: 'Cornelia Rau (Australia)': Chris Rau, sister, and Harry Freedman, solicitor.

Page 253: 'The federal government ... in compensation': '$4.5 m payout to Alvarez', *The Advertiser*, 1 December 2006.

Page 253: 'Mohsen', the Iranian... bid for legality': Damien Lawson.

All websites were accessed on 4 August 2008.

INTERVIEW LIST

Quotes in the text without endnotes come from either recorded interviews or phone conversations. All formal interviews were supplemented by extensive phone calls and quote verification. In some cases, as with Petro Georgiou and Russell Broadbent, there were also extensive unrecorded discussions. Below is a list of the tape-recorded interviews conducted for this book.

Paris Aristotle, 9 February 2007, 27 March 2007
Bruce Baird, 8 April 2008
Julian Burnside and Kate Durham, 26 March 2007, April 2007
Pamela Curr, 4 March 2008
Jacquie Everitt, 23 February 2008
Anne and Gerard Henderson, 28 March 2008
Trish and John Highfield, 21 March 2007, 11 June 2007
Michael Kapel, 6 March 2007, 27 March 2007
Damien Lawson, 27 June 2007
Marion Le, 10 February 2008, 27 February 2008
Judi Moylan, 15 February 2008
Louise Newman, 19 March 2007
Ian Rintoul, 29 March 2007, 8 May 2007, 28 May 2008
Ngareta Rossell, 22 March 2007, 2 April 2007
Philip Ruddock, 29 February 2008, 19 April 2008, 14 June 2008, 24 June 2008
Zachary Steel, 12 March 2007, 19 April 2007, 5 June 2007
Aamer Sultan, 10 June 2007
Jo Szwarc, February 2007

Index

www.ingramcontent.com/pod-product-compliance
Lightning Source LLC
Chambersburg PA
CBHW020510270326
41926CB00008B/816